GEORGE O'BRIEN

A Man's Man in Hollywood

BY DAVID W. MENEFEE

GEORGE O'BRIEN
A MAN'S MAN IN HOLLYWOOD
©2009 DAVID W. MENEFEE

ALL RIGHTS RESERVED.

No part of this book may be reproduced in any form or by any means, electronic, mechanical, digital, photocopying, or recording, except for in the inclusion of a review, without permission in writing from the publisher.

Published in the USA by:

BEARMANOR MEDIA
P.O. BOX 71426
ALBANY, GEORGIA 31708
www.BearManorMedia.com

ISBN-10: 1-59393-473-4 (alk. paper)

BOOK DESIGN AND LAYOUT BY VALERIE THOMPSON

TABLE OF CONTENTS

Introduction 1
Acknowledgments 3
Foreword 4
Preface 6

Part One: Biography

Chapter 1	A Rough Beginning 7	
Chapter 2	Football Fields and Battlefields 27	
Chapter 3	Mixing Up Careers 40	
Chapter 4	Iron Wills and Iron Horses 60	
Chapter 5	Fig Leaves 69	
Chapter 6	Sunrise and Success 81	
Chapter 7	Noah Speaks 99	
Chapter 8	From a Ford to a Stagecoach 118	
Chapter 9	Marguerite and Marriage 131	
Chapter 10	In the Navy Again 152	
Chapter 11	Sunset on the Trail 163	

Part Two: Filmography 175
Part Three: Portrait Gallery 325
Appendix: George O'Brien Defends Movies for Children 385
Bibliography 389
Index 413

Introduction

Fate placed George O'Brien on the edge of many major events of the 20th century, and then added dozens of incredible adventures in-between. George's actual birth records were lost during the 1906 San Francisco earthquake, and some people have debated whether his birthdate was on April 18, 1899 or 1900. In taped interviews, George recalled many details about his family's survival during that 1906 earthquake and fire. He distinctly remembered the event taking place just before his seventh birthday, which places his birth year at 1899. Orin O'Brien, his daughter, also recalled him telling her that his birth year was 1899. Because of their recollections, this biography records his birth at that year.

During World War One, George joined the millions of young men responding to the call-to-arms, and he enlisted in the US Navy. After the war, he found work in silent motion pictures as an assistant cameraman on motion pictures starring Tom Mix. He appeared in small roles in silent movies with Rudolph Valentino, Pola Negri, Hobart Bosworth, Wallace Reid, and many other films that went unaccredited and unrecorded. After his first starring role in John Ford's *The Iron Horse*, he achieved above-the-title status as one of Fox's most popular actors during the 1920s.

George successfully survived the chaos of Hollywood's transition from silent to sound pictures, and then he chose to abort his film career to again answer the call-to-arms and rejoin the navy during World War Two. After that war, he returned to civilian life only to discover that an entire generation of young people had grown up never seeing him in the movies. He found occasional work in films, notably with John Ford in *Fort Apache, She Wore a Yellow Ribbon*, and the Technicolor epic, *Cheyenne Autumn*. Never stopping, he took part in several early 1950s television series, and then he left the film industry again to return to the military to serve during the Eisenhower administration. By the 1970s, George was busy producing films about underwater demolition experts known as "frogmen," and he enjoyed the first restrospectives of his early work.

This book explores his personal life, military career, and work in Hollywood with a detailed and richly researched biography. A Filmography explores each film with production notes, contemporary reviews, examples of advertising art, and photographs. Finally, a portrait gallery reveals the many expressions of George O'Brien as he was seen through the eyes of accomplished photographers in his time.

Until now, the full George O'Brien story has never been told. In spite of an intriguingly varied life, George held fast to privacy. He was never plagued by any scandal. He avoided Hollywood parties and nightclubs, and he enjoyed working out in the gymnasium at the Hollywood Athletic club. A celebrated physical culture enthusiast before Charles Atlas made the hobby an American obsession, George served as a role model for many young men in the 1920s and 1930s.

His life spanned nearly nine decades, and in his film career, his wistful, Irish smile graced more than seventy-four major motion pictures, many of which are still seen today. Had he appeared in no other film besides *Sunrise*, his place in Hollywood history would be secure. Fortunately, most of George O'Brien's films have survived. I hope this book serves to stimulate the memories of those who recall his work when it was fresh and charms those who have recently discovered him.

Acknowledgments

This book began with a prayer because all things are possible with faith in Jesus. The monumental task of compiling the story of the life and career of George O'Brien required the help of Orin O'Brien and Suzanne O'Brien, his family members, as well as archives, friends, collectors, and fans. My gratitude goes to the following organizations:

Janet Bergstrom from the UCLA Department of Film and Television

Greg Kelly from the San Francisco History Center

The staff at The San Francisco Public Library

The staff at The Dallas Public Library Fine Arts Division

The staff at the Margaret Herrick Library Academy of Motion Picture Arts and Sciences

The staff at the American Film Institute

The staff at the New York Public Library C. L. Brown Collection

The staff at the Univeristy of Southern California

The staff at the Huntingdon Library

I also am grateful to the following individuals for their help, encouragement, and memorabilia:

Kevin Brownlow, Maurice Daly, Dennis Doherty, Robert Edwards, Ed Hulse, Randy Jones, Marty Kearns, Eunice and Doyle Menefee, Ron Raburn, Larry Rayl, Robert Seifried, Sam Sherman, Russell C. Sweeney, Lou Valentino, and Michael Yakaitis. I would also like to thank publisher Ben Ohmart at BearManor Media, and Valerie Thompson, the book designer. Without these wonderful people, this book would not have been possible.

FOREWORD

I love watching George O'Brien in films. He never achieved legendary status, but his performances in the film classics, *The Iron Horse, Sunrise,* and *Noah's Ark,* as well as the dozens of other films he made during Hollywood's "golden age," ranks him as an equal to Tom Mix, Roy Rogers, Clark Gable, Gary Cooper, and other top stars.

George was a college athlete, sailor, boxer, assistant camera man, film extra, bit player, featured player, and finally, a star with a tremendous following with both men and women. He was one of the most remarkable men in Hollywood. He had the wistful look of a little boy, the physique of Adonis, and six feet of Irish flesh burned by sun and wind to the color of an Indian. In his time, he was the idol of millions of people.

He worked in silent movies with Tom Mix, Rudolph Valentino, Wallace Reid, Pola Negri, Dolores Costello, and other big stars, survived the film industry's turbulent transition from silent pictures to talking pictures, and he later appeared in wide-screen Technicolor epics and early television shows.

His life was more than roles in motion pictures. He and his family barely survived the great San Francisco earthquake of 1906, and later, he served as an American soldier in World War One, World War Two, and the Korean conflict. He was good son and a devoted husband and father. George's experiences were varied and many.

In a letter to this author, Orin O'Brien, George's daughter, wrote:

> "My parents tried to be good parents. They wanted both Darcy and me to have a good education and

plenty of exposure to the arts: music, theatre, ballet, art, literature, and poetry. They must have succeeded, because Darcy had a very good career in both teaching and writing, and I have enjoyed my life in music and teaching. George was a kind and friendly person: he enjoyed the company of fellow actors, and regretted not working any more when he retired from film. He told me that he enjoyed being on location, sitting around the campfire at night, telling stories, and partaking in the camaraderie of an acting troupe. He had a beautiful bass-baritone voice, and sang very well in tune. I used to tell him that if I had met him early enough, I would have encouraged him to be an opera singer. He was part of the early time in Hollywood, when the budget was not as important as the script and the vision of the director. His favorite director was F. W. Murnau, and *Sunrise* was the film he was proudest of, I believe. He told me that Murnau had a string quartet playing on the set, to inspire the actors in their emotional scenes. I believe my father was a very good and carrying man who remained dignified and aloof from the world in later years. I hope this book is useful to readers in some way."

George loved his time in the Hollywood spotlight, but in his later years, he most wanted to be remembered as a man who served his country. This book explores both sides of his life. I hope readers enjoy the many facets of this remarkable man. He was truly a man's man in Hollywood.

PREFACE

All information in this biography can be traced to a variety of sources, including many interviews given by George O'Brien, reminices by his surviving relatives, and historical records relevant to the San Francisco earthquake of 1906, World War One, World War Two, and the conflict in Korea. In addition, many people who were close to him in his motion picture work shared their memories of filmmaking experiences when they wrote autobiographical articles and books. These manuscripts were extremely important in revealing how George was accepted in his time and how he affected their lives and work. Their personal stories are poignantly juxtaposed with his, including the early death of Rudolph Valentino, the tragic demise of Wallace Reid, the suicide of Lou-Tellegen, and the sorrowful decline of Olive Borden.

The author makes no judgment of George's work, but reveals many contemporary reviews gleaned from a wide selection of sources. They include excerpts from prominent magazines like *Photoplay, Screenland, Motion Picture,* and *Motion Picture Classic.* The *New York Times* offered insights from the perspective of major metropolitan critics, and *Variety* revealed opinions from a film industry point of view that often differed from others. In addition, the appeal of his many films has been gauged by the reviews found in small town newspapers across America, often countering the jaded opinions expressed in more prominent publications.

Chapter 1
A Rough Beginning

The genealogy of the O'Brien family can be traced back to Ireland, beginning with Turlough O'Brien (1000-1086), the king of Munster. Turlough's many descendants all bore names such as Conchobhar, Brian, Conor, Murrough, Dermod, Donough, Daniel, Charles, Henry, and James. Their names carried forward into the next generations.

In 1870, at least one member of the O'Brien family joined the thousands of immigrants leaving their Ireland homeland to explore the new world in America. Among them was James O'Brien, who had a son, Daniel Joseph O'Brien, born on August 8, 1875 in San Francisco, California.

Daniel first established himself in San Francisco as a journalist. In 1899, he met and married seventeen-year-old, French-Irish Margaret L. Donohue. They were both Catholics, and they shared a common desire to raise a family in San Francisco.

On April 19, 1899, Daniel was nervously pacing the floor of their home at 443 Clementina Street. Margaret was about to give birth to their first child, and for once in his life, he was unable to do anything to help ease her suffering. Thoughts came fast and in disconcerting waves. He could only wait for word about the momentous occasion. He thought about the recent past, and felt more than a little fear for the present. For the future, he already has his eye on a position with the city of San Francisco as an engineer in the Flood Building. With a new family, he wanted to provide a stable home and future for Margaret and the new child.

As Daniel O'Brien waited for news about his wife and the birth of their first child, hurrying footsteps reached his straining ears. Their child was born, and they named him George Joseph O'Brien.

George rapidly developed into a sturdy youngster, but he was not destined to be an only child. In 1902 when he was three years old, his brother, Daniel "Jack" James O'Brien, Jr., was born.

In 1904, Daniel Sr. joined the city of San Francisco as an Assistant Engineer. He was well on his way to providing a stable home environment in which to raise the family he and Margaret wanted. Their futures seemed full of growth and rich with possibilities.

"It was my luck to have a wonderful father," George recalled years later. "He knew how to manage a boy. He showed me what was what, and then gave me my head, with full liberty to make an ass of myself if I felt like it. His life and standards gave me plenty to live up to. My father weighed 220 pounds and was six feet tall. He had been an amateur boxer in his younger days when the West Coast was a rough and ready place."

Daniel's codes of conduct, poise, and athletics were emphasized in the way he handled George. Before his son could read, he often took the boy to the movies. George listened to his father quietly reading the silent movie subtitles so that he could understand the stories.

During these years, Tom Mix, an athletic and hard-working cowboy, performed stunts in Wild West shows staged by the Miller brothers, owners of the 101 Ranch in the Oklahoma Territory. The Miller's recreated a working replica of the American West, employing hundreds of cowboys and a thousand Indians. They put on daring reenactments of horsemanship, marksmanship competitions, buffalo hunts, and Indian attacks on a wagon train. Tom and the Miller's elevated the American West to a mythical level where cowboys were kings, and audiences ate up these shows that presented an idealized image of the American West.

In April 1906, George was excited about his upcoming seventh birthday. He was in the middle of the first grade at school, and as the days slowly turned on the calendar, his big week finally arrived. George went to school on Monday, April 16, and he eagerly anticipated the following morning of Thursday, April 19, when he would wake to a new year as a seven-year-old.

That week, San Francisco was alive with activity. In the world of the Arts, excitement was in the air. Enrico Caruso, the Italian tenor, was due to arrive and perform with the New York Metropolitan Opera. The next day, he blustered into San Francisco both tense and excited. Having been born in the shadow of the Vesuvius volcano, he arrived in town upset from shocking news that the ancient volcano had just erupted again. Thousands of people had died, and many more were homeless. Although he did not want to lead the Metropolitan Opera of New York on a tour across America, the $1,350 they were paying him for each performance motivated him to embark on the exhausting trek. News in the April 17, 1906 San Francisco *Examiner* testified to the devastating lava flow threatening Naples, his hometown, with extinction. "Maybe it was God's will after all that I should come this far," he told Alfred Hertz, his conductor. After a brief interview with newspapermen, the thirty-four-year-old Italian settled into rooms at the Palace Hotel.

That same day, Leonard Ingham, one of Daniel O'Brien's fellow police officers, began patrolling the Mission District. He had slept fitfully the night before, tormented with a recurring dream in which the Palace Hotel had been gutted by fire. As he left the Mission Police Station, he was weary from repeatedly having the same dream for the past two months. In his nightmares, he saw the entire city engulfed in flames, and the recurring nightmares had been increasingly vivid. As he walked through the cramped wooden frame houses and factories of the Mission District, he dreaded the long day on his beat. He decided to report his apprehensions to Jeremiah Dinan, Chief of Police, and to quell his gnawing fears, he obtained an insurance policy on his home on Dolores Street, just six blocks from the Mission Police Station.

In town, the renowned stage actor, John Barrymore, was dressing in his room in the St. Francis Hotel. He had been playing with Willie Collier's company in the Richard Harding Davis play, *The Dictator*. Their season had closed the previous Saturday, and he was set to sail for Australia on Wednesday, April 18. For his last night in San Francisco, he had in his pocket coveted tickets for a box in the Grand Opera House on Mission Street to see and hear Enrico Caruso in *Carmen*. As he dressed, he could see from his hotel window that children were returning home from school. The afternoon sun was sinking low over the bay, and Barrymore looked forward to joining San Francisco's elite at the opera.

(LEFT) John Barrymore, famous member of America's premier acting family. (TOP RIGHT) Daniel O'Brien, George's father, as Chief of Police of the city of San Francisco. (BOTTOM RIGHT) Enrico Caruso as he looked at the time of his appearance in San Francisco in 1906.

George arrived home from school, and a few hours later, his father returned home from work. They settled in for the evening, and George noticed the extra groceries his mother was placing in the pantry. He wondered if the new bags of flour and sugar were going to be used two days later for his birthday cake.

That evening, more than 3000 people occupied seats in the Grand Opera House. In office for about a year since April 5, 1905, Chief of Police, Jeremiah Dinan, and his wife occupied one box. They could not help but see John Barrymore in another. The rear of the auditorium was lined with other police officers, an arrangement made by the management to quell any potential riot scenes. The curtain rose, and Caruso gave a towering performance in *Carmen*. He came back for nine curtain calls, and finally, he left the stage exhausted and exultant. As he made his way to his dressing room, the bell in the tower of old St. Mary's Church chimed midnight.

"After the opera, I went to a supper party," recalled John Barrymore, "and then I walked home with a friend to his house. He insisted that I look at some pieces of old Chinese glass that he had just received. Upon this collection, my friend lavished all of his leisure and a great deal of money. It got so late that I decided to sleep there and not go back to the St. Francis Hotel."

Just after 2:00 in the morning of Wednesday, April 18, James Hopper, a newspaper reporter for the San Francisco *Call*, had finished writing his review of the Caruso performance in *Carmen*. He left and began to walk home to the Neptune Hotel on Post Street. He noticed the sea breeze had become unusually calm, and he looked forward to eight hours of uninterrupted sleep. As he passed the horse stable between Powell and Mason Streets, he observed one horse baying shrilly.

A stableman lolled in the darkened doorway. "The horses are strangely restless," he commented. "They've been kicking the stalls during the last few hours."

Hopper could hear gunshots ringing from the Barbary Coast, which was not an unusual sound in the middle of the night. He ignored the ruckus, and he went to his room to sleep.

A few blocks away, horses belonging to millionaire James Haggin were tethered at the rear of his wooden mansion on Nob Hill. Their unusual snorting and stamping disturbed those having dinner with him.

"It must be the odd weather," the millionaire said, and he continued entertaining his guests.

Shortly before 5:00 in the morning, policeman Leonard Ingham awoke with a gasp. His sinister nightmare had not returned to torture him. The sound that woke him was the rattle of a milk cart rolling down the streets and the voice of a milkman struggling to quiet his overly excited horse. Ingham heard the reassuring rings of the city clocks striking five bells, and then he again lay down to sleep.

In the O'Brien household, Daniel sat on the edge of his bed slowly putting on his slippers, as he rose to begin another day. In the distance at Chinatown's edge, he heard the bells ringing five times from St. Mary's Church.

At the same moment, artist Bailey Millard sat on the terrace of his villa on the summit of Russian Hill, and he faced a blank canvas mounted on an easel. He could see the great San Francisco Bay spreading before him and the two-hundred-foot cliffs lining the water's edge. He planned to paint the misty mood of Telegraph Hill with sunrays lacing through the fog at dawn. Miller's watch indicated that the time was 5:15 a.m., and he began to paint.

In the Bay 150 miles west of the Golden Gate, the schooner *John A. Campbell* suddenly shuddered in the water. The bow of the small vessel rose sharply, exposed the waterline on its hull, and then crashed back into the waves, knocking the crew from their bunks. The force of the jolt was as if they had struck a whale. Startled crewmembers bolted to the rail, as the schooner repeatedly bobbed in the water. Captain Svenson thought the jolt felt like they had scraped the soft seabed, a puzzling sensation because the bottom of the ocean was some 2400 fathoms below. Unknown to him, an earthquake had begun.

In that same second, the earthquake struck land. Svenson and the crew of the *John A. Campbell* rode a shockwave kicking back from the rip of the tremor traveling at two miles per second. The quake raced from the sea at a speed of more than 7,000 miles per hour, tearing into land ninety miles north of San Francisco and directly beneath the lighthouse on Point Avenue. The lantern and lens from the 110-foot structure cracked along with the brick and fell to the rolling ground in a shower of fragmented glass and debris.

Baily Millard lay stunned on his terrace beneath a pile of smashed canvas and scattered paints, while below him, the hills heaved billions of tons of earth and shifted masses of rock into new cliffs where a moment before there had been flat land.

The entire O'Brien house shuddered at 443 Clemintina Street.

Daniel was knocked flat onto the wood planks of the buckling floor. In the next second, another jolt threw George from his bed to the other side of the room some fifteen feet away. He blinked his eyes in the pre-dawn darkness and barely saw his mother hurrying to the window in her nightdress.

"My brother and I were in an old-fashioned double bed. My father, very calm, said, 'Lie down and go back to sleep, George. Cover up your head.' Well, he no sooner said that than I did it. There was a big, wonderful picture on the wall, and this picture tumbled over. You know the old saying, 'Did it kill you?' 'No, it missed me.' So, it came tumbling over, and at that, my mother jumped up and came in."

Mrs. O'Brien glanced outside and shrieked, "The street has burst open! People are running from their houses!"

"She looked out the window and saw this terrific catastrophe that was going on," George remembered. "She called to my dad, 'Dan, quick, get up! We're being swallowed up!' because the entire street had opened up. How long I stayed in bed, I don't know, but I know that my father was very calm. We got up. He shaved, dressed himself completely, put on a white collar and shirt, and said, 'Margie, now just be calm now. We'll see what the plans are.'"

The quake packed more energy than all the explosives used in World War Two, as it ripped along its journey, crumbling the nearby Russian Church like a stack of children's building blocks, and then plowing through beaches, sandstone bluffs, houses, and hotels. At Point Reyes Station, a locomotive and four cars jackknifed under the twenty-foot-wide crevice, sending the train toppling on its side. Then, it continued along the trails of ancient fault lines through the Bolinas fishing village where it cut into the Mussel Rock cliffs.

As the tremors sheared through the San Juan Mission and burrowed through the San Francisco reserve water supply in the lowlands south of the city, one police sergeant on duty actually saw the earthquake. Jesse Cook recalled years later in *Earthquake in California*, "There was a deep rumble, deep and terrible, and then I could see it actually coming up Washington Street. The whole street was undulating. It was as if the waves of the ocean were coming towards me, billowing as they came."

In the heart of San Francisco, buildings danced on their foundations, while chimneys and cornices snapped from the walls of their structures and the earth rolled in waves along Market Street. Inside homes, furniture, pianos, and bookcases danced through their rooms as if possessed by demons. Crockery and chinaware dashed from their snug closets onto floors. The frame of the City Hall administrative headquarters building shook its stone and brickwork off as if they werescales. The whole skyline of San Francisco staggered.

The old-fashioned O'Brien house had sliding doors between the rooms, and by the time the second wave of quakes were rolling under their home, the doors of George's bedroom began dancing back and forth as if they had come alive.

"Put on your clothes," Daniel sternly directed, seemingly undisturbed.

George recalled in a *Motion Picture Classic* interview with Dorothy Donnell, "I remember my Dad even combed his hair, but mother was hysterical. He put the jacket of his evening suit on her over her nightdress. By the time we went into the upper hall, the stairs were already twisted out of shape."

Firemen ordered them out, and threw up a ladder to the upstairs window. Margaret grabbed the only possession nearby—a pet bird in its cage. Daniel carried her down their stairs while she held Daniel, Jr., in her arms. "This was an incredible feat, I remember," George recounted. Daniel deposited his wife and son on the ground, and then he returned to retrieve George.

The large, five-story Brunswick Hotel on Sixth and Howard Streets held three hundred rooms and all were occupied when the entire structure suddenly collapsed to the ground. The Portland House, which was located on Sixth Street between Mission and Market, buckled, fell, and entombed about sixty people under the ruins. Their heart-rending cries for help could be heard a block away.

Then, as suddenly as it began, the shaking stopped. The bell in the tower of old St. Mary's Church continued to swing wildly, beating its unnerving clang into the abruptly stilled atmosphere that was choked with dust and rubble.

For ten seconds, an eerie silence and ungodly calm lay over the city. A pale, crescent moon hung silently in the greenish sky.

The uncanny quiet suddenly split with a sound of giant nails prying out of stubborn wood. The earthquake returned in an explosion of

San Francisco wrecked by an earthquake in 1906 just as George O'Brien was about to have his seventh birthday. Lower right, crowds on Mission Street near the O'Brien home watch the outbreak of unstoppable flames in the immediate aftermath of the tragedy.

discord, hurling through the city with an audible roar. Occupants of homes found themselves suddenly buried beneath falling ceilings. Inhabitants of the St. Francis Hotel heard the roar and crash of bricks breaking free from twisting girders and raining onto the street below.

In the Palace Hotel, Caruso bolted upright in bed. Still in his nightshirt, aghast and weeping hysterically amid a room filled with toppled furniture, he stared horrified at bureau drawers flinging open and a chandelier tearing from the ceiling and scattering to the floor. Alfred Hertz, stumbled into the room. Caruso fell out of bed and embraced him like a confused child.

"We're doomed!" he shrieked. "My vocal cords have been damaged!"

"Did you try your voice?" Hertz asked the hysterical singer.

Caruso could only shake his head. They moved to the window and looked out onto the grotesque chaos of people fleeing their rooms in undergarments. Some of the men still had shaving cream lathered on their faces.

Hertz tapped commandingly on the windowsill. "Sing!" he ordered.

Caruso hesitated a moment between sobbing gulps, and then the tenor opened his mouth and sang at the top of his voice. Below the window where he stood, people stopped in the street and stared bewildered at the opera star testing his potent voice, yet adding more confusion to the surreal chaos. With the help of his valet, Caruso threw on what clothes could be gathered from the heap of debris in the dark, and they made their way into the hallway.

Not far away, John Barrymore ran to James Haggin's bedroom and shouted to him, "Come see what has happened to the Ming Dynasty!" Haggin jumped from bed and saw his rare collection of oriental artifacts reduced to little more than a heap of powder and chips.

With nothing more to do, they left the hotel and walked toward town where whole sides of houses were gone. The effect was as if someone had lined the streets with gigantic doll houses of the sort that have no fronts. People were hurriedly dressing and gathering their valuables. More prudent persons put up sheets to shield themselves from passers-by. The square, into which so many oddly dressed persons and their belongings had been hastily thrown, presented a strange and almost uncanny appearance.

John Barrymore passed the remains of the St. Francis Hotel. He ran into Enrico Caruso standing beside his packed trunks loaded on a van. Having forgotten his key, Barrymore went to the desk clerk standing under a split in the middle of the hotel and asked if the structure was safe enough for him to go back to his room.

"Perfectly," the clerk answered with the trained assurance of a professional. "There isn't the slightest chance in the world of it ever happening again."

No sooner had he spoken than a new shockwave rocked the hotel. The terrified clerk jumped across the desk in one leap and disappeared into Union Square. Barrymore went behind the desk, retrieved his key, and then walked upstairs to his bed where he calmly went to sleep while chaos reigned in the street below. He was awakened hours later in the afternoon by the general excitement in front of the hotel, and he smelled the pungent odor of burning wood. While he had slept, fire spread throughout the whole city.

The O'Briens huddled with their sons in a neighbor's house. Mrs. O'Brien gripped her husband's jacket at her neck, as she looked out the window at the spreading devastation. She saw people in various stages of undress running in panic and carrying little possessions. Across the street, a family was hauling furniture from the remains of their home and depositing them on the front sidewalk. Suddenly, Mrs. O'Brien gave a wild scream.

"Dan—the manicure box with my things! My wedding ring! My marriage certificate! Oh, Dan!"

Her distress was so great that her husband was forced to return to their crumbling house to retrieve the cherished possessions Mrs. O'Brien feared she would lose forever. When he arrived at their house, a soldier barred him from entering.

"My wife's precious things are up there," he said sternly to the armed soldier, pointing to the upstairs room. "Man, maybe you've got a wife yourself. Then you know what a wedding certificate means to a woman."

Together, they crawled up the quivering ladder to the second floor window and into the unsteady house. Daniel walked across the slanting floor of what remained of the room and found the manicure box belonging to his wife. As he returned to the window, the brownstone house heaved and buckled. He hurriedly threw his legs over the sill, and then descended the wobbly ladder to the earth below.

While he was upstairs, soldiers herded Mrs. O'Brien and her two sons away. For some time, they walked through the broken streets with Margaret carrying little Daniel, the caged bird, and George tagging along.

"I remember passing houses with people pinned underneath, screaming to be shot and done away with," George said. "I remember buildings falling as we passed them."

That day, Daniel never got back to his family. Next door, soldiers had cleared everyone from the neighbor's house. He looked around and saw the streets filled with frenzied people clutching worthless household treasures. His family was nowhere in sight.

Mrs. O'Brien, bare-footed and still wearing her husband's evening coat, led her boys through the ruins. George stumbled along at her skirts carrying his brother. He saw things no child should see: people screaming from beneath mounds of rubble, dead bodies laying in twisted positions, and his friend's home crumbled into unrecognizable heaps of brick and wood. His main concern was that the earthquake had spoiled the birthday party he was going to have the next day.

George and his family were separated from Daniel for some time. They were unaware that he and all the other able-bodied men were taken by the National Guard to dig through rubble. Hours passed, and while Daniel worked, he thought of the handsome home he had been able to afford with his good position as a City Engineer. At about twenty-seven years of age, he was one of the youngest consulting Engineers for the State of California, and in a single moment, his home and career had been swept away.

Then, some of the official city fathers came by and recognized him. "Dan, what are you doing there?"

Daniel answered, "Ask that man with the rifle over there."

They explained that he, as an Engineer, would be better off planning how to handle the excavation rather than digging, so he was taken away, and someone else put into the trench.

At 1:00 a.m., St. Mary's Hospital at First and Bryant streets was abandoned to the fire. Patients were loaded aboard the ferryboat, *Modoc*, and taken to Oakland, as the entire financial district behind the Hall of Justice went up in flames. The blaze posed such a threat to Portsmouth Square that the General Manager of the Department of Electricity abandoned the Central Fire Alarm Station at 15 Brenham Place in Chinatown.

Brigadier General Funston saw panic taking control of the city, and he had appointed himself head of the crisis. Across the city, not one fire bell clanged because the central alarm system had been wrecked.

Police officer Leonard Ingham grimly surveyed the black smoke drifting languidly through forks of flames and he realized his recurring dreams during the previous months had been horribly realized. He calmly joined the thousands of men marshaled under arms by General Funston to maintain a semblance of order in the chaos.

Policemen, busy conveying the wounded to temporary hospitals, had no time to arrest the many thieves ransacking unguarded homes. There was no place to incarcerate them even if one was arrested. In response to the widespread looting, the Mayor issued his first order to Chief Dinan under the "law of necessity," which stated:

> April 18, 1906.
> "As it has come to my attention at thieves are taking advantage of the present deplorable conditions and are plying their nefarious vocations among the ruins in our city, all peace officers are ordered to instantly kill any one caught looting or committing any other serious crimes. E. E. SCHMITZ, MAYOR."

Mayor Schmitz issued another public notice at 3:00 a.m. from the Hall of Justice:

> "Let it be given out that three men have already been shot down without mercy for looting. Let it also be understood that the order has been given to all soldiers and policemen to do likewise without hesitation in the cases of any and all miscreants who may seek to take advantage of the city's awful misfortune."

All day, landmarks and buildings crumbled, offices perished, and homes were destroyed. In their place, fire had begun devouring the still-standing structures. Flames quickly advanced from street to street, while bodies of the unfortunate dead began lining the roadways in sheet-covered piles.

John Barrymore was forced at gunpoint to join all the other available men in rescue efforts. Still clad in his dapper evening attire, the theatrical star labored sorting through stones and rubble for survivors buried alive. Prisoners from the city jail were herded into the square, given shovels, and ordered to dig graves. While ash fell like rain, the men began the grim task of burying bodies. They sorted through crushed buildings following the sound of weak voices emanating from the unseen victims. At one wreckage site, a man had been trapped for hours with crushed legs. Unable to move, he shouted for someone to shoot him. A policeman approached, and in a moment of mercy, shot the man twice, but failed to hit him properly. A young man snatched the gun from the officer's hand, took aim, and instantly killed him.

On Third Street near Mission Street, a building collapsed in such a manner as to pinion an unknown man to the ground. His cries attracted people on the street who attempted to rescue him, but by that time, fire had reached the rear end of the building. Realizing that he would soon be burned to death, he begged bystanders to kill him. A large, middle-aged man hesitantly stepped forward, and after exchanging a few words with the unfortunate prisoner, he whipped out a revolver and shot him through the head. He then requested the witnesses to accompany him to the Hall of Justice. The Mayor, after hearing the circumstances and seeing the man's distressed appearance, commended him for his humane act.

In many other streets, a panorama of equal horrors passed like scenes from one of Leonard Ingham's nightmares. His worst fears had come true.

Daniel finally caught up with his family after having been separated from them for the entire day. Together, they went back to their neighborhood, which was now a burned relic smoldering with smoke. They found George's bicycle still standing, leaning dejectedly against a section of area railing.

By evening, dynamiting had been initiated to stop the spreading fires. Unfortunately for San Francisco, untrained members of a demolition squad administered the blasts. Raw black powder was used in most cases, doing little to stop the spreading fire, and causing more ignitions in the process.

As night fell, looting broke out in the few stores remaining intact. The fire reached Van Ness Avenue during the evening. In an attempt to build a firebreak, mansions were dynamited along the street on orders from Colonel Charles Morris of the Army Artillery Corps.

By 6:30 p.m., Chinatown was in flames, a casualty of the inexperienced hands entrusted with the task of igniting raw dynamite. By evening, the advancing curtain of flames had progressed beyond all control. As block after block of wooden buildings were consumed by the spreading inferno, the enveloping darkness was lit by a hellish, glowing red color. Chinatown was filled with leaping flames and tens of thousands of rats running out of the conflagration. People began to flee the city in droves.

Army troops from Fort Mason first reported to Mayor Schmitz at the Hall of Justice between 7:00 p.m. and 8:00 p.m. The 10th, 29th, 38th, 66th, 67th, 70th, and 105th Companies of Coast Artillery, Troops I and K of the 14th Cavalry, and the 1st, 9th, and 24th Batteries of Field Artillery arrived Downtown to take up patrol.

Seventy-five soldiers from Companies C and D Engineer Corps were assigned to the Financial District, and another seventy-five were positioned along Market Street from Third Street to the City Hall at Grove and Larkin Streets. The second major aftershock had caused the collapse of many already-damaged buildings, and there was widespread panic.

Shortly after the troops began patrolling the streets, the first looter was caught while he was making an attempt to burglarize Shreve's Jewelry store at Post and Grant Avenues. He was turned over to a soldier who killed him and left his body to be consumed by the fire.

Makeshift refugee camps sprang up in city parks and Union square where people were sleeping on the grass. Mrs. O'Brien was one of the many women cooking outdoors for the thousands of refugees lined up for free meals. While the bizarre events played out before him, six-year-old George sadly saw that his dismal fears for the loss of his birthday party had been realized.

While the city smoldered, George said to his mother, "Well, I guess I won't have a birthday party now."

"George, you *will* have a birthday," she vowed.

She scrounged around with the help of other men and women in the camp and the Red Cross, who were feeding them at the time, and found enough ingredients to bake a huge, cream-filled strawberry shortcake, so big that one tottering old gentleman in his late 80s thought the confection was a chair and accidently sat on it.

"Now look what you've done!" Margaret shouted. "Just for that, you'll eat every piece of that cake that you sat on!"

George remembered thinking, "I wished that I had sat on it so I could eat everything!"

By 8:00 p.m., Mayor Schmitz was still confident that a good part of downtown could be saved. His optimism deflated when an arsonist set fire to Delmonico's Restaurant in the Alcazar Theatre Building, and the ensuing blaze spread wildly into the downtown and Nob Hill. Thousands of angry flames shot high into the sky. The cracking timbers, falling buildings, and the terrific roar sounded like a dozen cyclones.

At 8:40 p.m., the War Department received a telegram from General Funston asking for all available rations and thousands of tents for the fortunate survivors. At that time, he placed the unofficial death toll at one thousand.

That night, George slept on a mattress in the park among hundreds of other people, old and young cradled together in haphazard piles of human wreckage. Not even a candle was allowed to burn. Firefighters attempted to make a stand along Powell St. between Sutter and Pine, but it was unsuccessful in keeping the fire from sweeping up Nob Hill.

On his birthday, Thursday, April 19, George woke to the smell of burning wood ash choking the atmosphere. To everyone's astonishment that day, a new newspaper made its way into the streets. Normally the fiercest of competitors, the *Call, Chronicle,* and *Examiner* newspapers were burned out of what was called "newspaper row" in the area of Third and Market streets, and were forced to Oakland to publish on the nearest presses large enough to print thousands of copies of a combined newspaper with the masthead, the *Call-Chronicle-Examiner*. This article from the front page was published on the presses of the *Oakland Herald* and distributed free in San Francisco on the morning of George's birthday:

> "Death and destruction have been the fate of San Francisco. Shaken by a temblor at 5:13 o'clock yesterday morning, the shock lasting 48 seconds, and scourged by flames that raged diametrically in all directions, the city is a mass of smoldering ruins. At six o'clock last evening the flames seemingly playing with increased vigor, threatened to destroy such sections as their fury had spared during the earlier portion of the day. Building their path in a triangular circuit from the start in the early morning, they jockeyed as the day waned, left the business section, which they had entirely devastated, and skipped in a dozen directions to the residence portions. As night fell they had made

their way over into the North Beach section and springing anew to the south they reached out along the shipping section down the bay shore, over the hills and across toward Third and Townsend streets. Warehouses, wholesale houses and manufacturing concerns fell in their path. This completed the destruction of the entire district known as the "South of Market Street." How far they are reaching to the south across the channel cannot be told as this part of the city is shut off from San Francisco papers."

People found it difficult to get word out by mail, and telephone communication was impossible. The US Post Office at Seventh and Mission streets was dreadfully damaged by the earthquake. Walls had been thrown into the middle of various rooms, destroying furniture and covering everything with dust. In the main corridors, the marble was split and cracked, mosaics were shattered, and chandeliers were rent and twisted by falling arches and ceilings.

John Barrymore managed to escape the mayhem by boarding a ship bound for Australia with a troupe of actors. As soon as the ship temporarily docked in Vancouver, he scraped together what funds he had and wrote a long letter to his sister, Ethel Barrymore, describing in great detail what he had seen the harrowing day before.

"I confessed to having seen people shot in the street, spiked on bayonets, and other horrors so great that the imagination was almost blunt from contemplating them," he later inscribed in his memoirs. "I wrote that I had been thrown out of bed by the earthquake and almost miraculously escaped injury from falling bricks and plaster, and then, with much pathos and resignation, I described the terrible scene at the Oakland ferry where, weak from exhaustion and privation, I had been cruelly put to work sorting stones by the soldiers."

When the letter reached Ethel in New York, she read it to their uncle, actor John Drew. As he read, he was so strangely quiet that she stopped and asked: "What's the matter, Uncle Jack? Don't you believe it?"

"I believe every word of it," he answered, looking up. "It took a convulsion of Nature to make him get up and the United States Army to make him go to work."

By mid-day on Friday, April 20, the fire had burned as far as Franklin Street, and by 5:00 that morning, it then attempted to circle south. At the foot of Van Ness Avenue where the historic mansions had been dynamited into heaps of charred debris, sixteen enlisted men and two officers from the *U.S.S. Chicago* supervised the rescue of 20,000 refugees, the largest evacuation by sea in history and as large as the evacuation of Dunkirk during World War Two.

After darkness again settled on the devastated city, the homeless numbered into uncountable thousands, who were making their way with blankets and scant provisions to the beach and to Golden Gate Park to find shelter. Those in the homes on the hills just north of the Hayes Valley section piled their belongings in the streets and waited for express wagons and automobiles to haul their things away to the sparsely settled sections.

Under a special message from President Roosevelt, the city was finally placed under martial law. Hundreds of troops patrolled the streets and drove the crowds back, while hundreds more were set at work assisting the fire and police departments. Strict orders were issued, and in true military spirit, the soldiers obeyed. The curious were driven back at the breasts of the cavalrymen's horses, and all the crowds were forced from the level district to the hilly section beyond to the north.

Everybody in San Francisco prepared to leave the city because they were certain that it would be totally destroyed. Downtown was ruined, and hardly a business or house stood. Theaters were crumbled into heaps beside the smoldering sites where factories once operated. The total earthquake death toll by then stood at more than 3,000 from all causes. Damage was estimated at $500 million dollars, a staggering sum in 1906.

In the dreadful days to follow, the O'Briens found refuge in the unburned home of one neighbor. People crowded into its rooms where they slept on floors and mattresses hauled in from the remains of other dwellings. No one dared light a candle inside the structure for fear of starting another fire. "Once we lighted one to hunt for a nursing bottle that belonged to a baby," George later chuckled, "but the soldier outside shot a bullet through the window."

For many weeks, George lived among the ruins, stood in breadlines, and attended classes on a hillside. His father lost everything he owned, a circumstance that would have defeated many a man under similar calamity. Daniel never lost his positive morale, and he refused to allow his responsibilities to slip. He sturdily began life anew and found work as a night watchman. George was put to work driving a cart through acres of ruins and miles of militia posts to the Red Cross depot for their daily food supplies.

"We moved from the refugee camp into a dance hall," he recalled in an interview with Harry Brundidge. "We were crammed together with fifty-five other people. I remember the night that Dad came home and said, 'Well, Margie, we got to eat, so I'm joining the police force.' He passed the examinations and became a patrolman."

In time, boxes of clothing came from other cities and were apportioned according to need rather than by such trivial details as size or sex. People that once had appeared trim and stylish wore bizarre outfits: women in pants, men with mismatched coats and trousers, and children in oversize shirts and rolled pants legs. George drew a streetcar conductor's cap and thought he was lucky to wear it. His baby brother wore a man's derby over his long flaxen curls.

"After months of this kind of life, we were allowed to go down into the city again, though all cooking had to be done out of doors and the houses were unlighted," George remembered. "We found some relatives and all started housekeeping together in a few rooms—six or seven kids to a bed. My mother was the cook all along—this was a fantastic thing to me—there was mother cooking for everything they needed and watching out for the baby bottles that were needed because of the women coming down, and she had nothing but a wood stove outdoors! Miraculous as it was, she came through all right. Certainly, it wasn't ordained that she should be the cook for fifty-five people, but I find that the mothers and the fathers and the worthwhile people of those days always came through in an emergency."

George also remembered, "We moved back into the old neighborhood, on a street near St. Vincent's parochial school. My father had a job as a night watchman. He went to work at midnight and did not come home until morning. A lot of men just ran out, but he took care of all of us, including his mother, who was there, and all our relatives."

His father had gone back to engineering with a private firm to try to bring some stability to their lives, but the earthquake had destroyed his sense of security. He was afraid to be away from his family for too long for fear of what might happen next.

Chapter

FOOTBALL FIELDS AND BATTLEFIELDS

In 1907, the O'Briens moved into a home at 414A Tehema Street. St. Vincent's Parochial School educated George for the next several years. Between the ages of eight and twelve, he went to Columbia Grammar School and spent many days at the Columbia Park Boys' Club enjoying tumbling, acrobatics, hiking, boxing, and swimming. As a nine-year-old, George got a job trimming the wick and lighting a coal oil lantern in front of a warehouse each night for $1 a month. After eleven months, he had saved eleven dollars, and his mother took him out shopping. He bought a suit, a book called *The Green Mountain Boys*, and a baseball bat.

Vacations found him hiking through the open woods and the mountains of Utah and Nevada. On one of these trips, George and three other boys became separated from the rest of the party and soon found that they were lost. They wandered into the arid Carlton Valley in Nevada, where they stumbled over the crunching white alkali for two days without food. His knowledge of woodcraft saved them from death when he led the boys along a trail following the crests of the "hog-backs" until they emerged onto recognizable terrain. By that time, his friends were too weak to go on, but George stayed the course. In time, he came across a government surveying party, and led them on a return hike back to his stranded friends.

"I'm a tramp at heart, I guess," he grinned, when telling of the experience later. "I've always been curious about people and the way they live and what they think about things. I ran away from home a good many times when I was a kid, but it was the kind of running away where you can always send home for money for a return trip ticket. The folks knew where I was and I knew they'd be glad to see me back whenever I came. So I had the sort of life that every kid dreams of, traveling, ranching, and living in a lumber camp between while I went to school."

When they were back at home, the Columbia Park Boys Club started George on his life-long sports and physical fitness activities.

"My brother and I put on boxing gloves when we were around nine years old," recalled George. "I weighed eighty-five pounds then. My father taught us what he knew about boxing, including how to use the left hand. One person I knew in those days was Jim Corbett. I learned a lot from him. He was a swell fellow, a great fighter and a fine gentleman. He encouraged my brother and me to hook up with the Columbia Park Boys Club. It had a membership of 500, and the idea of it was to build up strong and healthy youngsters. We were taught calisthenics, military drill, boxing, wrestling, tumbling, pyramid building, working on the bars, and games. And we camped in the summer time."

At the boys club, George also took part in some plays performed for the enjoyment of family and friends. A group of boys played some musical instrument, sang, or recited, and every summer, they tramped around California on foot and gave concerts from town to town. After proving his abilities for several years in their summer camps, George was fifteen years old. He went with the dramatics club on tour giving shows. They performed charades, tumbling acts, and sang opera selections in many little towns and at big resorts such as Lake Tahoe.

"I played in many mountain towns where there were no chairs. They bought a ticket, and brought their own chairs. They brought rockers. If you've ever given a performance and looked out at a man with a pipe watching you while he rocked back and forth, you would think, 'Why doesn't he stop that?' But we were too young to complain about the noise."

In 1909, Tom Mix took part in the making of a Western film, *The Range Riders*. In early 1910, the Chicago-based Selig Polyscope Company signed a deal with Will A. Dickey and his Circle D Ranch Wild West Show. After seeing Tom Mix perform, Dickey hired Tom to locate stock and wranglers for Selig's Western films. He was given a part in a bronco-busting scene in *Ranch Life in the Great Southwest* (1910), a semi-documentary. William Selig was so impressed with

Mix's on-screen performances that he signed him to a one-year contract and sent him to Florida to act in a series of jungle movies in supporting roles with Kathlyn Williams, their female star. Tom thought the steady income would go a long way to providing a means to buy the ranch of his dreams in Oklahoma. He never thought that his stint in front of the cameras would become a new, full-time career. In 1910, he made twelve films for Selig, all of which were among the company's biggest moneymakers.

In December 1910, Marguerite Churchill was born in Kansas City. She began a life that would be a fantastic adventure in itself. She and George were destined to cross paths about twenty years later.

Also in 1910, Daniel again found work as a policeman, and the family moved into a slightly larger home at 2951 Harrison Street. At the age of twelve, George first became interested in barbell lifting. The Columbia Park Boys Club featured weight lifting equipment, and George began developing the physique that would win him much admiration.

"Back in those days, we kids didn't have the instruction they have now," George told Lew Pike of *Strength and Health* magazine. "If you wanted to lift, you had to trust to luck that you didn't hurt yourself, because only a few knew how to handle the iron bells property. Fortunately, my dad knew lots about weight training, so he gave me my early pointers."

Daniel considered barbells and dumbbells excellent for his growing sons. "There's nothing better for a lad of fifteen," George later stated. "It gives the young man a chance to test his strength and build up a powerful body in a short time. Under the right supervision, he can lay the foundation for a healthy, husky, physical being which will pay dividends in later life. The boys of today are more fortunate than I was when I was a kid who wanted to grow big and strong. Now, magazines like *Strength and Health* offer the best in exercise instruction so that anyone who trains with weights or wants to go into lifting can readily learn the right way quite simply and know that he's going to get splendid results in a short time without the danger of hurting himself."

"My father wanted me to become a professional man, preferably a doctor, not a journalist like himself," he recalled. "He liked being a journalist and respected his work, but found little solace in the low

Three pictures of George O'Brien taken from the San Francisco Polytechnic High Annual of 1918. PHOTOS COURTESY OF THE DARCY O'BRIEN ESTATE.

pay it rendered for his long hours of endeavor. I wanted to please my father because I both loved and respected him, so I studied hard to become the doctor he wanted me to be."

In 1915, George graduated from grammar school, and then he attended San Francisco's Polytechnic High School. While there, he became a popular athlete endowed with a fine physique, and he distinguished himself in all forms of athletics. He was captain of the baseball team, played basketball as all-State guard at the end of his last season, was on the swimming teams, and earned letters in four sports.

(TOP) George O'Brien in navy uniform shortly after enlisting during World War One, posed beside his father, Daniel O'Brien. (BOTTOM) Marguerite Churchill as a girl in one of her first stage roles. PHOTOS COURTESY OF THE DARCY O'BRIEN ESTATE.

"I went in strong for high school athletics," he later remarked. "Did the quarter mile in fifty-six seconds—considered good in those days. And I played football. I had a leaning toward medicine and specialized in chemistry and biology, developing my muscles with the blacksmith machine-shop courses so I could get on the football team, which I did."

While playing football, George was on the receiving end for Reynolds "Ren" Kelly, who later was with the St. Paul team of the American Association, and who was the brother of George Kelly, the first basement of the New York Giants.

George learned horseback riding, roping, and bulldogging from a family friend who owned a ranch near his home in Los Gatos. In return, he did odd jobs around the city stables.

During his high school days, George struck up a friendship with George Merchant, a cowboy hired to instruct the San Francisco police in horsemanship. They became great pals. The police had a riding arena, and during odd hours away from athletics, George rode the police horses. At the end of a year, he was almost as proficient a horseman as his tutors. He could ride, rope, and break horses with the best of them.

At this time, certain people and events were simultaneously converging in a way that affected George's ultimate destiny. In 1913, another youth on the other side of the world was trying desperately to leave Castellaneta, Italy. Rodolfo Alfonza Raffaelo Pierre Filibert Guglielmi di Valentina D'Antonguolla begged his mother to help him find some way of making the journey across the sea. Finally, borrowed money barely made possible his passage in steerage class for the trip. After buying the cheapest ticket, he converted the remaining money to American currency and found it equaled exactly one dollar. With the bill pinned to the inside his shabby coat and the prayers of his widowed mother, the eighteen-year-old set out alone for America on December 13, 1913. Rodolfo landed among the teeming immigrants of New York City.

In 1914, Marguerite Churchill's family moved to Peoria, Illinois. She made her stage debut as a four-year-old in a play performed at a theater built by her father. At her mother's urging, Marguerite appeared in many roles at her father's theater that year.

Another important man in George's life was just beginning his first

George O'Brien, his mother, father, and brother Dan at a family funeral ca. 1917.
PHOTO COURTESY OF THE DARCY O'BRIEN ESTATE.

work in Hollywood. Sean O'Feeney had left Maine University to go to California where his brother, working under the name Francis Ford, had become a successful actor and director. Sean changed his name to "John," and he found work as property man, stunt artist, actor, and assistant director. In 1917, John Ford got his chance to direct his first film, a western called *Cactus, My Paul.*

While George was playing football in San Francisco, newspaper headlines announced a nationwide call to arms. "All Eligibles Face Military Service—Every Young Man Who Can Pass Physical Examination May Be Conscripted," screamed the headline of the *Elvira Evening Telegram* in early 1917. In a Washington news release circulated around the country, young men were told, "Every man within the conscription age who can pass the physical examinations faces military service in the immediate future. As the result of the President's and General Crowder's appeals for strictness in exemptions and in view of the known plans for the steady maintenance of an armed force of nearly two million men in France, this idea began to develop strongly here. Many of the men chosen may never see a trench under fire...."

George's main interests were sports of every kind, and he grew into a stalwart youth. In 1917, the country plunged into war with Germany. He heard the news while at school, and when the students were dismissed, he left to find his father. Downtown, a marching band had gathered, and crowds were rallying in the streets, talking excitedly about the astounding news. The infectious pounding of drums and the enticing strains of popular war songs lured young men from all walks of life to enlist that day. George ran to the police headquarters to tell his father that he wanted to join the assembling ranks.

"That's fine with me, but have you told your mother?" he asked.

"No, I'm going to wait until after I sign up."

His father gave instant consent, and in just three hours, George was duly examined, weighed, measured, and enlisted in the United States Navy. He was just a few months past seventeen at the time, and he enlisted as a Radio Signalman.

He later remarked. "I could have remained in college and obtained my degree and then gone into medical school, but decided to enlist and serve my country instead. I tried to enlist in the Marine Corps, but they wouldn't accept me because their quotas at the time were full. So I tried the navy and they accepted me."

At that same time on the other side of the world, Friedrich Wilhelm Murnau, a twenty-nine-year-old actor studying with Max Reinhardt's theatrical school, passionately dreamed of artistic achievements in the fledgling motion picture industry, but when war gripped the nation, he was called up to join the First Regiment of the Foot Guards at Potsdam. He was not a military man by choice, but within a short time, he participated in heavy fighting. He was quickly promoted from a position as an officer to a position as company commander at Riga. The fields of battle were not far from the German stages on which he had acted in *The Miracle* and *Henry IV*.

George first trained for eight weeks as a seaman assigned to Goat Island, the Pacific Naval Station at San Pedro. After boot camp, he was asked if he wanted to go into the US Navy Reserves or the "regular navy," as it was called. George chose the regular, US Navy. He soon found that scrubbing decks for his country was too tame for his energies, so he trained for and received a Gunner's Mate rating.

At that time, they were looking for men to go as stretcher bearers to France. The lure of adventure drew him, and he went through a training series at the hospital school. He trained for and received a Third Mate's rating, and then a Pharmacist's Mate 3rd Class. He received orders to transfer to *Subchaser 397*. One of George's responsibilities while on the subchaser was to pick up the crew's daily mail. One day while they were still in port, he and another sailor left for town, and while they were away, a fire sparked near leaking gas chambers and the subchaser exploded. He heard about the tragedy while they were driving in their jeep, and he and his companion raced back to the docks. There, the horrible wreckage of the ruined subchaser languished in debri-strewn water. Many sailors had been burned, and some had been killed. Had he been at his post at the time of the accident, there was a good chance that his name might have been listed among the dead.

After completing his training, he was sent to accompany Marine Corps troops to France. There, he saw first-hand the terrible cost of what bullets and bombs did to those at the frontlines. In June 1918, George was transported to frontlines located some fifty miles southwest of Paris. In the Battle of Belleau Wood, US forces were intent on taking back the woods near the Metz-Paris road at Château-Thierry, an area held by the German Seventh Army since the end of May. It was not one solid forest, but a mass of one to five acre patches of oat and wheat fields.

In a spirited action together with the French 10th Colonial Division, the task they faced was perilous. While capturing the town of Bouresches, the Americans had been unable to secure the rocky strongholds in the woods. They passed by, leaving the Germans lurking in wait among with their nests of machine guns. When the Americans returned, they found the Germans waiting for them with murderous intentions.

On Sunday, June 9, they crossed an open wheat field while Germans swept the area from end to end with machine gun fire. The barrage kept up into the next day, and by Monday night, the Germans redoubled their efforts, fiercely defending the woods from well-placed positions behind trees and rocky caves.

Civilians were caught up in the horrible conflict between warring nations. In a letter to her parents, Hester Titman Kennedy, a young woman who happened to be at Belleau Woods at that time, wrote,

"Here, in God's providence, some former king of France had the forethought to preserve the forest, and God, through nature and Foch, saved us. It was not the French, English, Italian, American or any of the Allied forces. At our very best we all bungled. It is human to bungle . . . the American forces had been put in charge of the battle lines at Belleau Woods . . . this evidently gave Foch some of his mightiest forces and his hardest seasoned veterans . . . Foch let the Germans' come right on, through an open wheat field, he evidently retreating, but at twelve o'clock one night they marked into a bombardment that lasted only ten minutes . . . the slaughter was terrible . . . Belleau Woods is a high elevation that extends in a circular direction. The woods were full of machine guns and Germans, which neither French nor American airplanes could bomb, as the foliage of the trees and the underbrush concealed them completely. It was across a broad sweep of valley, right through a wheat field, that our boys went on right up through Belleau Woods, fighting hand to hand . . . ."

When the Americans seized machine guns, bayonets, and hand grenades, the Germans responded in a headlong fight. Some Americans began surrendering, but the Marines chased them around the woods. For three days, German food and other supplies had been cut off from their reach. More than 300 German prisoners from the crack 5th Guard Division were taken by the end of the third day.

Six times during June 6-26, control of the woods switched from the US Marines to the Germans, and then back again. Because they were in the open, casualties on the first attempt were the highest in the history of the Marine Corps at that time. 9,777 men were wounded, and 1,811 of those died. 1,600 German troops were taken prisoner.

George and the other stretcher-bearers raced under machine gun fire at the frontlines, picking up the wounded where possible. They were instructed to carry the maimed men to a clearing station located in an old church on the outskirts of a nearby village. Illumination was provided by the light of candles and lanterns flickering over walls that were gray with age. The windows, once adorned with stained glass, were covered with blankets, canvas, and bits of carpet tacked over their openings to prevent the light from betraying their location to the German bombing planes. From the ground, they could hear the planes buzzing in the black sky overhead.

They placed stretchers over the floor where a number of pews had been pushed aside. An operation table had been crudely erected in front of what had been the church altar. Ornate candelabra of brass and gilded wood surrounded the operating table, where surgeons wearing bloodstained, white gowns labored at the grim task of saving those men near death. Anti-tetanus serum, the all-important inoculation that prevented lockjaw and killed the germs found in gangrene, was running out. In desperation, they sent word to the Red Cross in Paris of their dire need. Within hours, limousines requisitioned for the war arrived bearing the much-needed serum.

"I was scared stiff all the time," George later revealed, "but not so badly that I wasn't mindful of my duties or trying to save a life. I saved many a marine from dying, and luckily didn't wind up a casualty myself."

By the battle's end, the Marines succeeded in pushing the Germans back across Marne to Jaulgonne, bringing an end to the last major German offensive of the war. In honor of the Marine Corp's tenacity in retaking it, Belleau Wood was subsequently officially renamed Boi de la Brigade de Marine, the name the region holds today.

George miraculously survived and returned to America. His original hitch was for four years plus additional time for the duration of the war. After the Armistice was signed in 1918, he remained enlisted for nearly a year, and he was stationed at Goat Island and San Diego. Unfortunately for his eager and restless reserves of energy, he saw no action during this time. As a way of putting into motion his pent-up strength, he agreed to train for boxing and spar with another sailor, Bob Ferguson. After a series of tough fights, Bob won several titles. Two weeks later, George challenged Bob at a benefit boxing show and he defeated him. He went through a series of elimination bouts, won them all, and ultimately won the Light Heavyweight Championship of the Pacific Fleet. He was affectionately called "Rock 'Em and Sock 'Em O'Brien."

"My father's trick of taping my right hand behind me to teach me to use my left bore fruit," he remembered. Defending the title was a constant challenge, and he often took to the ring with opponents who considerably outweighed him. Seven times, he battled to maintain his title, and through it all, his ring tactics were clean-cut and sporting. He was the idol of his shipmates.

In September 1919, he was discharged. At the end of the war, George told Harrison Carroll, a writer for the *Monessen Daily Independent*, "... in the war, I wore a life preserver for years. When I left the navy, I took it off, walked over to the edge, and threw it over ... it sank."

He emerged from the war with five decorations for bravery under fire, two from the French, and three from the Americans. He also earned a Navy Commendation Medal, Marine Corps Commendation Medal, and the Silver Star. Many promoters offered him opportunities to become a professional boxer, but he still had ambitions to be a doctor. His friends urged him to aim for a professional boxing career and they pointed out that the purses were large and the glories great. They assured him that he had a good chance to win a world championship. When he expressed this possibility to his parents, his father was silent. His mother objected, saying that he was born for better things. To George, his mother's wish was law, and he squelched his championship hopes. His love and respect for her kept him from accepting any of those offers.

He returned to San Francisco where his father was rising in the police ranks. Daniel had been promoted from Police Patrolman to Corporal, from Sergeant to Lieutenant, and in 1920, he was elected from his position as Captain to the prestigious office of Chief of Police of the city of San Francisco. By that time, nearly a thousand officers filled the ranks of law enforcers. The Chinatown Tong Wars were fomenting with eruptions of violence between rival gangs. Chief O'Brien, with the help of Inspector Jack Manion, took bold steps to bring Chinatown leaders together with an early form of community policing. He persuaded the Chinese leaders to sign an agreement ending the violence. Because of his department's new ruling philosophy, the Tong Wars effectively ended, and the Chinese community came to respect and admire him. In addition to this achievement, in 1923 Chief O'Brien instituted the first Police Academy in the nation.

The 1920s were a time of great change for everyone. "The war made everybody stop and think," George thought back. "I got to wondering what it was all about. My father was Chief of Police by now and, proud as I was of him, I didn't want to go through life just the son of the chief.

The boss understood me—he always understood."

The west coast was alive with filmmaking activity. Every day, camera crews crisscrossed the scenic wonders of southern California, filming stories at every possible location. Taking advantage of the nearly year-round sunshine the state afforded, every major filmmaking company had outfits at work. Westerns were especially popular, and Tom Mix was among the biggest Western stars. Handsome, masculine, and seemingly fearless against all odds, Tom had developed an amazing, worldwide following, and his films were among the most popular.

Hollywood, California was a wide-open city of orange trees, and the city rapidly became a booming town of almost 400,000 people spread over a flat plain extending from the mountains to the sea. Tom Mix was given a studio in Glendale. For the next six years, he ground out at least one two-reel Western each week. His films proved enormously popular, especially in small towns across America and abroad. As the industry grew, audiences became more sophisticated and demanded an ever-increasing attention to detail and production values. Films expanded from the early one and two-reel lengths into hour-long feature films. By 1917, Tom was a top star fully entrenched in manufacturing regular releases. He found success and wealth, but his dream of settling down on a ranch became impossible to achieve.

Later in 1917, the Selig-Polyscope Company disbanded, and William Fox signed Tom to make films for his larger organization. Tom's Fox films realized the potential the company had expected of their new star, and they provided an organization to create Western films aimed at youngsters. On a special studio lot covering twelve acres near Edendale, California, Tom assembled a team of splendid people, and produced films more elaborate than those he had made with Selig. There was a mock Indian village nestled on a flat piece of land near the rear of the acreage where many convincing raids were filmed, and over another lot, a simulated desert spread out where Tom and his famous horse, Tony, wandered looking for bad men. This filmic vista was named Mixville. Mix was always on the lookout for new locations, as well as talented, attractive, young men and women to enhance his films. He made plans to do some filming in San Francisco.

Chapter 3
MIXING UP CAREERS

After the war, George returned to his home in San Francisco. He tried to decide upon a definite career, and he looked to his father for guidance and inspiration. An arrangement was made where he could attend a prep school in Santa Clara and catch up on the credits he needed. He was to earn tuition by washing dishes, waiting on tables, and assist the coach with boxing.

"The Captain," as George called his father, "was an innovator, inaugurating unique programs for police recruit training and examinations." Among his ideas was a program compelling all new members of the department to attend a fourteen-week course consisting of instructions in the proper methods of breathing, walking, talking, running, jumping, swimming, life-saving, resuscitation, boxing, wrestling, military drilling, and instructions in the handling of revolvers, rifles, and shotguns. He also prescribed compulsory *singing*.

With the purpose of inoculating recruits with poise, Chief O'Brien's officers were compelled on their first appearance in the school to go before the class and sing a song. This proved especially difficult for those not in the habit of singing before an assemblage. With his course, recruits acquired sufficient poise to enable them to later sing without nervousness. It was not unusual for many of the newly poised and confident singers to later organize into quartets and perform before public gatherings.

In an article for the *San Francisco Bulletin,* Daniel O'Brien boasted his singing recruits "handled themselves very well before local audiences, and we find that public appearances enable the men of the department to handle practical police work in a creditable manner when they are called upon to do actual police duty. Like the actor on the stage, they learn to appear before audiences without nervousness, and when confronted with a police problem, they are able to step into the breach and handle the situation as it should be handled, forgetting entirely or ignoring the crowd or audience before whom their little drama is being enacted, paying attention to themselves and the principals in the drama, with a coolness that is entirely foreign to those who have not had this particular form of training."

In addition, Chief O'Brien devised training for a system of locks and holds for the handling of prisoners in a humane manner, assuring safety for the officer and security for the prisoner. Recruits were compelled to master his system of locks and holds in order to graduate from the school and join outlying companies of the department. Chief O'Brien also encouraged athletics in the police department with annual track and baseball events to insure the men remained physically and mentally alert.

The same year while George was working odd jobs, Friedrich Wilhelm Murnau completed his wartime service, returned to Berlin, and devoted his work entirely to expressing his conception of art in the newfound freedom of post-war German cinema. Together with several associates from the Max Reinhardt School, he began working on pictures at his own company. The Murnau Veidt Filmgesellschaft boasted the names of several people who would soon achieve renown in the cinema: Conrad Veidt, Ernst Hofmann, Alfred Abel, Eugen Klöpher, Paul Hartmann, Werner Krauss, Olda Tchechowa, Lya de Putti, and Adele Sandrock. Critics appreciated the unique artistic quality and humanity of their subject, and American producers began to take notice.

While George was at Santa Clara College to resume his studies to become a surgeon, his father arranged for him to do some work handling police horses for the city. "He was proud of his Mounting Department and used to take me, along with men of the department, to the rodeos, but I was more interested in athletics," he pointed out. "Pretty soon after about a year of it, I became restless. My wonderful father didn't oppose me. Whenever I got that way he'd say, 'All right, have your head; and write me a postcard when you need me.'"

As his success soared higher in athletics, his scholastic achievements plummeted. He was quarterback of the football team, and a star in baseball, basketball, and handball. He finally had to agree with his professors and face the fact that as a student, he was a great athlete, and a career as a surgeon seemed unlikely.

Motion pictures had become the leading form of entertainment for the masses. Nearly everyone was trying to get into the movies. "I had long been a movie nut," George reminisced. "I became a fan of the first Western action films of Bronco Billy Anderson, Bill Hart, and Tom Mix. Fox Studios was not far from the college, so I used to spend a lot of time there, watching them make the Western films I would later see on the screen."

In those days, one reel of film was screened and the show lasted about fifteen minutes. Silent films matured in the 1920s. Feature-length films became the standard, and Tom Mix's films were as valuable to Fox as Mary Pickford's were to Famous Player-Lasky and United Artists. Across America, thousands of small towns welcomed the arrival of a new Tom Mix picture. He had a tremendous influence on the youth of America, and for many children, the appearance of one of his films was a great event in their lives. Mix took the responsibility seriously. Press agents ground out reams of copy for the burgeoning fan magazines, dictating his personal mode of living, his uninhibited enthusiasm, and his dedication to maintaining a clean reputation.

George O'Brien enjoyed handling horses for his father's Mounted Department with the San Francisco Police. On one occasion when Daniel took him to a local rodeo, he had an opportunity to see Tom Mix in person. George later observed, "It was at one of those rodeos, given for the Red Cross, that I met Tom Mix. Mr. Mix told me if I ever got to Hollywood to look him up and he'd give me a job—'not as an actor,' he said, 'but as a camera man.'"

"What do you do, young man?" asked Mix when he met George.

"I'm a student."

"A student of what?"

"Oh, I play football at Santa Clara, but I want to be a doctor. I'm taking a pre-medical course. I've got a long way to go—maybe eight years, and then, I don't know."

"I understand you were in the navy?"

"Yes sir."

"Well, if you ever decide to go to work and want to get into the movies, just look me up," Mix told him. "There's some pretty good jobs on the camera. We teach fellas how to become cameramen."

He had plenty of time to consider Mix's invitation. In a football game against Santa Clara's rival, Stanford, the opposition nailed him at the start and he did not stand a winning chance. He was tackled, pummeled, crushed, and left on the field in a broken heap. Days later while he languished in a hospital bed, taped and bulging with bandages from injuries he had received in the game, his mind wandered, and he began to seriously consider the movies as a possible future career. He mulled over Tom Mix's offer. While lying on the hospital cot, he decided the movies would be easier on him than football. He returned home with a suitcase in hand and met his father. Daniel sized him up instantly.

"What did you do, quit?" Daniel asked. "What are you going to do?"

"I'm going to work with Tom Mix."

His father was surprised. "Work for Tom Mix? Doing what? Not acting, I hope! You don't know anything about acting."

"No, working on the camera."

"Are you a cameraman?"

"No, but Mr. Mix said I can learn."

George went to Hollywood, but he found that Tom Mix was gone on a location trip to Oklahoma. He boldly insisted to his staff that Tom had sent for him and wanted him to join the organization. They responded by putting him to work for Frank Burns doing what was called "slopping hypo" in the developing tanks and making prints in the dark room at night. During the day, he went out with the Buck Jones company and worked as a second assistant cameraman. From what Mix had told him about the business, he thought his job was good for at least $125 a week, and was unpleasantly surprised when his first envelope contained only $15.

"And if you think living in Hollywood on $15 a week is easy, you are mistaken," declared George to John Parker in a later interview. "But it was wonderful, just the same, and I would not have missed it!"

Mix finally returned, and George met him as he was driving through the Fox Studio gate.

"Hello, George, what are you doing here?" asked Mix.

"Hello, Mr. Mix. I came down to accept your offer," George smiled.

Four early film stars who helped George O'Brien. (TOP LEFT) Wallace Reid gave George O'Brien a part in his 198th film, *The Ghost Breaker* (1922). (TOP RIGHT) Tom Mix, enormously popular cowboy star, hired George as an assistant cameraman. (BOTTOM LEFT) Richard Dix, arranged many auditions for George. (BOTTOM RIGHT) Western actor Art Accord.

"Tom looked me over," explained George, "and with a rather long face, explained that his own unit was pretty crowded, but he would see what he could do with some other unit."

Another cameraman was promoted to taking still pictures, and George got a chance to operate a camera and assist with every type of grunt work imaginable. He buckled down and tried to earn their esteem, carrying cameras and doing whatever they told him. At night, he went into the laboratory and dove into the mysteries of film developing. At other times, he was allowed to crank a Pathe camera filming additional angles during dangerous stunts.

"The cameramen were really wonderful," he recalled in an article in *American Cinematographer*. "They apparently liked me and gave me all the advice in the world, with the result that I eventually became a regular assistant and found myself being allowed sometimes to crank the camera myself. It was here that Dan Clark and I formed a remarkable friendship. Dan, at that time, was getting $25 a week. I was getting $15. Between us, we didn't have much, so we decided to get a room together at the Y.M.C.A. The room cost us $11 a month. It had two army cots and one small rug. As the floor was concrete the rug was a nice thing in the morning when you stepped out of bed. We used to toss the rug across the floor as soon as we had finished with it so the other fellow could use it to step on. Dan and I had one topcoat between us. And when I went out on a cool night and had announced my going early, I wore the coat and Dan stayed home, or was cold. We shared the neckties the same way. When we both had to go out the same night, one wore the coat, the other the good necktie."

George also became good friends with Charles Gebhart, a rugged army veteran, who was a stuntman and a double for Tom Mix. While George was working on the Tom Mix lot, Dan Clark was promoted from Assistant Cameraman to shooting stills, and George got the assistant cameraman job. Tom began production on *Just Tony*, an action-packed film built around Tom and his famous horse. When the company moved to locations in and around San Francisco, horses from the local city police corrals were recruited for a few days. The Western star liked George's outgoing personality and gung ho athleticism. He let George play small, extra parts.

"I never was a stuntman with Mix like Charley Gebhart was, but was good enough to play tough-guy parts and play Indian parts, that sort of thing, and make good death falls when shot," George thought back. "I got banged up several times, but nothing serious. I learned to ride horses and this later came in handy when I also became a Western star."

When the *Just Tony* unit moved back to Mixville, George returned to extra work, hauling cameras, and any odd jobs needed behind the scenes. For a year, he was a second cameraman for Tom, lugging a 95-pound Pathé camera around, and on some occasions when more than one camera was needed for an especially important or difficult scene, he

The production crew of the Tom Mix film, *Just Tony* (1922). Assistant cameraman, George O'Brien, center.

was allowed to operate it. He also closely observed and learned the filmmaking trade.

In a letter to Buck Rainey, he told of the military-style organization of the Mix production team. "Every department in Tom's company was organized, and a Number One Boss, or Foreman, or Honcho gave his crew their orders, which came down directly from Tom Mix or the director . . . we assistants were all learning the business in those days . . . a great opportunity, hard work physically, but years later when I had my own company, the knowledge and experience was most valuable."

George O'Brien, center with back to camera, and Tom Mix, far right, are setting up a shot for one of his cowboy films.

One event during his work with Mix stood out vividly in his memory. While serving as a cameraman on a film shooting in Prescott, Arizona, he was helping on a steer-riding scene that involved a cowboy jumping onto a horned steer while the animal dashed from a chute. Cameras were set, and he expected the animal would run out in a straight line. Instead, it wheeled sharply and charged directly at the camera George was cranking. He dropped the camera when the steer was six feet from his face and dove to one side, intending to side step like a bullfighter. In turning to avoid the steer, he fell directly in its path. The steer's hooves just missed his head and completely demolished the camera he had been operating.

George and Dan took full advantage of the food line provided by the studio. Tom always had a chuck wagon on their daily locations, and the two ate bountifully from the tremendous, noontime free meals. To save money, they ate a light supper.

Among those aspiring filmmakers was Lewis Milestone. He bunked with George and Dan at their rooms at the Y.M.C.A., as did

Tom Mix with Daniel O'Brien ca. late 1920s.
PHOTO COURTESY OF THE DARCY O'BRIEN ESTATE.

Richard Wallace. After two years, Fox gave George a raise of five dollars a week, and he was then able to move from the Y.M.C.A. to a slightly better place.

"I had a little corner room in a boarding-house, one of those places where you stand in line for your turn at the tub and grab at the word 'go' when the food is put on the table," George remembered. "I got along for the next two years without sending home for money, and at the end of the twenty-fourth month, was being paid $20 a week. I quit, disgusted...."

He left the Mix company, and for $35 a week, briefly went to Mexico to work with cowboy star Art Accord, but at the end of the third week, the company went broke and George was out of a job. He was almost penniless, but he got into a dice game with a couple of other boys and won enough money to catch a day train to San Francisco.

"After a while I decided that I would not make a good cameraman, anyway," George told John Parker. "All that time I had been working, I had been watching the actors and directors, and my heart lay in that direction, but I suddenly packed up and went back to 'Frisco, intending to go to sea."

He went to work as a deckhand on the *Wilhelmina*, sailing to the South Seas for a six-month stint. Then, he returned to once again look for an opportunity in film work, but found that the film capital was anything but glad to see him return. Opportunities were few, and he again became discouraged. His ambitions were thwarted, his hopes shattered, and out of it all sprang a dogged determination to sail away to the South Seas. He gave up on ever making a career in motion pictures.

George signed on as a seaman with the crew *The Raven*, a weather-beaten schooner. While waiting for the ship to leave port, he sat broodingly on a packing box on the San Francisco wharf alongside of which *The Raven* rose and sank slowly with the rolling waters. In his meditations was the unhappy memory of his failure to break through the barriers that surrounded Hollywood. He was unsure if he would ever return. He was ready to sail, and his eyes slowly scanned the horizon, peering intently over an endless expanse of blue-green sea.

Excited voices suddenly shouted him out of his daydreams. He looked up to see a melee of men in a fistfight, and he strolled over to get a closer look. Then, someone yelled for him to get out of the way. George turned and found that he was looking right into the lens of a motion picture camera while an irate cameraman gesticulated wildly and hurled epithets that turned the air blue. Nearby, film star Hobart Bosworth supervised the making of this waterfront scene. George did not realize until that moment that he had wandered into the middle of a staged, movie fistfight.

Since 1908, Hobart Bosworth had been a pioneering film producer, writer, director, and popular, veteran star of action and adventure films. On that day, he was working on his ninety-fourth film, a seafaring picture called *White Hands*. George had known him for some time, having crossed paths with him while they were on the Fox lot.

"Why the sea-faring get-up, George?" asked Hobart. "Working on a picture?"

"I'm shipping for Honolulu."

Hobart did not ask any more questions. George's downcast expression told him everything. The star realized that he was facing a young man who had given up on the movies.

"Get in there and show those birds how to fight," Hobart ordered. "This picture will last three weeks."

George went into action, joining the melee with the sort of action for which he had made a name for himself. *The Raven* sailed without him, and after three weeks, he had earned a small bankroll.

Hobart had also cast him in bit part in *White Hands* as a fighting sailor, paying him $7 a week and a daily box lunch. In another scene, George earned an extra $12 playing a shark. He wore a black covering with a tin shark's fin mounted on his back, and then swam around under water with only the fin exposed and pulled down the villain, played by Robert McKim. When the picture was finished shooting, he was again out of work.

George was only one of many young men trying to get into the movies. In 1921, after eight years of struggle to get a foothold in motion pictures, the young man who sailed from Italy to America in 1913 had changed his name to Rudolph Valentino and finally scored his breakthrough role in *The Four Horsemen of the Apocalypse. Uncharted Seas, The Conquering Power, Camille,* and *The Sheik* followed in quick succession that same year, placing him in the fore-

The dramatic change in Rudolph Valentino (LEFT) at age 13 when he came to America, and (RIGHT) eight years later in Hollywood as a top star of silent films.

front of the new male stars and creating an unprecedented furor of passionate idolatry among female fans.

In 1922, production began on the first of four films Valentino was to make, *Moran of the Lady Letty*. He appeared as the scion of a noble Spanish family, a petted society favorite. Shanghaied above a vessel, he proves beneath his lavender kid exterior he is a real man. In the end, he even conquers the intrepid Moran and wins her heart. In this role, Valentino's robust qualities were brought forward with splendid effect.

The company faced many difficulties producing that film. Fighting on the foretop of the schooner with the vessel rolling and pitching and the mast swaying was no easy task. The scenes were filmed in San Francisco Bay, the original locale of the novel by Frank Norris, and the director expected to return with a finished film in three weeks. Instead, they were in the Bay City more than five weeks just making the exteriors.

Many scenes were taken aboard two schooners, a three-masted ship and a four-masted ship. Towing these vessels took four to five hours. In the morning as they were going out to sea, the tide was coming in; in the evening as they turned the noses of the ships homeward, the tide was going out. It was necessary to buck the tides on both trips, which accounted for the extreme time delays. Then, when they got out to sea, if Dorothy Dalton or William Marshall were not seasick, a few of highly dramatic scenes were film. Due to these hardships, the five-week adventure tested everyone's resolve.

For the story climax, Walter Long, playing the captain of the hell-ship, and Valentino were at least sixty feet above the deck engaged in a fight that continued up the rigging until they reached the foretop. From there, they fought on out to the end of a spar. After a final struggle, the villain dropped into the ocean. Not willing to risk dropping Walter Long sixty feet into the sea, a daring stuntman was needed for the dangerous dive. Director George Melford had given George a small role in the film as a sailor, and he was picked to double for Valentino in other shots. When the risk of throwing Walter Long into the ocean loomed, George volunteered for the treacherous stunt dive.

After filming Long taking the final punch, the camera stopped, and George took his place. A camera was lashed to another spar, and George fell the sixty feet into the ocean for the spectacular end to the climactic fight.

In *Moran of the Lady Letty*, George is also seen in the early shots at the beginning of the film strolling around on the deck of the ship with a masculine swagger, and wearing shirtsleeves rolled high enough to show his prominent biceps. He is in another close shot lounging around happily on the deck, and later in a fire sequence, he is visible beating out the flames of the doomed ship. In these fleeting moments, a future star was born. Some audiencs members noticed the unusually handsome sailor, and they wrote to write to the studio about him.

"Then the real fun began," George reminisced. "I haunted the casting offices without success—weeks passed—broke—hungry—a job now and then as a cowboy—a prehistoric man with a hatchet—the owner of a Tux in a café scene—and then, I began doubling, and eating with regularity though at the risk of my neck. Another year rolled by . . . ."

His apprenticeship was thorough. He learned from watching the stars work. He was a furtive figure in a Limehouse street scene in one film, one of the denizens of a Long Island party in another film, and an idolatrous reveler in the orgy scene in Cecil B. DeMille's *The Ten Commandments*. In another DeMille film, *Manslaughter*, he can be seen as a man in a leopard skin carrying one lady on his shoulder and dragging another by the hair. Audiences barely saw him in the Lila Lee film, *Is Matrimony a Failure?* As the Apache with the black beard in a nightclub scene for the Pola Negri film, *Shadows of Paris*, he finally had a few moments up close to the camera.

"These were small, little bits, so small that if you closed your eyes for a moment you would miss me, but it was enough to pay the room and buy food, you see," George explained. "We were all very bohemian in those days...."

Some days he worked, but many days he did not. When the idle intervals became alarming in duration, he was not above laboring on the studio lot as a lumber hauler, prop boy, or sixth-assistant electrician. Officially an actor, he had little difficulty in finding odd jobs around the studio. To hire him was economy, and production managers enjoyed seeing him run cheerfully about with props tucked lightly under his arm, work that would have normally required two men to accomplish.

"Well, from then on I was determined to be an actor," he told John Parker, "but there were times when I wondered if it would ever pay me to spend the best part of my life wandering around Hollywood waiting for a job. Jobs came here and there as an extra, and finally I became a $25-a-day man doing bits and small parts that required riding and athletic ability."

Few chances came for him to be in front of the camera. Modest and unaware of how good-looking he was in the opinion of others, the truth only surfaced when he met a famous star that did not hesitate to show outright enthusiasm for the impact he made on people.

Actor Richard Dix, a star making scenes for *The Woman With Four Faces* with Betty Compson, received a letter from Daniel O'Brien inviting him to a party he got up for the cast and crew.

Dix recalled to Helen Klumph, a writer for *Picture-Play*, "We met George there, and Herb Brenon was so impressed with him he told him we would try him out in pictures if he would come to Hollywood. George came to Hollywood all right, but he was too shy to look up Brenon and remind him of his promise. I ran into him at the Athletic Club where I was working out—ran into him is right. He nearly knocked me out. You know, I'm no modest violet about my boxing. I wouldn't be afraid to take on any of the Tearles or Dennys or other athletes in this business, but deliver me from George. After once meeting his fist, you never forget it. He's got the finest build of any man in the business. He reminds me of Wallace Reid when he played as the fighting blacksmith in *The Birth of a Nation*. And he is always in training. I used to argue with George trying to get him to go to Brenon, but he wouldn't do it. Instead, he hung around Hollywood getting extra work whenever he could. Finally, I went to Brenon about him myself, and he gave George what chance he could. Of course, as luck would have it, he was making a picture that didn't have a single bit in it that George could play. But George worked pretty regularly as an extra out at the Lasky lot, after that and got some good experience. It was a rotten waste of talent, though. He should have been playing parts. Why, he was one of the extras in *The Ten Commandments*, running around during the Worship of the Golden Calf carrying a 200-pound ingénue. He was so good looking that they were afraid he would distract attention from some of the principals, so they put whiskers on him."

Richard Dix felt sure that George would impress the producers of *Ben-Hur*. In 1922, the Goldwyn Company purchased the motion picture rights to film the popular stage success in an unprecedented arrangement involving a percentage of profit rather than money up front. The play had already been a huge success for years, and once the film rights were secured, Samuel Goldwyn settled into the challenge of adapting the story into silent motion pictures. A massive hunt took place to find the perfect actor for the once-in-a-lifetime role of Ben-Hur. Nearly every actor in Hollywood tested for the role, including George, and he was a serious contender. With his finely honed physique, he had the robust good looks required, and he spent about eight hours one day testing for the title role.

"I went out there," George remembered. "Everyone was most enthusiastic. I had been out on the beach and had a good tan, and obviously, I looked like what I hoped they thought Ben-Hur would look like. So they all told me, as far as they were concerned, I could have it. I came back again for some other tests in scenes for *Ben-Hur*. On the third day, I got the terrible news. Both Miss Mathis and Mr. Hogan said, 'George, we're both terribly disappointed. We believe that you're absolutely it.' I said, 'Well, thank you very much!' But they wanted a name. If they can, they want to get Rudolph Valentino, if they can get him.'"

(TOP) George Walsh was MGM's first choice to play the title role in *Ben-Hur* opposite Francis X. Bushman as Messala. Walsh was replaced by (BOTTOM) Ramon Novarro in the title role, and Francis X. Bushman retained as Messala.

George O'Brien, ca. 1920s.

"I felt sure that George would get the part of *Ben-Hur*," Richard Dix later recalled. "He was obviously ideal for it. George not only had his wonderful build, but he had great charm and a lot of character in his face. The day they made tests of him out at Goldwyn, there wasn't anybody there to show him how to make-up. He probably looked like an Indian chief or the victim of some strange disease."

Goldwyn was hoping for someone who also had delicate acting

skills and proven experience. George lost the role to George Walsh, another actor who was similar to him in physique and temperament, but also had a long list of film credits to his name.

Losing the coveted role in *Ben-Hur* proved to be a blessing in disguise. Cast and crew moved to Italy, where director Fred Niblo struggled with an inability to communicate with Italian workers building sets. Further frustrations mounted for him, as political turmoil fomented within rival factions of the local citizens. As a result, construction of the ships on which to stage the sea battles stretched from weeks to months. George Walsh waited idly for nearly an entire year without ever filming any scenes. The production experienced additional, unheard-of delays and ran up millions of dollars in expenses without creating much useable film. By all accounts, *Ben-Hur* was shaping up to be a collasal disaster.

George O'Brien could not have anticipated the unmanageable debacle. When Metro merged with Goldwyn, the year-long production was recalled from Italy back to California where the watchful eye of Irving Thalberg and the MGM executives could shepherd the expensive epic to completion. With the change of studio management, George Walsh was replaced with Ramon Novarro, a protégé of Louis B. Mayer.

Ramon recalled the experience in an interview with Margaret Chute. "It was a great chance; a wonderful thing for me," he said. "And yet—it was bad. It kept me off the screen for practically two years; and two years is a long time. The public forgets so soon. There are ways, I suppose, of keeping oneself in front of the public, but I don't believe in them. I think a man should be judged by his work; I believe that his private life is sacred. To me, such a thing as a personal appearance is terrible; it must be avoided."

George was so disappointed in failing to obtain the role in *Ben-Hur* that he was ready to give up on film work. The failure capped what had been years of struggle to gain a foothold in the industry, and he finally believed that he would never get a real chance at a meaty role. His friends, Ricardo Cortez and Richard Dix, worked out with him at their gym, and they pleaded with him not to give up. They reminded him of all the cases they had known where a sudden break brought a man to prominence. Finally, Dix bet George $100 that he would be a popular film star within one year.

"He had about made up his mind to go back to San Francisco and join his father's police force or work for his brother," Dix thought back, "but he finally said he'd risk my bet."

George appeared in a series of small parts in quick succession. He appeared with his real-life roommates, Mervyn LeRoy and Richard Arlen, as one of four sheet-covered ghosts in *The Ghost Breaker*, a film starring Wallace Reid, the most popular leading man in the movies.

"Wallace Reid had inherited his father's gift for storytelling, had a keen sense of humor, a good singing voice, played the saxophone and piano, and was altogether the most magnetic, charming, personable, handsome young man I've ever met. And the most co-operative," wrote Jesse Lasky in his book, *I Blow My Own Horn*.

George found his small role in *The Ghost Breaker* a great experience. Associating with the most popular leading man in films was fortunate, although George went unseen by audiences. As a "ghost," he was covered with a sheet.

On New Year's Eve 1922, George sailed to Panama with Thomas Meighan to work on *The Ne'er-do-Well*. While filming in Panama, someone was needed to fly in an airplane over Culebra Cut with an Army pilot and stage a recreation of a man falling from the cockpit to his death. A dummy was to be thrown from the plane from a thousand feet high, and the cameramen below were to capture its plunge. George volunteered. He was strapped into the seat, and then the plane ascended to a thousand feet. At the appropriate moment, George leaned over to drop the dummy, but the seat belt broke and he slipped over the edge. He was about to plunge into the wind, but he desperately managed to grab the side of the plane and pull himself back into the seat. When he reached ground, he commented, "You nearly had two dummies to pick up!"

While making *Thirty Days*, his last film for Lasky, Wallace Reid was barely able to stand, let alone act. Cecil B. DeMille remembered many years later the brave determination in Wallace's voice just before he entered a sanitarium for the last time. "I'll either come out cured," the heroic man said, "or I won't come out at all. He was under treatment for more than a month, attended by Dr. G. S. Herbert. As the weeks passed, his normal weight of 185 pounds had reduced to 135 pounds. His personal descent into the secret agony of morphine addiction was accidental and born at the insistence of the film producers, who initially plied him with the drugs to keep film production moving after he suffered an injury while making a film. On January 18, 1923 while George O'Brien was busy making *The Ne'er-do-Well*, Wallace Reid died at the age of thirty-one in the arms of his wife while trying to beat the grip of morphine addiction. The public understood the tragedy of his decline, and wept all the more because of the unfortunate circumstances. After his death, they still thought he was the most magnetic, charming, personable, and handsome young man in the movies.

They cast and crew of *The Ne'er-do-Well* returned to New York in the winter of 1923. Later that year, George had a bit part in *Woman Proof*, another Thomas Meighan film. Meighan, a tall, handsome Irishman like George, had also studied medicine, but at an early age, he decided the stage offered a more promising career. He had been on the stage before he was twenty in London and America, and he had scored a personal triumph in 1919 in the film, *The Miracle Man*.

When the spotlight on Wallace Reid dimmed, the beam began to move toward George.

Chapter 4
Iron Wills and Iron Horses

In 1924, while the film industry and the public reeled over the death of Wallace Reid, George tested for the lead role in *The Leather Pushers*. His friend, Ricardo Cortez, joined him in a boxing exhibition for the screen test. In a later interview with Leonard Maltin, George recalled, "When we got the report from the studio, the man in charge, who I assume didn't know too much about boxing and probably very little about *The Leather Pushers*, told me that he thought it was very good, but what they wanted was an actor who could look like a boxer, and not a boxer who could look like an actor."

Richard Dix recalled in another interview with Dorothy Herzog, "George had tried to get the job Reginald Denny vacated in the *Leather Pushers* series when Denny was made a star. He didn't get a look-in because he wasn't considered photographic material! I was working in *The Stranger* on the Lasky lot, when George dropped around to the set and announced he figured he was a flop and was going to give up pictures. He was discouraged. After all, he had been an extra for three years, and it looked as though that was as far as he would get."

While George was doggedly playing what small parts he could obtain, as well as working as prop boy, stunt man, stand-in, assistant cameraman, and extra, director John Ford had been busy establishing himself as a quietly competent director of Westerns for Universal. Although the New York critics virtually ignored his unpretentious program films, *Cameo Kirby, Kentucky Pride,* and *The Shamrock Handicap,* among others, he kept cranking them out in a hectic schedule. He managed to instill some notable touches of originality in his work, and as the film industry grew, he was able to entertain offers from other studios.

From modest earnings in 1917 of $125 a week, Ford had increased his earnings to $300 a week in 1919. When William Fox signed him in 1921, his salary rose to $13,618 a week. By 1922, he was earning $27,891 a week and he was a vital part of Fox's aim to establish his studio on equal footing with Adolph Zukor and Paramount.

When Ford arrived on the Fox lot, Buck Jones and Tom Mix, the studio's two biggest Western stars, were cresting at the height of their careers. In 1923, *The Covered Wagon* was an unexpected blockbuster for Paramount. Audiences and critics alike were impressed by the scope of its story, and the film provoked a great interest in Western epics.

William Fox wanted to top *The Covered Wagon* with an epic Western of his own. The building of the Pacific Railroad connecting the eastern half of America with its western half was a story of incredible engineering and pioneering spirit unequalled among historians. Ford had amassed considerable experience directing, and his youth had been filled with stories from his uncle about the workings of the transcontinental railroad. His imagination was already fired, and in August 1924, after the release of his fifteenth film, he was gnawing to be taken more seriously as a director. Fox agreed that he was the best choice to make a film of the historic story.

The Iron Horse was the title given to the proposed movie of the building of the transcontinental railroad, the epic event that rendered wagon trains obsolete and sped the development of the west. Ford tested fifty-eight actors for the lead role, but remained unsatisfied. When George was asked to report for a test, he met Ford, and the two of them proved to be a good match.

"How about taking the test today?" Ford suggested. "You haven't got a chance, you know that, George," said the crusty director, as they headed to the camera set-up.

"Yes, I know," George replied. After three years of trying, he planned to give himself only six more months to make good, and then if his hoped-for career failed to develop, he was going to move on to another kind of work.

"You mustn't set your heart on it," Ford continued kindly. "You know, we've tried out about fifty fellows, all experienced actors."

"Yes, I know."

Years later, he told Harry Brundidge, "Jack Ford told me I looked like a sheik, and asked me if I could muss my hair. I did, and then made a love scene screen test with Gertrude Olmstead."

With Gertrude, he improvised a short love scene impersonating a man with only five-minutes to say goodbye to the girl he loved. After the test was sent to Fox's New York office, word came back to Ford: the young actor looked good enough to try an additional test. The Fox executives veiled their comments with doubt. They were unsure about whether to trust such an important role in their proposed epic to a relative beginner.

"Well, we'll kill him or cure him in the first scene," said Ford. "If he gets through the first day, he'll do."

"So I went on going about my work," George later told Leonard Maltin, "looking for extra work or stunts, came back about three months later, and I figured they must have forgotten me. I was number 59 of the actors he'd tested. Then, another call came to come down."

Ford shot a second test of George in a fight scene with Fred Kohler, and included some footage of him vaulting onto a horse. At the moment he hit the saddle, the cinch broke, sending George sprawling into the dust. To Ford's delight, he bounced up unhurt and was eager for more action. As far as Ford was concerned, George had the role, but the final decision rested with the Fox executives.

While waiting to learn if he had the part, George had to earn a living. He took an extra job as one of the galley slaves in the Milton Sills epic, *The Sea Hawk*. Directed by Frank Lloyd, the ambitious production was an expensive, handsomely mounted epic of the sea. Two gigantic vessels, replicas of 16th century pirate ships authentic in every detail, were employed. More than a thousand sailors, galley slaves, corsairs, and officers managed the ships. Several sea battles were staged with the pirate ships ramming each other head-on and lashing themselves together to engage the sailors in hand-to-hand battle.

Although George is indistinguishable in the film, he reveled in his role as one of the galley slaves, later commenting to Leonard Maltin, "It was a wonderful job in Catalina a few months earning ten dollars a day and all you could eat, all the time watching behind the camera, because I really wanted to be a director. I came back from Catalina, and Frank Lloyd and the rest of the company were going to do some

George O'Brien while filming John Ford's *The Iron Horse* (1924).

interiors, then they were going to pick us up again. In other words, we were off salary, but they still had us signed for the job. So I went home to our little house, where Mervyn LeRoy and I were renting a room from a nice man and his wife; Gary Cooper was living there. I walked in the door, and Mervyn yelled at me, 'George, quick! Fox wants you!' So, I got on the phone, with a very nice gentleman from the casting office, Jim Ryan. He said, 'George, I've been trying to reach you. Hurry up down here. Have you seen Ford?' I said no. I went down to Ryan's office and he took me to Ford's office."

"Have you talked to Mr. Wurtzel?" asked Ford, as he stood up.

"No."

Ford took him to Sol Wurtzel's office and read him a five-page letter from William Fox that said to sign him for five years with a six-month option. He warned Ford this plan was entirely untried, and he still felt concerned about employing a new, unknown actor in a major role. He said Ford would be forced to film ninety takes of each scene if necessary.

Had George O'Brien won the title role in *Ben-Hur*, he would have missed the opportunity to work with John Ford in *The Iron Horse*. He also would have lost the *Ben-Hur* role to Ramon Novarro, as happened to George Walsh, and the O'Brien career might never have happened.

The Iron Horse started with George in the leading man role and Madge Bellamy and Gladys Hulette playing the two feminine leads. The entire cast and crew spent many months together on arduous locations.

George and Ford quickly became close friends. They were united by their religion, love of the sea, and their heritage. The director insisted on authentic atmosphere, and he required the actors to live like pioneers among the elements in Mexico. Filming began with nothing but a small crew photographing cattle herds roaming from dawn to dusk, footage to be later cut into the finished film.

From there, the production moved to New Mexico and a location in Dodge, Nevada. The 300 people in the film company lived in compartments of a train rented from the Al G. Barnes circus. The train was parked on railroad tracks lying adjacent to the track that served for the story. A circus tent was erected to provide a makeshift mess hall. Conditions worsened when snow fell on the area, blanketing the outdoor sets and train tracks in immobilizing, frozen

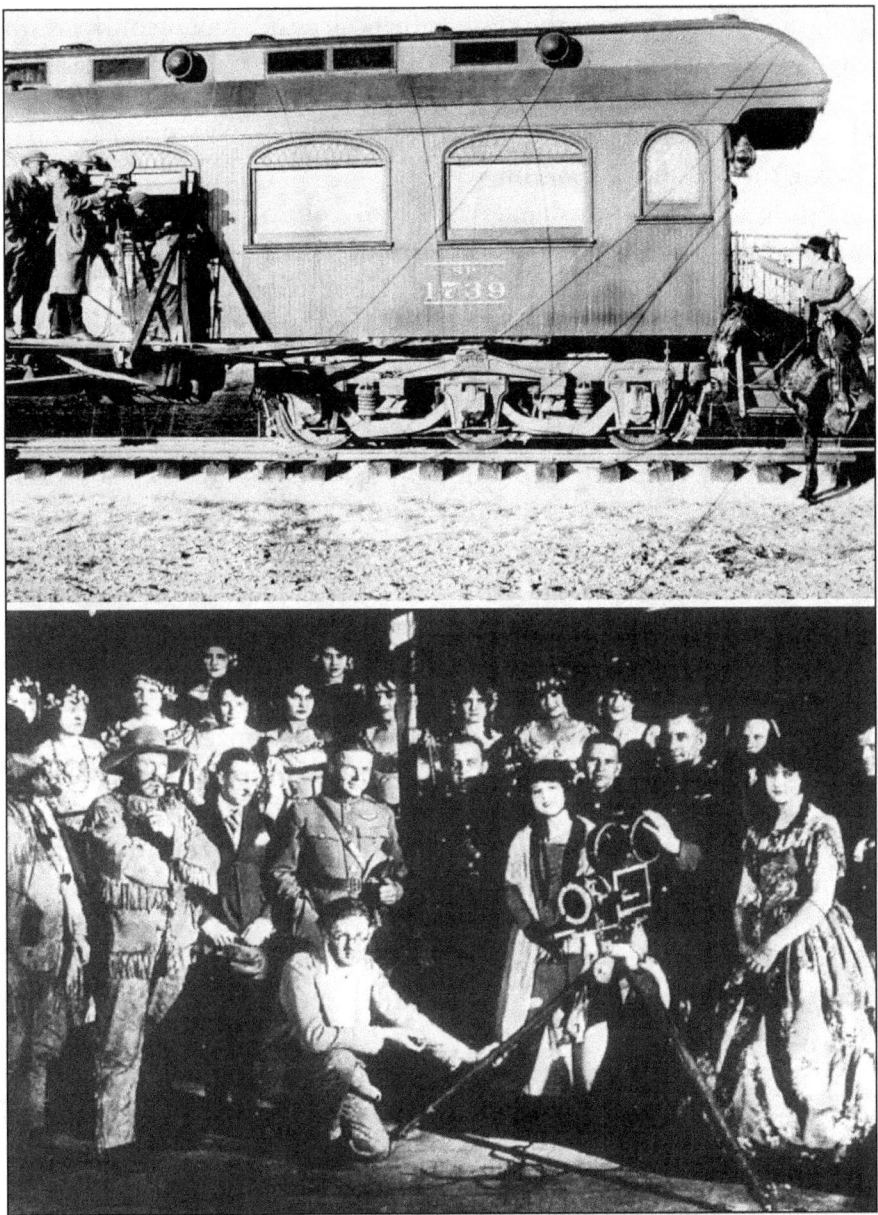

(TOP) *The Iron Horse* (1924) filming a difficult camera set-up. (BOTTOM) Director John Ford with some cast members of the film, *The Iron Horse* (1924).
PHOTO COURTESY OF THE DARCY O'BRIEN ESTATE.

drifts. Actors were oblidged to perform in the freezing temperatures, and after a day's work, return to sparse accommodations that were little better than the outdoors. Outhouses were set up behind the sets and some distance from the train. The boiler tank on one of the train engines supplied hot water. The deadly conditions began to take a toll on everyone involved in the production. One member of the crew, a circus steward named Kelly, died from pneumonia in a Reno hospital during the making of the film.

While shooting continued, fights broke out between Ford and his brother Eddie. During one argument over Ford's use of live ammunition in a scene, the two threw punches inside a train car. George was nearby when the altercation erupted, and he tried to come between the battling brothers. In the melee, an alarm clock was thrown, shattering glass and parts over the floor and injuring J. Farrell MacDonald, as he also tried to stop the fight.

While *The Iron Horse* crew fought against the weather and each other, Charlie Chaplin was nearby just over the California border in the town of Truckee. He was shooting scenes for *The Gold Rush*, his comedy about gold prospectors snowbound in the Sierra Nevada Mountains. Eddie Sutherland, Chaplin's assistant director, met Ford on a break, and after a night spent drinking, they removed all the furniture from Chaplin's room at the Summit Hotel, replacing the furniture with empty liquor bottles. After disappearing for several days, George and others from *The Iron Horse* crew found the two men drunk and asleep in a boxcar with a gang of Irish extras.

The Iron Horse production also experienced unscheduled accidents during a buffalo stampede. Camera operator Arthur Lund, positioned in a pit with a camera poised to record spectacular low-angle shots, barely survived when a buffalo tripped on a wood plank over his head and crashed to the ground with such force that the the animal was killed.

After several months of tedium, freezing temperatures, rough terrain, and difficult weather, the cast and crew wore down, but Ford still had to stage the climactic scene of the driving of the Golden Spike, a grand finale linking the two locomotives on the tracks running between the Atlantic and Pacific coasts. Once he completed photography, and the cast and crew disbanded to return to their former lives, final production costs mounted to about $250,000.

Publicity drums began to beat even as the film was being edited. Billboards were erected in New York with teaser ads, and ballyhoo mounted in anticipation of the film's premier long before its release.

When the film did premier in New York on August 28, 1924, public and critical reception was immense. A reviewer from the *New York Times* was at the Lyric Theater with the prominent representatives from the film and railroad worlds. The following day, he wrote:

> "Gray-haired men, whose fathers had constructed railroads in the pioneer days, were much moved by the spectacle in shadows that passed before their eyes. And some of them wept, not so much at the story interspersing this gigantic accomplishment of the '60s as the sight of the men working with sledge hammers on the spike nails, as tie after tie and rail after rail were laid down. They wept also when they saw the slow moving old engine with its ungainly funnel, which to the folk of the olden days, ran so smoothly on its quickly constructed path of iron. Sometimes, people in the audience wondered why cattle figured so often in the picture, forgetting that these railroad builders had to eat. One is also impressed by the fact that in every halt of any consequence, they founded towns as they went along, and usually the first sign painted was that for a saloon. Of the many scenes which drew applause last night, were those on the desert, where hosts of men were scampering along with a will in laying their ties, while others equally handy wielded their sledge hammers and riveted the rails to the wood. It looked like a slow job even if it were merely a score of miles, but to realize the immense distance that had to be covered almost made one cover one's eyes with one's hands."

Advertising for the film proclaimed:

> "FROM THE LAND OF ROMANCE
> COMES THE GEORGE O'BRIEN SMILE
> THAT IS SPREADING THE SPIRIT OF HAPPINESS OVER SEVEN SEAS!
> SEE THE O'BRIEN SMILE IN *THE IRON HORSE*!"

The Iron Horse played for about a year in New York as a "roadshow" special presentation, and many critics proclaimed the film a masterpiece. It was shown in a special process that enlarged the screen image. William Fox thought the public reception from the rest of the country would score the much-anticipated success he so desired. He astutely saw that Ford was signed to a new contract, upping his salary to $1,500 a week with increases over a three and one-half year period to $2,250 a week. For George, public reception was frenzied. He attracted legions of fans, and many of them became lifelong admirers that followed his career for the next thirty years.

The Iron Horse premiered in Los Angeles on February 21, 1925 at Grauman's Egyptian Theater. Although director Ford skipped the New York premier, he attended the Los Angeles opening and participated in ceremonies staged with Colonel Tim McCoy, parading twenty-five Shoshone and Arapaho Indians in a prologue, recreating war dances, and enacting several scenes from the movie.

His mother and father came down to Los Angeles to see the opening of the picture. After the last scene had shown on the screen, George turned anxiously to his mother.

"Well, Mom," he asked, "how was I?"

"You were splendid, George," she said placidly, "I'm proud of you, son, but—my favorite movie actor is still Tommy Meighan!"

"Obviously," George later said, "I was good enough in my part in the film, because it not only launched my screen career, but got me a ten-year contract with Fox, as well. I remained with that studio most of my career."

"I saw the opening in New York," remembered Richard Dix. "The next day, I clipped the reviews and sent them to George. He wired me back: 'I owe you ten bucks.'"

Chapter 5
FIG LEAVES

After the release of *The Iron Horse*, George scaled the ladder of fame almost overnight in one mighty bound and landed solidly at the top. Everyone liked the big, genial young man with the Irish grin. In fact, George was about the only person in Hollywood who was not aware that he had arrived at a career height undreamed-of by most actors.

"He's not a sheik or a cave man or a lounge lizard—he's a man's man and an idol of women!" proclaimed advertising copy released from the Fox publicity department.

While *The Iron Horse* ran in New York, Fox knew they had a potential star in the making. They chose a powerful, dramatic story for his second starring appearance, a role that reminded many of the recent Wallace Reid tragedy. George played Henry Potter in the title role of the film version of Jules Eckert Goodman's play, *The Man Who Came Back*, a story about a young man's struggle with alcohol and drug abuse. In that serious and sordid story, George went to incredible lengths to create a realistic characterization.

"Emmett J. Flynn, the director, thought I did not look like an emaciated alcoholic, you know, a man who goes down the pipe," George explained, "and he was quite honest about this. I would have said the same thing."

Although Flynn did not initially want George for the role, Fox reminded the director that George was box office and the film had already been pre-sold to exhibitors, so he had to use him. George responded by taking dangerous steps to insure that he convincingly looked the part.

"I quit eating for six weeks before the picture started," he recalled, "with the exception of tea and toast, or tea and cookies once a day. I almost dehydrated myself. What make-up did for other actors, nature did to me. At the end of the picture, I was so weak! Oh, I boxed every day, too. I sweat myself out. A lightweight boxer just bumped me one day and I fell to my knees. On top of that, I broke out with a horrible skin infection. My condition was so low that something in the bottles we were using to make believe that it was liquor on the set were dirty or something, and I caught a cold, and I really wasn't acting. I was down so far. Well, it did the trick. I got terrific notices."

His performance won great praise around the world. In Germany, F. W. Murnau watched a screening of the film, and he thought of George for a story he was planning. The director knew he had to take a giant leap to gain access to a prominent American actor under contract to a leading Hollywood studio. Murnau began to think of a way to achieve his dream.

Dorothy Mackaill, a blonde beauty who went from the Ziegfeld Follies to Hollywood, was a gorgeous 1924 Wampas Star, a title bestowed on a bevy of beauties each year who were earmarked for future film success. She made her first picture, *Torchy*, in 1920, and by 1924, was a veteran of eighteen films. In *The Man Who Came Back*, she was paired opposite George in his second starring role, and as quickly as that effort was completed, the two immediately made their next film together in the remaining months of 1924.

The Painted Lady, a romantic melodrama, put George opposite Dorothy Mackaill as a character named Luther Smith. In the story, Mackaill, playing a woman of easy virtue, meets up with George on a South Sea island cruise and finds redemption in his love.

In the same film, Flo Ash, an infamous exotic dancer, performed a sanitized version of her renowned fan dance, a risqué display she had performed for some time. For years after the release of the film, she capitalized on her screen appearance by noting in advertisements for nightclub appearances that she was doing the fan dance "as seen in *The Painted Lady*."

George's popularity increased rapidly. The studio tended to capitalize whenever possible on his athletic prowess, and his physique was often displayed for no other reason than to show off his body. He was

Max Mun Autry physique portrait of George O'Brien, ca. 1920s.

flooded with fan mail, especially from youngsters who wanted to know how they could build a physique like his.

"It got so bad I had to make a form letter to answer such requests," he later told writer, Lew Pike. "I would tell these zealous correspondents that I couldn't suggest how to build their bodies unless I know more about them, and I advised them to visit a gym and seek a competent instructor."

George deliberately fanned the flame of interest in his physique. Along with Tom Tyler, George Walsh, Norman Kerry, and Douglas Fairbanks, he was one of several prominent screen players who were athletes in their own right. George had the physical build of a Greek Hercules, the lithe grace of a dancing master, and the hitting power of a Missouri mule. He was one of the few motion picture actors holding a membership card in the American Athletic Union. His record was a genuinely impressive one, and he held enough amateur medals to fill a sizable cabinet. He trained with a program as rigorous as any professional athlete, and he enjoyed showing off his physique.

Personally, George was modest, unassuming, shy, and quiet. He still thought of using his boxing prowess, and sought to qualify for the Olympic boxing tournament. The studio hastily stopped him, pointing out that his contract forbad engaging in any hazardous undertaking.

Many reviewers at this time, notably in *Variety* and the *New York Times*, observed the frequent display of his biceps and chest in his films. George also posed for number of photographic portraits that were taken of him in the 1920s that flaunted his muscularity in a manner befitting a Rodin statue. He was posed artistically in the nude throwing a discus, aiming a bow and arrow, and in full-figure with strategically positioned fig leaves attached to his anatomy. These images, though shocking in their time, were widely circulated on postcards and in various magazines. They served to motivate many a young man to aspire to similar physical accomplishments.

"Max Mun Autry and I did those shots over a period of about a week," George explained. "There was a request from the Fox office over in Paris. Somebody wanted these for some gallery. He did these at Fox. Also, when I was at school in Budapest, there was a photographer over there. I spent an entire day doing torso shots. You see, these people demanded these things, and I gave them. The request came, and I did these things, and that was that. We spent hours doing the lighting."

His popularity was partly caused by the circulation of these beefcake nude portraits. He was one of the first, prominent men to pose naked, and those portraits started the male physique portrait wave that ultimately became an industry of its own.

The following year, George was busy turning out four films in a row: *The Dancers, Havoc,* and two more films directed by John Ford, *The Fighting Heart,* also known as *Once to Every Man,* and *Thank You.*

In 1926, *The Roughneck,* also released as *Thorns of Passion,* gave him another opportunity to show off his boxing skills. He insisted on performing his own fighting in the boxing scenes, as well as other dangerous stunt work. The public could always bank on George doing his own stunts, whether rolling over a cliff, falling from a horse, or swinging a heroine from a moving train onto his saddlebow. When his fans heard that he doggedly performed his own stunts, they were amazed.

"Don't you ever get hurt?" asked Bernarr Macfadden from *Physical Culture* magazine in an interview some years later.

"Oh, now and then," George answered. "I've been in the hospital twice from stunts that went wrong. Diving from the top deck of a ship, fifty-five feet high, into the Pacific Ocean. That was in *The Roughneck.* It was understood that in about a half hour a speedboat would pick me up, and that I was to keep out of the way of the picture. If I drowned it would be too bad, of course, but the important thing was to keep out of the picture. They finally got around to picking me up."

"Weren't you afraid of sharks?" asked Macfadden.

"No, I didn't think of that. I'm something of a fatalist," George revealed, "but when I made that dive, I hit the water with such force that I tore off both pants legs and both sleeves out of my shirt. Sometime I'll have to try it in the Atlantic to see if the water there is any softer."

In the film, he was to be saved from drowning by a girl. The actress playing the role told the film's producers she was a good swimmer, but, she could not swim at all. "She didn't want to lose out on the role," George explained to writer Alma Talley, "so she said she was a good swimmer. It wasn't until we got out to Catalina and the scene was about to be made that we found she couldn't swim at all. Oh, just a few strokes, that is. She was supposed to be a South Sea Island girl; she wore tights, to look like no clothes at all, and an enormous wig. Well, as soon as we got in the water, the tights shrank. 'I can't move in these things,' she said. I kept pulling at them trying to stretch them. And then she got a cramp in her leg, and her long wig, when it got wet, kept getting into her eyes and winding itself around her arms. She got pretty scared, and she was supposed to save me!"

George went on to say, "So I told her just to lie flat on my outstretched arm and keep her own arms moving, as if she was swimming, and then I'd take us both in, swimming on my back. It was all right until we got nearly to shore, when she suddenly became panicky and clutched me, and of course, we both went down. Her wig came off and we got tangled up in it; it was all I could do to get us both on land. I'd give her a push—try pushing something through the water some time, and see how much luck you have—and then, I'd swim after her and push her again, and finally we got to land. I was just exhausted, believe me! And when I got there, I was met by a frantic prop man. 'Hey,' he said, 'go back and get that wig. It cost twenty dollars!'"

Also in 1926, while George was making waves in Hollywood, sixteen-year-old Marguerite Churchill achieved her first measure of national prominence. Out of 20,000 Camp Fire Girls, she had been selected for the title of "The Ideal American Girl." Her photo appeared in some national magazines, and she soon received her education in both New York City and in Los Angeles.

Shortly after his initial success with his first starring roles, George began work on *Fig Leaves* with Olive Borden, a Southern girl born in 1907. She first gained attention as a Wampas Star. She signed a long contract with Fox, and then she paired opposite George in two of his best silent films. *Fig Leaves* was her tenth film.

The story of *Fig Leaves* parallels the domestic problems of Adam and Eve with a contemporary couple known as Adam and Eve Smith. For *Fig Leaves*, director Howard Hawks wrote a rough story and then turned it over to two other writers, Hope Loring and Louis D. Lighton, to elaborate it into a screenplay with strong appeal to female audience members.

While shooting progressed, visitors to the Garden of Eden set were shocked to see the weird virgin forest constructed by the Fox designers. Adam and Eve's tree bungalow had a sign in front, "No. 780—No Peddlers Allowed." A crude streetcar track ran nearby, a sort of Stone Age edition of the Toonerville Trolley, with the train drawn by a one-ton brontosaurus. Seven men operated its mechanism with startling realism. George roamed the set wearing a bearskin tunic and a flowing wig that would have shamed Samson. Olive Borden wore a gorgeous leopard skin fur. Much of the action was worked out with improvisation.

"Howard Hawks was more or less getting his footing, or getting his stride, at this time," George recalled. "It was one of the far-out films, but of course the studio was behind it, or they wouldn't have let Hawks make it. But the work that went into the prehistoric scenes! There's one scene where I'm reading the 'newspaper' and Olive Borden is trying to read the ads on the back of it, and I rip the stone in half, terribly annoyed, and give her half. Then, we go out on our way to work and a dinosaur comes by like a subway."

George enjoyed his role and his appearance on the exotic *Fig Leaves* set. "Where else would you find a scene like that?" he asked Scott Pierce from *Motion Picture Classic*, shortly after work on the film completed. "And where else in the civilized world would I get a chance to dress like this and play Adam, without landing in some nice booby-hatch? In pictures, I never know what I'll be doing next. Today, I'm Adam. Next month, I may be playing a lumberjack up in Oregon. The month after that, I may be a prospector over in Arizona. In this game, you never know what's around the next corner. That suits me in every way. I don't even want to know when I get up in the morning what I'm going to do that day. I hate routine. And I never make plans. They take all the kick out of life. I'm glad I've managed to get across in pictures, of course. I worked mighty hard in doing it, and success has brought the same feeling of satisfaction to me that it brings to any normal man who has finally won it after a hard pull upstream. I like the acting and the other things about the game. If I didn't, I wouldn't be in it."

The light sexual sparring in the film was buoyantly handled, and the finished effort perfectly found approval with its intended audience. Silent-era romantic comedies, along with Westerns, were the staples

Fox ad for "Youth in Pictures," appearing in the December 1926 issue of *Photoplay*.

of the film industry, and *Fig Leaves* contained many plot elements that would work their way into future Hawks films: the defining of relationships by sexual role-playing, good-humored give-and-take between men and women, and instances of female impersonation

Photo of George O'Brien. COURTESY OF THE DARCY O'BRIEN ESTATE.

The picture features prehistoric sequences with striking production values and endearingly weaves exaggerated animals into the scenes. The fashion show sequences were planned to entertain female audience members, and lingerie models provided tantalizing glimpses for male audience members. The costumes by Adrian paraded through the extravagant sets in startling two-color Technicolor photography. Advertising copy from the Fox publicity department proclaimed that $50,000 was spent on Borden's costumes alone.

Fig Leaves opened in July 1920 and was such a strong box office draw that it was said to have made back its cost in one theater alone.

At this time, Janet Gaynor, a beautiful young actress, was making her initial foray into films with Fox. Born Laura Augusta Gainor on October 6, 1906, in Philadelphia, Pennsylvania, she grew up in George's hometown and attended high school in San Francisco. Shortly after graduation, she moved to Los Angeles hoping to find work in films. Her life was much like the character she later portrayed in *A Star is Born*, for Janet believed she was destined to be a film star. With no qualifications other than an unshakable dream, she pestered the various film studios for a chance to appear in any role.

After working as an unaccredited extra and bit player in seventeen films, she finally earned a lead part with George in *The Johnstown Flood*. She was signed to a contract with Fox, and the studio was impressed with her beauty and ability to project naïve vulnerability.

For sheer spectacle, *The Johnstown Flood* was on a par with *The Iron Horse*. Many of the special effects were created with clever miniatures, but as George recalled in an article by Joe Collure, the actors were involved in dangerous situations. "As for the flood scenes, they were especially hard on Janet Gaynor, who, soaking wet, is all of ninety pounds. Once, I pulled her out of the water unconscious. I carried her to her dressing room. There was a woman on the set with Janet whom we called Lady Thompson. She and I managed to get Gaynor into a hot shower, clothes and all. Then, I started pulling Janet's dress off, knowing she had on heavy underwear, because the director, Irving Cummings, had warned us it was going to be a cold night and we'd better dress warm."

George went on to explain, "The studio doctor came in while we were trying to bring her around. I told him she had been in the water for three hours and was suffering from a little shock. The doctor looked at me funny and asked if I was prescribing—actually, I am a frustrated medical student. Anyway, after Janet came to, he asked if I wanted a drink of whiskey. I told him, 'No, but some black coffee would be good.' He advised me to get some rest and I went back to the set to report to Cummings on Janet's condition. He asked me how she was, and I said, 'Okay.' Then, he said to me, 'Alright, George, now let's get your close-ups.' The money thing, you know—keep the studio working."

"He made *The Man Who Came Back*, and they starred him in *The Roughneck*," Richard Dix recalled in 1925. "If he were only a freelance now, he could go out and get about $1,500 a week and have his choice of a lot of big parts. But he is signed up with Fox at a comparatively small salary. He isn't kicking the way most actors do when they get caught in a situation like that. No. George is like a stray pup that follows forever the first guy that gave him a friendly pat. He's downright grateful to William Fox for giving him a chance. George doesn't realize how popular he has become."

Dix clipped the New York reviews of George's pictures and sent them to him, trying to give him some idea of the way people raved about him, but George only saw how he was received in Los Angeles. Out there, William Fox had no big theater, and George's pictures were shown in the less important houses. He erroneously thought of himself as a second-rater.

After Janet and George experienced their first successes, Fox was impressed with the couple as a romantic team. They were both tabbed for roles in *Seventh Heaven*, but director F. W. Murnau thought George would be the best actor for the lead role in his proposed film, *Sunrise*, with which he was deep in pre-production work. Charles Farrell took over the role of Chico in *Seventh Heaven*, and George was slated to work with Murnau on *Sunrise*.

Richard Dix feared that George had succumbed to the depressing thoughts that often hit actors after their initial success. He did not have anyone to share his triumph with him. He had worked for something, and now that he had achieved it, he wondered what it was all about. "Our work has brought us money and a certain amount of public acclaim," Dix revealed, "but there is something lacking. The first time you see your name in electric lights you get a great thrill, and after that, you realize it doesn't mean a thing. Maybe I'll be able to find what it is we're looking for, and maybe George will. I hope he does. It would be terrible for him to lose interest now, when he is just at the beginning of his success, for he has the makings of the greatest popular idol the screen has ever had."

Charlie Chaplin, Mary Pickford, and Rudolph Valentino were the greatest popular screen idols at the time Valentino was near death. The world watched with mounting fear while his life hung in the balance.

Chapter
Sunrise and Success

On Monday, August 23, 1926, Rudolph Valentino lay ill with peritonitis. His condition took a turn for the worst. Father Joseph H. Congedo, a native of Castellaneta, administered the last rites of the Roman Catholic Church. At 12:10 that night, Valentino died.

The ensuing hysteria reached undreamed-of proportions. Valentino's body was laid in state at Campbell's Funeral Home at Broadway and 66th Streets, and the public was allowed to view it. A crowd of 30,000 people immediately gathered. Rioting began, the worst in the city's history, as police attempted to order the lines into a controllable mass. Store windows were smashed, while dozens of mounted policemen repeatedly charged into the crowds. Some women rubbed soap on the pavement to make the horses slip, causing pandemonium on top of the rioting.

On the day of the funeral, more than 100,000 people, mainly hysterical women, lined the streets around the church where the rites were held. As the funeral procession left the church, the throngs became ominously silent except for the weeping women. Valentino, idolized by so many, led a lonely, sad life, made more mysterious by his tragic, untimely death. His final film, *The Son of the Sheik*, played in theaters after he was gone.

In the fall of 1923, George shared a room with Richard Arlen at Mrs. Grover's Boarding House on the southeast corner of Sunset Boulevard and Vine Street. Another roommate, Mervyn LeRoy, joined the fledgling actors. The three young bachelors, living on their own in the growing movie Mecca, blossomed in the exciting Hollywood atmosphere.

Around June 1925, Fox Film Company underwent reorganization, and for the first time, raised capital by issuing $6,600,000 in common stock. Their goal was to form the Fox Theater Corporation and build thirty first-run theaters. With a projected investment of $200 million, they planned a four-year period of unprecedented construction of a chain of 4,000-seat to 5,000-seat theaters in key cities that would give them venues in important markets and enable them to compete with positions held by Paramount and MGM. Producing films to feed this expanding exhibition circuit was vital. Some actors and directors who were proven effective were already passing away by this time. The industry had lost Wallace Reid, William Desmond Taylor, and Robert Harron, and the business needed new stars like George O'Brien to lure patrons into the new theaters.

After making *The Iron Horse*, John Ford planned to direct *3 Bad Men*, another big Western. The story by Herman Whittaker followed three outlaws who redeem themselves while protecting pilgrims on their way to the 1877 Dakota land rush. With this film, Ford again planned to celebrate the pioneering American spirit. Spectacular locations near the Grand Tetons at Jackson Hole, Wyoming, were chosen as sweeping panoramic background for scenes of outlaws and wagon trains journeying through the Badlands of Dakota. Ford wanted George, Tom Mix, and Buck Jones to portray the three outlaws, but executives at Fox thought Mix and Jones too valuable to waste on one single picture. Ford was allowed to retain George, and other actors were recruited to replace Mix and Jones.

The film's climax was a land-rush sequence, and one particular moment proved especially thrilling. A couple pausing over a broken wagon wheel stop for repairs and then venture back into the land-rush, forgetting that their baby sits idle in the dirt a few feet behind. In the midst of the onrushing mayhem, as wagons, horses, and every known vehicle of the day rush by at breakneck speed to stake their claims, the couple resume their race with the others and accidently forget that the child has been left behind. At the very moment when onrushing wagons and horses threaten to trample the infant, a galloping rider snatches the child into the air and out of danger. The moment is highly suspenseful, made the more so by realism. Ford paid one of the film's stuntmen to place his child in harm's way, and the frightful rescue often caused audiences to gasp.

Actor Lou-Tellegen, who had been working as a star under contract to Fox for several years, appeared with George in *3 Bad Men*. Having spent his youth as a wandering bohemian, pugilist, circus acrobat, and leading man to Sarah Bernhardt and Eleonora Duse, he achieved enormous fame. With Bernhardt, he toured the world in her 1910-1914 itineraries that transported them to every large city around the globe. Also with Bernhardt, he had starred in the milestone film, *Queen Elizabeth*, which propelled the 1912 American film industry to leap from predominately one-reel films to feature-length productions. After two more films with Bernhardt, Goldwyn had acquired him for a series of starring vehicles capitalizing on his fame. As a matinee idol, he was extremely popular with women audiences, but by the 1920s, he had aged. He continued working in pictures in the roles of older lovers and villains.

"Lou-Tellegen was a great matinee idol, a great boxer in France years ago," George said. "He had a fantastic romantic life. He was married to Geraldine Farrar, the opera singer. He was a real man's man . . . fantastic physique. He posed for Rodin. The statue is in Paris. I've seen the statue in the Louvre many times. He not only took care of all his wardrobe, but he sewed on buttons when things would go wrong. He didn't just toss it off to the wardrobe people. My first experience knowing Tellegen the man was when we were cast in *The Silver Treasure*. We were at Catalina. But you should see him in a big whale boat, which we used in these scenes. He sat down and rowed. He could row! Oh, he was really he-man!"

3 Bad Men proved to be one of Ford's best films, a masterpiece of the silent era and a triumph for George and the other actors, Lou-Tellegen, Tom Santschi, and Frank Campeau. Released on August 28, 1926, *3 Bad Men* was successful and added more luster to George's burgeoning career.

Despite his incredible success, George never strayed from his core values. One of his hobbies had long been weight lifting, and he had built himself into a 240-pound giant, enhancing his prestige more than ever. No scandal of any sort was ever associated with him. He realized the influence he had with children, and he resolved to furnish them with an example of the kind of man he wanted their

(TOP LEFT) A lobby card for the John Ford film, *3 Bad Men* (1926), starring George O'Brien, Lou-Tellegen, and Olive Borden. (BOTTOM LEFT) George O'Brien and Lois Moran on the cover of *Picture Show*, July 13, 1929. (RIGHT) George O'Brien in *Rough Romance* (1930). PHOTO COURTESY OF THE DARCY O'BRIEN ESTATE.

parents to encourage them to emulate. The strategy paid off, both at the box office and in his personal satisfaction. In the vacancy left by Valentino, up and coming stars like George were vying for engaging newfound attention.

By the mid-1920s, Fox Film Corporation occupied a middle position in terms of product prestige and economic power. Long thought of as a producer of unpretentious films for mass appeal, William Fox longed for the high regard of major critics. Fox production facilities were upgraded and he began acquiring new talent as part of a carefully orchestrated plan to elevate the status of his studio to one of preeminence. To achieve this goal, he turned to director F. W. Murnau. His proposed film, *Sunrise*, was planned as a highly artistic picture worthy of critical attention. Fox also thought sound would add to its allure.

In the January 2, 1926, issue of *Moving Picture World*, William Fox placed a full-page advertisement announcing his signing of F. W. Murnau, saying he was acquired to ". . . put subjective thought on the screen, to open up the mind, the heart, the soul." Fox needed a profound director to add to his stable because Raoul Walsh, Frank Borzage, and John Ford simply could not make enough pictures to carry the studio. Fox had a strong eye for talent, but he had a problem competing with the polished productions of MGM and Paramount. He had actually signed Murnau the previous year, long before Murnau's *The Last Laugh* had been released in America and caused a revolution in the value of a moving camera in the visual construction of a film. Murnau's lavish, four-year contract provided for a salary of $125,000 the first year, escalating to $150,000 the second year, $170,000 for the third year, and $200,000 for the fourth year. If he was able to make more than one film each year, he was guaranteed an additional $125,000. Murnau was the sort of man who watched people and situations with quiet reservation, noticing eyes, watching feet, and gazing into faces. He had noticed George O'Brien.

Long before he set foot in America, Murnau was well-known for *The Last Laugh* and *Faust*. His works were highly regarded as part of the phenomenon of the German cinema, characterized by a consistent set of stylistic traits begun years earlier with *The Cabinet of Dr. Caligari* (1921), *Siegfried* (1925), and *Metropolis* (1927), among others. German films received attention in the press in part because they were products of a recent military adversary, but also because of their aesthetic effects, a type that mainstream assembly-line Hollywood studios were unable to create.

D. W. Griffith, considered by many to be the greatest of film directors, did not hold the German technique in awe. "Motion pictures haven't changed," he declared in a 1926 interview. "The technique of telling your story varies with passing vogues, but the photoplay remains essentially the same. It has remained unchanged since the Biograph days. Yes, I know, it has become the custom to say that the Germans are pioneers in a new technique. Why, they are doing the things that we discarded long ago. A certain primitive virility comes of that, but it is absurd to talk of a new technique. They do things long prohibited over here . . . mugging, for instance. Long scenes played right at the camera. We did all that in the beginning. The fact that this primitive stuff has been dressed up with superb camera work has confused observers. The Germans have a fine mechanical mind. They have perfected the camera. In fact, after the war, we found that they had gone beyond us in cameras, camera equipment, and in lighting, too, but this new German technique is all bosh. We make better pictures in America."

Sunrise: A Song of Two Humans was the first film Murnau was to make in America, and much was expected of this new effort. In July 1926, he arrived in New York. William Fox feted him at a banquet at The Ritz-Carlton Hotel. More than a hundred members of the press and prominent members of society were present, including justices, admirals, generals, professors, bankers, and editorial writers from many publications. The event was broadcast to thousands over radio station WNYC. Covering the affair was a correspondent from *Moving Picture World*. In the July 17 issue, he wrote, "It was a proud night for him. He realizes the move on which he is embarking will have a tremendous influence on pictures as an international art."

While they were still in Berlin, Carl Mayer and Murnau began to write *Sunrise*, an adaptation of Hermann Sudermann's *A Trip to Tilsit*. He planned the picture to treat the congestion of the city and an escape from it as the basis for a romantic triangle of destruction and redemption. From the city would also come the vamp that threatened the happy marriage of the young couple, and in the end, the city and its hundreds of anonymous passersby would be the balm for their damaged love.

In Berlin with Murnau was cameraman Charles Rosher. According to him, Murnau completely planned the film and the sets before signing

(TOP) Margaret Livingston, George O'Brien, Director F. W. Murnau, and Janet Gaynor while filming *Sunrise* (1927). (BOTTOM) F. W. Murnau and the production crew of the 1927 film, *Sunrise*.

Portrait of George O'Brien in *Sunrise* (1927).

a contract with William Fox.

"He had, as they said then, far-out ideas on camera techniques, and Charles Rosher and Karl Struss, who I knew very well. I would sit for hours while they were lining up a shot. It was all closed in," George told Leonard Maltin in a 1971 interview. "We worked about six months on it; Janet Gaynor, Margaret Livingston, Murnau, and I had lunch and dinner every day when we worked at the studio. He had it like a family."

Murnau's agreement with Fox guaranteed that he would be given a free hand in carrying out his preconceived vision for the picture, and Fox kept his word. A unit manager was assigned to handle business details, but Murnau was the final decision maker. He was given virtually carte blanche to produce whatever his imagination conjured.

An article in *Fortune* magazine revealed the spirit of cooperation between Murnau and William Fox: "The slogan around the Fox plant was 'when Murnau wants anything, give it to him.' If anyone had any ambition for an increase in salary, an actor, cameraman, property man, clerk, or in any capacity whatsoever, it became the usual thing to say, 'But that is impossible; Murnau is spending all Fox's money, the company can't afford any raise even for the most unimportant office boy; we must wait until *Sunrise* is completed.'"

Murnau wanted George for the important lead role in *Sunrise* because he was handsome, gregarious, and one of Fox's most popular contract players. At the time, George had seen the play, *Seventh Heaven*, in New York, and thought he could give a good performance in the lead role. The script had been purchased by Fox for him, and he was working with director Frank Borzage on the script, but then he was told that he had been personally selected by Murnau to be in *Sunrise*. George recommended Charles Farrell to take over his role in *Seventh Heaven*, and he eagerly plunged into work.

In late 1926, filming began. Murnau believed that each set had to be created for a specific shot with a single perspective. An entire village was built at Lake Arrowhead, including the interior of the church, the dance scene, and Luna Park. The sets were built to slant upward in a forced perspective, creating a stylized impression of depth. "We danced on a slanted floor, if you recall the peasant dance," George pointed out.

Newspaper reports of the time noted that the erection of the city set with streetcars and buildings that were a mile and a half wide. 2,000 extras were required to run the streetcars and taxicabs and fill out the crowds, the biggest call for extras in the studio's history.

Murnau was demanding of George and pushed him to new depths as an actor. He said, "I try to make the actors understand the minds of the characters they are asked to portray so that they will know their very thoughts. I talk to an actor of what he should be thinking rather than what he should be doing."

George remembered those moments. "In order to help me with my mood, Murnau would explain each situation." Murnau went to great lengths to maintain a mood between himself and the actors. The effort was a great strain on those involved.

"I lost my voice in the scenes calling for the girl out on the water," George remembered. "This was done at two or three in the morning when there was already a mist and heavy fog on Silver Lake where we shot the close-ups. With the yelling all night long and Murnau coaching, I lost my voice completely and absolutely couldn't say a note."

In February 1927, *Variety* reported the costs of producing the film had soared to $1,200,000. Murnau asked the studio to release no publicity on the film until it was ready for consumption. This cloak of secrecy only added fuel to the mounting interest.

Finally after many months of shooting, Murnau finished principal photography on *Sunrise*. In addition to directing, Murnau appeared in a bit part as a vacationer on a boat. In March 1927, while the film was being edited and titled, anticipation began to build for the release of the picture. On March 5, *Moving Picture World* noted, ". . . reports and photographs filtering through from Hollywood indicate that the distinguished German director has created an unusual picture." The magazine went on to add that "John Ford had seen the rushes and declared the film to be the greatest picture ever produced," publicity ballyhoo that may not have been real. According to Charles Rosher, no one but himself, Murnau, Karl Struss, and the film editor saw the completed picture before it was finished.

In an interview with Kevin Brownlow, Rosher recalled, "We had many problems. My assistant was excellent and very helpful—Stewart Thompson, later cameraman for Bing Crosby. For some scenes, such as the swamp sequence, the camera went in a complete circle, creating enormous lighting problems. We built a railway line in the roof, and then suspended a little platform from it, which could be raised or lowered by motors. My friend and associate, Karl Struss, operated the camera on this scene. It was a big undertaking; practically every shot was on the move. The German designers built an enormous set on the Fox lot, with false-perspective buildings. Real streetcars were brought in and streetcar rails laid. For the forest scene, a mile-long track was built out at Lake Arrowhead; the end of the track came right in to the city. All of it was specially built, including the streetcar, which was mounted on an automobile chassis. On those big scenes, such as the fairground and café, I think I used more lights than had ever been used before."

"They say that I have a passion for camera angles," Murnau stated in *McCall's Magazine*, "but I do not take trick scenes from unusual positions just to get startling effects. To me, the camera represents the eye of a person, through whose mind one is watching the events on the screen. It must follow characters at times into difficult places, as it crashed through the reeds and pools in *Sunrise* at the heels of the Boy, rushing to keep his tryst with the Woman of the City. It must whirl and peep and move from place to place as swiftly as thought itself, when it is necessary to exaggerate for the audience the idea or emotion that is uppermost in the mind of the character. I think the films of the future will use more and more of these camera angles, or as I prefer to call them, these dramatic angles. They help to photograph thought."

Photographically, *Sunrise* appeared rich with European flavor and infused with delicate visuals obtained by Rosher. "I found it difficult to get Murnau to look through the camera," he later told. Murnau trusted the veteran cameraman implicitly, having proven his worth many times over in his many memorable works with Mary Pickford.

Another reason the film looked beautiful was due to the making of the film with the new Fox Movietone process, which required a standard speed bearing the sound track. Where silent films were usually made to project at varying speeds usually at about eighteen frames per second, sound film ran at a regulated twenty-four frames per second, the optimum speed for the best quality of sound reproduction. This was an increase of six frames per second over the old method, which added a noticeable smoothness to the projected image.

Variety paid particular attention to the Movietone effects:

> "Nor should be neglected credit as a detail contributing vastly to a satisfying whole, the accompaniment of the Movietone," the publication noted. "Here is a sound obbligato that contributes subtly to the effect of sight drama instead of detracting from the essential pantomime by its distracting blare. Here the incidental music blends smoothly, suggesting the mood of the scene, but without intruding into the conscientiousness. In

many scenes (honking autos, when dreaming lovers block a street, is a case in point) sound effects are introduced. This has been managed with skill. One accepts the sound as part of a real situation. It never suggests its own mechanics, and herein is the whole difference. Perhaps one reason is that the sounds have been handled judiciously. They do not attempt too much. One passage has to do with a young couple honeymooning in a sort of sublimated Luna Park. The sound effects here have full swing. On the other hand, one of the dramatic high lights was a terrific storm far out on a lake. There was almost no attempt to get sound effects here, probably because sound would have seemed foolish by its inadequacy. The musical accompaniment was reproduced with flawless delicacy and under absolute control, merging into the entertainment and apparently disappearing as a separate element."

Lured to Fox in July 1926, Katherine Hilliker and Captain H. H. Caldwell specialized in writing titles. They approached their work on the film with agonizing thoroughness. Each title was subjected to multiple drafts, and they labored on titles for each sequence that struck just the right universal feeling. Filming title cards proceeded, and by the time they were finished, the final version contained almost twice as many titles as were in the original script.

Superb acting and stunning visuals characterized *Sunrise.* The subtle sensuality of the moving camera, the use of distorted artificial and natural settings, and the stylized blending of light and shade achieved genuine beauty, and few films displayed honest emotions as effectively. Due to Murnau's direction, the performances of O'Brien, Janet Gaynor, and Margaret Livingston were outstanding.

Murnau elicited the best performance of George's career. He forced him to wear twenty-pound weights in his shoes so that his heavy, clomping tread physically expressed his emotional state. The remarkable and daring effect proved especially effective in the film's first scenes, as he trudges with head down and shoulders thrown forward to emphasize his brooding, hulking body. In the later scenes, freed from the shoe weights, his character changes to an exhilarated and enraptured husband, bounding from street to subway and freely enjoying the excitement of the fairgrounds with his wife.

There were at least four different versions of *Sunrise*. One used a happy ending that was made for the American market, and another featured a tragic ending that was made for the European market. Both American and European versions were released in silent and sound prints because not many theaters were initially equipped to handle the new sound film technology. For the European silent and sound versions, *Sunrise* ended with a tragic scene depicting the man choking the vamp, and then he drops her, letting her slowly slip from his hands until she sinks beneath the water.

"Then, there's a scene where he walks down the street with this wonderful weird lighting," George remembered, "and you see the man searching with the light on the lake while some of the village women watch him. That was the European ending. I remember doing the scene twice." In that version, the wife remains lost, the vamp dies, and the man lives on alone with their little baby, forever haunted by his horrible deeds.

For the American silent and sound versions, *Sunrise* ends less dismally with the man choking the vamp while other men call him with the joyful news that they have found his wife. The couple reunites for a happy ending.

The silent versions of *Sunrise* were shipped with a sheet music score. George had a hand in the creation of this score along with Carli Elinor, the Director of Music at the Carthay Circle. "I worked with Carli Elinor and several other composers," he recalled. "Each evening when they finished their shows, we started working at midnight composing this with a piano and writing down everything." That score was also the one performed live by an orchestra at the original New York opening.

The film industry found that the growing emergence of radio diverted audience's attention. For the first time, people were *listening* to shows and becoming attuned to the spoken word as a means of dramatic expression. Broadway actors were being recruited to appear in spoken dramas in the burgeoning radio industry, while technicians at Warner Bros. were quietly experimenting with a new process to merge spoken words with motion pictures. The studios finally realized the potential of talking pictures, the kind that so many had experimented with some years before.

William Fox invested $60,000 in the rights to the Tri-Ergon sound process and Western Electric's Vitaphone technology. He encouraged his engineer, Theodore Case, to implement the Fox Movietone News, a weekly newsreel of current events presented in selected markets with synchronized sound.

For the sound versions of *Sunrise,* Hugo Riesenfeld made use of the Fox Movietone process to compose a subtle but memorable new musical score. In climactic moments, some creative and symbolic sound effects were employed, such as the ringing church bells. For many viewers, the Movietone process was an even bigger hit than the film. The Movietone newsreels were advertised in New York with notices listing the theaters in Manhattan and Brooklyn that were showing it with *Sunrise.* "Hear the news as well as see it!" proclaimed an ad in the *New York Times.* A Movietone newsreel of Benito Mussolini and the Vatican Choir also accompanied *Sunrise.*

By the fall of 1927, the Fox Movietone News reported many world events shortly after they occurred. William Fox scored one of his greatest coups with a Movietone newsreel of Charles Lindbergh taking off for Paris. Shown in theaters as early as the day following the event, Lindbergh was seen and heard talking from the screen on the dim, misty morning of his historic journey. Audiences also heard the thin, ratchet buzz of his fragile, single-engine plane, and for the first time, viewers felt as if they were experiencing the event in person.

Mordaunt Hall reviewed *Sunrise* in the *New York Times,* writing, ". . . Mr. O'Brien shares honors with Miss Gaynor, for his actions are governed by the character, whether listening to and being caressed by the Siren, or in those moments when, with staring and seemingly glazed eyes, he is on the point of committing murder. He gives one a clear idea of the man's stodgy brain, also of his fury at the Siren for having considered the taking of his wife's life."

A reviewer in the December 1927 *Photoplay* described George's characterization as, "the Golem's little boy", referring to the lumbering Frankenstein-like monster in *The Golem.*

Unfortunately, *Sunrise* elicited limited enthusiasm with exhibitors. It suffered from poor promotion, partly due to Murnau's veil of secrecy during and after production, and from the hoopla surrounding the release of *The Jazz Singer*. Teaming the film with Fox's Movietone newsreel further distracted attention from the subtle nuances of his silent masterpiece. In New York, sweltering summer heat kept people away from theaters for the entire first week. Those who did venture out into the heatwave to see a film had many choices including *Sunrise, A Student Prince in Old Heidelberg, Wings,* and *The Jazz Singer,* all formidable competitors.

The first week in New York, the film drew capacity crowds and $19,450; the second week it earned $16,900. By the third week, *Variety* reported its grosses had fallen to half that and tickets were being given away by the handfuls. According to *Moving Picture World,* by November it was slipping into oblivion, and in its tenth week at the month's end, it struck rock bottom, earning only $1,500. Despite falling receipts, *Sunrise* ran for a total of twenty-eight weeks.

Sunrise played with more success in cities far away from New York critics. The general release of the film also featured the Movietone score composed by Riesenfeld. A reviewer for the *Sheboygan Press* wrote: "The direction and camera work of *Sunrise* are the two outstanding factors, but the action, too, is superb. Janet Gaynor gives an inspired performance in the role of the wife, and George O'Brien as the husband does far and away the best work of his career. Margaret Livingston is the siren. Murnau is said to have fought with the studio three weeks to get Miss Livingston. He won out, and proved that he was right. Weird camera angles give the film a very artistic touch, and the titles—very few of them are right to the point. The spectator is swept away in the turmoil of a conflicting emotions that rush through a simple young farmer's head when, after being tempted by the girl from the city, he takes his wife out for a boat ride, determined to drown her."

In Louisiana, a reviewer writing in *The Motion Picture Almanac* said, ". . . Artistic, probably, from a directorial point of view, but the plot was too simple and dragged out to excessive length. Small town patrons not very enthusiastic regarding its merits and there were as many knocks as words of praise. The intelligentsia of the large cities may go wild over Mr. Murnau's art, but the people in small towns don't appreciate it quite as much. O'Brien's, Gaynor's, Livingston's acting was good."

On November 29, 1927, *Sunrise* had its gala premiere at the 1,510-seat Carthay Circle Theater in Los Angeles. Murnau attended, and the audience was treated to a live symphony orchestra performance of the score specially composed by Carli Elinor. Stars, directors, and producers arrived for the event, including Colleen Moore, Tom Mix, Charles Farrell, Mervyn LeRoy, Dolores del Rio, Frank Borzage, Cecil B. DeMille, Clara Bow, Norma Shearer, Irving Thalberg, Joan Crawford, Clarence Brown, and Tod Browning. Fox arranged to have William Farnum as Master of Ceremonies and a bevy of pyrotechnics and electrical displays greeted the stars, George O'Brien, Janet Gaynor, and Margaret Livingston, along with Charles Rosher and F. W. Murnau.

The Los Angeles, showings of *Sunrise* fared better when released as a "road show." The film attracted audiences for ten straight weeks. In Philadelphia, the film never fully recovered from the stigma of its New York opening, but the film ran for eight weeks. In Detroit, it ran for nine weeks. Reviews were mixed, and general attendance was unstable. The glittering effects, gliding cameras, and waves of dissolves could not overcome the general story line that some people found slight.

Critical reviews were mixed. Reactions to the acting tended to fall between praise and derision. *Photoplay* awarded one of its "Best Performances of the Month" citations to "The Camera in *Sunrise*." Regardless of opinion, the film sparked much discussion, and it was examined in-depth by nearly every publication of merit.

In the final analysis, *Sunrise* earned domestic rentals of $818,000, and was the third highest-grossing Fox release of the year, surpassed only by John Ford's *Four Sons* and Frank Borzage's *Seventh Heaven*. Its earning in terms of prestige was incalculable.

At the first Academy Awards ceremony for films released during the 1927-28 season, *Sunrise* won an award for the cinematography of Charles Rosher and Karl Struss, and bestowed on the film an award for "Artistic Quality of Production." A third award for Best Actress went to Janet Gaynor, who won for her combined efforts on *Sunrise, Seventh Heaven,* and *Street Angel. Wings* won the award for "Best Picture."

After seeing *Wings*, Murnau was optimistic on the future of talking pictures. "I think this new invention, the talking picture, is here to stay. Those who saw that great drama of the air, *Wings*, at the early previews without the Movietone attachment, and later at the regular performance with the roar of the motors, the whirr of wings, and the tatt of machine guns, will admit that the sounds increased the intensity of the action."

As a visionary, Murnau was sensitive enough to see into the future. In a *McCalls* interview, he stated, "There will be other technical changes in the next ten or twenty years. The three-dimension movie will be the usual thing instead of the occasional effect. I produced an appearance of depth in the marsh sequence of *Sunrise* by a trick arrangement of lights and shadows. Other directors have experimented with sets in which the floors rise and fall, and the lines of doors, ceiling and furniture slant sharply according to the laws of perspective. But there is a simpler and less expensive device already in preparation which I may not explain now, but which will produce the same illusion of depth and distance as the old-fashioned stereopticon slides."

"Perhaps, too, there will be a radical change in the way motion pictures are projected. I understand one producer is experimenting in a method of showing a picture without a screen so that it looks as though the characters themselves were present in the room in which the audience sits! Television and the radio may bring the movies of the future through the air into your own home at the turn of a key."

Suddenly, talking pictures revolutionized the film industry. Warner Bros. staked the solvency of their company on the future of talking pictures, producing a series of shorts and a musically accompanied feature, *Don Juan*. The critical response was greater than they hoped. They immediately paid Al Jolson $25,000 to break from his stage show, *Big Boy*, and appear in a Vitaphone short titled, *A Plantation Act*. Jolson sang three songs in this short and even talked to the audience. The film was released on October 7, 1927, as part of a bill surrounding the feature film, *The Better 'Ole* starring Syd Chaplin, brother of Charlie Chaplin. The film was highly successful and paved the way for the film that transfigured the industry: *The Jazz Singer*.

George was quite pleased with the way his performance in *Sunrise* was received. For once, he had played in a film that was not built around a boxing bout, and he did not have to be the strong hero carrying a heroine to safety. He hoped to be in more films of the caliber of the Murnau masterpiece, but he did not know what Fox's future plans were. There were already rumblings of him being in a talking picture, using the Movietone process throughout to record dialogue.

William Fox nurtured his prized director. When Murnau sailed from New York after the completion of *Sunrise*, Fox went to the pier with $50 worth of flowers and a parcel of fruit. Murnau became one of George's closest friends. The two were often together for hours at a time, enjoying quiet walks and sailing together. In 1927, George sold his yacht to Murnau, who then sailed to Tahiti in the craft. "He was a pussycat," George described. "I was flattered Murnau wanted me, since he could have had any big name on the lot. One day, I was at the ocean with a couple of my fellow beach bums, Rex Bell and Joel McCrea, and I noticed Murnau coming towards us. He was very tall, about six-foot seven, and had red hair. So, I said to Rex, 'I've got to ask him why he chose me.' It turned out he had seen me in *The Man Who Came Back* where I played an alcoholic and dope addict. He told me he watched that film many times in Berlin. Well, I was twenty-six at the time of this conversation, and still a little insecure about my future in motion pictures, so this was the kind of verbal pat on the back I needed to keep going."

The two men planned on making other films together. George was looking for a new challenge. He wanted to branch out into directing and producing a series of films to be made in the South Seas. He became involved with Murnau's *Tabu*. George borrowed money from his father to finance the film score, music strikingly rife with drums and native, tropical conch horns. George was devoted to Murnau, and he wanted to again work with him.

Chapter 7
NOAH SPEAKS

Instead of working again with Murnau, George was rushed back into the boxing ring for a silent picture, *Is Zat So?* He appeared in silent films well into the first year that Fox produced sound pictures. *Paid to Love* (1927), *East Side, West Side* (1927), *Sharp Shooters* (1928), also known in the United Kingdom as *Three Naval Rascals, Honor Bound* (1928), *Blindfold* (1928), *True Heaven* (1929), and *Masked Emotions* (1929), all featured a silent George O'Brien. Since comparatively few theaters around the world were yet wired to accommodate sound films, this output of silent pictures actually helped to cement his popularity with audiences. George O'Brien pictures were everywhere, and legions of fans adored him.

While making *Paid to Love*, George first worked with Virginia Valli. Born in Chicago on January 19, 1900, she came to Hollywood by way of a convent, an unusual path for an actress in the "roaring twenties."

"Had my parents wanted to make me a screen actress," she told an interviewer for *Picture Show*, "they could not have gone about the job better. They disapproved of the stage, and had no use at all for motion pictures. Knowing that I had always wanted to act, they thought to remove temptation by sending me to a convent where studies and other interests would occupy every moment of my time; and they told me to lose all thoughts of ever becoming an actress when I grew up. The theory was all right, but the practice worked in exactly the opposite direction. Motion pictures were, of course, taboo in the convent. With the obstinacy for which our sex is noted, many of us girls immediately became thoroughly film-mad, and would go to any length to smuggle screen magazines and papers into our dormitories and furtively read them after 'lights out.' Some of the more daring of us used to hide photographs of our screen favorites in our school books."

As time passed in the convent, Virginia felt more enthusiastic about an acting career, and as she read about the successes of her favorites, she longed for the day when she could work with them.

After leaving the convent, she rushed to New York and applied for work at a film studio. Disappointed, she tramped about for a number of days applying at one studio after another, found her hopes dashed, and then returned to her home in Chicago, much to her parent's delight. They thought her little experience would have cured their daughter of her longing to become an actress, but they were mistaken.

Soon after she arrived home, she saw an advertisement calling for girls for a stage stock company, and immediately, she applied. Years later, she recalled, "I may not have had as much talent as I imagined, but I certainly was blessed with an abundance of nerve. I gave the impression that I had had previous experience, and so landed the job."

At the end of the run with the stock company, she had gained the confidence of a headstrong fledgling, and having tasted the thrill of acting, she took the first train to Hollywood. Amazingly, Virginia got a bit part in a film the very first day she applied at a studio. She quickly was promoted to bigger parts, and her chance came when she was asked to play the heroine in *The Storm*. After several films, including *The Unknown* with Lon Chaney, Virginia was cast opposite George in *Paid to Love*, the first of two they would make as a team.

In early 1927, George began work on *Paid to Love*. Fox was committed to filling theaters with a steady outpouring of new product. With director Howard Hawks on the staff and between assignments, he was given a script for *Paid to Love*. Hawks had only directed films of his own creation up to this time, and *Paid to Love* became a beautifully crafted but misunderstood romance.

The original thirty-two-page treatment came from the pen of Harry Carr, a columnist for *The Los Angeles Times*. In 1926, Benjamin Glazer reworked the story to angle the leading lady from a Frenchwoman to an American. From there, Seton I. Miller, a twenty-four-year old Yale graduate on his first assignment for Fox, wrote the decisive treatment.

Miller pleased Hawks with his treatment of the modern and racy story, adding into the scenario a character of a diplomat hailing from America who entertains a Prince and his playboy cousin by taking them to a sophisticated and bawdy Paris nightclub. William M. Conselman provided a final polish to the story, and Hawks went to work shepherding George through his paces as Crown Prince Michael, and Virginia Valli as his love interest, Dolores. William Powell was along for the fun as Prince Eric.

In *Paid to Love*, Hawks experimented with stylistic tracking shots and expressionistic lighting typical of Murnau. Once completed, Fox held up release of *Paid to Love* for almost an entire year. One reason could have been the abundance of George O'Brien titles in release during the late 1920s, but by the time it finally came out in July 1927, Hawks and other directors had imitated its plot elements repeatedly, and the film registered as a flop at the box office.

The single failure made little difference. By 1927, George was recognized wherever he went. While making the film, *East Side West Side*, he ambled around New York's garment ghetto in search of a realistic set of clothes to fit his character. In the film, George played a young man taken in by a family who operates a secondhand suit shop. He went in search of a worn suit of clothes and equally distressed shoes. Hester Street hosted a line of such shops, and with a friend in tow, he shopped for attire to wear in the film.

George told Alma Talley, a writer from *Picture Play*, about his amusing venture into the streets of east New York. At the first shop, a boy came out to wait on him and instantly recognized him from the movies. In the uproar of excitement caused by his visit, he was unable to haggle and purchase anything. Down the street he went, and soon found another shop where a local, ethnic proprietor, thinking he was a sailor looking for a cheap suit, grabbed his arm.

"Suit o' clothes? Suit o'clothes?" the young man asked, grabbing his arm. "Vat kind of suit you vant?"

"Oh, for Sundays," George nodded solemnly.

"And vat do you do?"

George told him he worked on a barge and wanted a Sunday suit for his day off on shore. "But I need two suits just alike," he added.

"Two suits? For vy you vant two Sunday suits? Two suits, maybe yes, but two suits alike? Vy vould you vant two suits chust alike? A gray one—all right; a black one, all right. But alike?"

George wanted two suits alike because, in the story, he ruins the suit he wears, and expecting that there would be retakes, he needed two. He explained that his brother wanted two suits so they would wear better. After much rifling through the proprietor's racks, the puzzled vender found two alike.

Later, George bought two pairs of secondhand overalls for a quarter, and a pair of heavy, round-toed shoes from an old woman for five dollars. He wore those garments in the scene where he comes off a wrecked barge and lands, a stranger, in New York.

Screenwriters took too seriously the advertising slogan proclaiming him "the most physically perfect young man in the movies." He found the strong man roles he was called upon to play amusing. Writers kept working boxing scenes into his films, and other strong man stunts cropped up with alarming frequency.

"For instance," he later recounted to Alma Talley, "I always have to carry the heroine across the room, or up the steps, or somewhere. The scenario writer calls me in, while he's working on the script. 'George,' he'll say, 'I've got a great stunt for you—this will go over big. You see, in this scene—well, you pick up Eloise and carry her up the hill.' So I say, 'Fine! Great! We'll do that again.' In every picture, it seems, I have to carry the heroine somewhere. You know, of course, what would happen in real life? I'd look at Eloise and say, 'Carry you? You're healthy, aren't you? Can't you walk?' But these movie heroines! For some reason, I always have to carry them."

In 1928, George starred in the film, *Blindfold*. The film was a happy one for him and his co-star, Lois Moran. For Lois, she found an opportunity to satisfy the desire she nursed to portray something untra-spophisticated.

"I was quite thrilled," Lois revealed, in an article in *Picture Show*, "at the prospect of reveling for the first time in screen wickedness. I had a slightly blasé part once before, but not so thrilling a role as in *Blindfold*."

In order to keep a steady ourpouring of product featuring their muscular, manly star, Fox attempted to craft pictures around his attributes, and at times, sacrificed quality for quantity. George's feelings about the kind of roles Fox was giving him began to surface. Rumors began to circulate of disputes over roles, as he was not getting any more opportunities of the caliber of *The Iron Horse, 3 Bad Men,* and *Sunrise.* Despite these objections, he performed admirably in every film, and his popularity only increased.

George was still working hard on silent films, while the studios experimented with the innovative possibilities of talking pictures. *Sharp Shooters* (1928) first paired George with the beautiful Lois Moran. She was born in Pittsburgh on March 1, 1907, and educated there until the age of twelve. When he expressed a desire to be a dancer, her mother sent her to Paris to study. After two years, Lois was admitted to the ballet of the Paris Opera, and within a month, performed her first solo dance in *Falstaff.* A French photographer displayed her portrait in the window of his shop, and the image caught the eye of a French film director. When she was sixteen, she auditioned for Samuel Goldwyn and made her American film debut in *Stella Dallas.* She soon appeared with George in three films.

The Fox expansion strategy paid off during the 1926-27 year. Along with *The Monkey Talks, The Cradle Snatchers,* and *What Price Glory?*, George's film, *A Holy Terror,* was listed among *Photoplay*'s best films of the year.

His work schedule was grueling. As a contract player, the studio thrust him into one picture after another. In-between films, George took a trip to Europe with F. W. Murnau as his unofficial guide. Together, they visited Paris, Budapest, and Vienna. They went to Berlin by air, and Murnau took him to Potsdam, the former Kaiser's palace. From there, they sailed down the Rhine River and through the lakes.

"When Fred came out to California," George told Alma Talley, a writer for *Picture-Play,* "he was always asking me, 'What's that building?' And I'd look—never having noticed it before—and, of course, I wouldn't know. 'You're a fine one,' Fred would say, 'you don't even know your own country.' But when we got to Germany I had the laugh on him. 'What's that?' I'd ask. And he wouldn't know. He kept getting more and more annoyed until finally he said, 'Do you have to keep asking *all the time?*'"

The two had a wonderful journey crisscrossing Europe, but the holiday came to a sudden halt when an urgent cable arrived. Executives at Fox sent a message demanding his immediate presence back in Hollywood. He was told that plans to work with Murnau on

4 Devils had changed. The film was created for George to make his talking picture debut. *Variety* had already reported on October 5, 1927 that Fox had tapped Murnau to direct *4 Devils* as their first synchronized sound feature. Suddenly, the entire scheme was scrapped. *4 Devils* was to be made with Charles Morton and Barry Norton, and George was ordered back to America because Warner Bros. had bought his services.

He was pulled back to work on a film with one of the most innovative and creative directors in Hollywood, one that some people thought was mad. The film was going to stage a cataclysm of Biblical proportions. George responded like a true professional, aborting their travel plans and journeying from Germany to California as quickly as connections could be arranged.

Once there, he found a bizarre wind blowing through Hollywood. He learned that Al Jolson had turned the industry upside down with his work in *The Jazz Singer*, and the surprise had turned the town upside down. Furthermore, Warner Bros. planned to stage the destruction of the entire world with a retelling of the famous Biblical tale of the Great Flood. Titled *Noah's Ark*, the ambitious project was planned to be a modern story with a comparable theme of love and struggle in Biblical times, lavish in the same manner as Cecil B. DeMille had done with *The Ten Commandments*. Ancient Biblical scenes of Noah and the events leading up to the Great Flood were to be expanded with a fictional story about his son, Japheth, to be played by George, who would be blinded by his enemies with a white-hot poker drawn from a fire. Japheth is then sentenced to hard labor on a chain bound to a grinding stone until the epic deluge washed away mankind. George joined into the project with enthusiasm, and production started on the grand project.

Interest in *Noah's Ark* began to spread in the summer of 1928. The name of Dolores Costello, when linked to the list of the cast, began to seep into reports in newspapers. The production was already touted as costing at least $2 million to produce, and the ballyhoo claimed that 5,000 extras were employed. The role of Noah was to be played by Paul McAllister, who was a matinee idol on Broadway back in 1906 and 1907.

In 1928, the *Santa Cruz Morning Sentinel* reported the film in progress:

"Closing three days of intensive and fruitful effort the "Noah's Ark" company returned Wednesday evening to the Warner Bros. studio in Hollywood. Director Michael Curtiz, known as one of the greatest of European directors, in conversation with a Sentinel scribe, summed up his opinion of local settings in one word: 'Marvelous!' Curtiz, a master of the art of accomplishing big things in movie production, was imported from Hungary by the Warners, especially for this super play. In "Moon of Israel," his greatest European masterpiece, recently shown in this country, Curtiz handled mobs of thousands of people in many of the scenes, making of it a stupendous and impressive spectacle. "Noah's Ark" is expected to rise to great heights as a film sensation. Already from 500 to 5000 people per day have been engaged in certain portions of the story, which takes in both ancient and modern times. Scenes will be included using sets and crowds of greater extent than ever heretofore engaged in the filming of a motion picture. In addition, it is admitted that the new sensation, the Vitaphone will be employed in many important sequences of the wonder play, which has been two months in production, and is now only about half completed. *Noah's Ark* will be given its world premiere in September. Director Curtiz with his staff of able assistants secured many extremely beautiful shots at the Big Basin locations in Governor's Camp. Panchromatic motion picture film is now used extensively and, with this, aided by special artificial lighting equipment, some striking results were obtained for the Biblical portions of the play."

Director Michael Curtiz drove the production to unheard-of lengths to achieve realism. Some of those involved with the project thought he was a madman.

"But I didn't think so," George later admitted. "When I was to be blinded with a hot poker, he said, 'George, I want to come very close,

(TOP) George O'Brien receiving medical aid for injuries suffered while filming the dangerous flood scenes for Michael Curtiz' film, *Noah's Ark* (1928). (BOTTOM) Director Michael Curtiz with Dolores Costello and George O'Brien while filming *Noah's Ark* (1928).

George O'Brien and Dolores Costello in *Noah's Ark* (1928).

my boy. I want the audience to scream.' And I'll tell you. I could feel the heat of that thing. I screamed bloody murder, and I went through the rest of the picture blind. That was an experience. The Westmores were wonderful; they hadn't yet developed whatever it is they use now for blind people, and they used spirit gum, the stuff you use to put whiskers on. I had fourteen sties in both eyes. I had to be led off . . . once you put it on in the morning it was murder to take it off, because your eyelashes would come off with it!"

Darryl F. Zanuck, a twenty-six-year old with ambitions in the film industry, began his career at Warner Bros. as a writer in 1924. *Noah's Ark* was his first film assignment, and he vowed to make it the greatest picture ever made.

Michael Curtiz planned and photographed *Noah's Ark* as a silent film. The flood was planned to be impressive. A huge tank containing more than a million gallons of water was constructed with access spillways leading to the top of the Babylonian temple set. In his zeal to obtain authenticity, director Curtiz was neglectful of safety precautions. "They're just going to have to take their chances," he told cameraman Hal Mohr.

Alligators and snakes were released onto the set, and oxen and sheep were herded into the gathered conflagration along with the actors and extras. At the director's signal, the deadly stunt was launched. Tens of thousands of gallons of water was released from the tanks and crashed onto the extras and animals from several different directions like tidal waves. The unexpected force of the blast broke apart the poorly constructed sets, and in the pandemonium, debris crashed into the watery onslaught injuring many extras and animals. Drowning bodies floundered along with the panicked animals and cattle. In the frenzy, Curtiz was even seen throwing 2x4 boards into the melee to add to the realism of the moment. Cameramen were horrified, but they kept their cameras running.

George remembered the nightmarish minutes. "I lost both my big toenails in the flood scene. He had me tied up. I was blind and chained to this thing when the first flood started, and rock and debris and wood from the top of the chutes fell down. Several boards tore into me and ripped two of my toenails off. Dolores Costello, who was wet so much, caught pneumonia from all the water. She fainted by the sheer force of the water hitting her into the stomach. She was out of the film for two months after that. Every day after that, my toes were bandaged. They were completely raw. It took months for the nails to grow back."

There were other mishaps during the making of the film. While making one scene from the Biblical sequences, Anders Randolf was supposed to hurl a collapsible spear at George. "The spear was supposed to disappear," George recalled, "but I guess it was rusty or something. It didn't disappear, except into me. Blood shot out. I was supposed to fall. So, he hit me, and I knew I had been hit. I fell back, and the blood started to roll out, and I saw Curtiz watching me. They wouldn't stop the camera in those days. Dolores Costello broke away and fell over me. She screamed, 'He's stabbed! He's stabbed!" Finally, they said, 'Cut!' and Curtiz said, 'Don't touch him! Are you alright, George?' 'Yes, I'm alright.' 'I want to get the close-up!' So they ground a few away of me really bleeding, and then I was picked up and the doctor came and he washed it out and so forth. I had a pretty good tan, but under the lights, the wound showed, and they had to keep touching it up with body make-up."

Disasters continued. A week later, director Michael Curtiz was on a raised platform shouting to a far-away actor on the set of a big scene. He did not watch where he was stepping, fell off, and broke both legs and ankles.

After principal photography wrapped up, Warner Bros. decided to further exploit their new sound recording capabilities and add spice to *Noah's Ark* up with a few talking sequences.

William Fox had long held ideas about talking motion pictures as early as 1908 when he presented, in the old Dewey Theater on 14th Street, one of the many early experiments with a talking motion picture. The voices were human, belonging to stage players who watched the action of the picture from behind a specially constructed screen. The film was *East Lynne*, and the stock company of players provided crudely synchronized speech from behind the screen that appeared to come from the mouths of the actors in the film.

He never lost his desire to make true talking pictures a reality. In a 1927 interview with the *New York Times*, Fox told reporters, "No producer in five years will think of making anything but talking pictures. It will take five years to permit us to perfect the sound and screen devices, to achieve the required results in recording the sound, without any flaws. We want this time just as we took time to get where we are today. Many of the present players who may still be popular then will have to take courses in elocution, and we will then be able to look at and listen to a motion picture, without a subtitle or a spoken title. The news reels will undergo a drastic change, for instead of seeing a statesman opening and shutting his mouth and a brief caption explaining what he is saying, the news reels of the future will show the distinguished person and his speech as he made it will be heard, and the voice will be recognizable. The showing of a present day news reel in five years' time will seem just as absurd as would the screening of stereopticon slides in this day."

William Fox invested a great deal of money in making his dream a reality. Soon after acquiring the Roxy Theater, he predicted there would be success for talking dramatic films and sound newsreels. He flung a huge fortune into the talking motion picture field because he discovered that while audiences had increased during recent years, their numbers had come to a standstill. At that time, 20 million people attended movies each week, and his aim was to see that number increase by 10 million with talking pictures.

Only ninety-six theaters were initially equipped for the reproduction of sound features, and a fourth of them wanted to have the equipment taken out. "Now, things have undergone a tremendous change," Fox said, "and we shall have about 1,000 theaters fixed up with the necessary wiring and so forth by the first of next year, and 4,000 by the end of the next twelve months. Those who were cold to the notion of the sound motion picture are now breaking their necks to make sound and talking films."

To provide a New York venue for the screening of the new talking pictures, Fox invested $15,000,000 in the Roxy Theater, and added wiring and speakers to make it the largest film theater in America and the first of his own to show the fledgling sound films.

"Hitherto, the Fox Corporation pictures have been in the position of a man in evening clothes who does not know what to do—all dressed up and no place to go," Fox said. "Now we have a Broadway outlet for our productions. The new theater will inspire the studio staff. It will make the work harder but much sweeter."

Sound was an imperfect technology in 1928 and was still in the experimental stages. The cumbersome recording equipment did not allow for the freedom of camera movement that had been perfected during thirty years of film production. Except for scenes in which speech is used to drive the narrative forward, the talking sequences added into *Noah's Ark* were made under primitive conditions. The entire experience was new to all of those involved in the revamping of the film. Michael Curtiz struggled with the newly developed sound film technology and the severe challenge to film some additional sequences with talking scenes.

George remembered, "Well, there was half a talking sequence in *Noah's Ark*. Dolores Costello, who had a delightful voice, said, 'George, have you had any tests?' I said no. She said, 'This is going to be a test.' We had already heard over at Fox that we were all going to be replaced by stage actors . . . and the directors were, too. So the scene was written, kind of a semi-love scene. They took the platter and went into the projection room. Jack Warner came in, the director came in, they ran it, and I was amazed. I thought it was my brother talking. You see, you don't hear yourself. Warner turned around, and said, 'It was great,' and Del Ruth said, 'Great.' So we went right back and made the whole sequence. It was a good sort of pat on the back."

At a cost of $10 million, Fox built a special Movietone studio on forty acres of land in Hollywood. There were eventually to be twenty-seven structures on this property. The first attempts at recording were handicapped by not having soundproof studios in which to make them, and with the new studio in place, Fox had great expectations for the pictures to be made. However, there was a problem with some actors who had never spoken on a live stage before. They were inexperienced at expressing themselves in anything other than pantomime, body language, and facial expressions. Panic struck the colony of actors in Hollywood with this sudden and unexpected change to talking films. Producers were worried that their beautiful silent stars would be unable to speak intelligibly and in agreeable voices. Some of the more ambitious ones frantically began studying under elocution teachers.

In an interview with Kevin Brownlow, Colleen Moore recalled how frightened she was the first day she appeared at the door of a cultured, former stage star that had quickly gravitated to Hollywood to train the erstwhile, "talkie film" actress. Her first day was spent reciting the proper pronunciation of the word "mother," and drawing out the intonations so that it sounded like "moth-ah." She returned to the studio head and reported her progress.

"How much did this lesson cost us?" asked the executive.

"One-hundred dollars," Colleen replied.

For her second lesson another day later, she spent the entire hour practicing to say the word "father" with similar instruction to pronounce the word as "fahth-ah." Colleen again reported back to the executive.

"How much did she charge us this time?" asked the worried executive.

"One-hundred dollars," Colleen reminded him.

"One-hundred dollars to learn to say 'mother' and one-hundred dollars to learn to say 'father.' By the time you learn a full vocabulary we'll be broke!"

Lou-Tellegen, George's co-star in *3 Bad Men* and *The Silver Treasure*, found himself falling victim to the sound revolution. Despite his worldwide successes in the theater, his Dutch/French accent threw casting directors into a quandary. He turned his back on the upheavals in Hollywood and emerged from the heartache with a vaudeville engagement, returning to work in front of live audiences. He hoped the exposure would show film producers he was more than capable of handling the spoken word. No one knew how the end result would be for him or any actors in talking pictures.

Despite the disasters and hardships, *Noah's Ark* was a monumental achievement and became another blockbuster success for George, establishing him as an up-and-coming player in talking pictures. His voice, untrained as it was, recorded beautifully, and his ease in front of the apparatus translated into a completely natural image with a voice that matched his personality.

George liked being a star, but he did not take it to heart. He wished all the pictures in which he appeared could be big successes, but if they fell short, he was not depressed. He maintained a healthy balance, a rarity in Hollywood, by virtue of the fact that he had outside activities that were just as absorbing as film work. Physical fitness was very important to him, and although he did not make a fetish of it, he followed a routine that was more than just a pastime. On the Fox lot, he played on the basketball team with Barry Norton, Charles Morton, and other actors. He was as pleased by the notices of his last film as he was by the team's victory against the Richfield Oil basketball team.

Dear to his soul was his boat and the time he spent cruising indolently up and down the coast, courting storms, and exploring seaways. He claimed to feel a kinship with all sailors, and one source of great pride was the unfailing Christmas telegrams he still received from those few men who, like him, barely survived the explosion on the *Subchaser 297* during World War One.

Sound pictures had come to stay, despite the fact that many people felt that talking pictures would have a brief vogue and then pass away in six month's time. With the first sound films, technicians were uncertain how to edit the film sound track. To cope, main characters would have one camera directed on their close-up, a second camera would film two or three people from further back, and a third would be set far enough back to record a master shot of the entire scene. Hiding microphones was a challenge. They were placed under props, behind furniture, strapped to the back of an actor, or wired into telephones. They presented limits on how far an actor could walk. At MGM, Lionel Barrymore solved the dilemma of recording Ruth Chatterton speaking as she walked across a room by dangling the microphone from a fishing pole over her head just out of camera range. In this makeshift fashion, Barrymore laid claim to inventing the first boom microphone to record Ruth Chatterton in *Madame X*.

The early amplification process was the cause of the microphone's immobility. It had an effective radius of about five feet, and sound ran through a cable to vacuum tubes build in a heavy wooden box. If the box was touched or moved, a loud "bang" would record. This technical malady resulted in many painstaking retakes.

F. W. Murnau was experimenting with the new medium of talking pictures when he finally began work on *4 Devils*. He reflected on the new technology. "They have experimented with the camera. It will do many strange and fine things now, most as much as I can ask of it. But one must keep a large and expensive cast waiting for hours while the lights are moved about. Then, when at last the scene is being made, perhaps a tiny bulb blows out, or a screw comes loose and there is a five thousand dollar a day cast held up again while the trouble is repaired."

"The present machinery of the studios will not be enough for the director of the future. Even now, I ask that they make me special equipment so that I can get my camera where I want it. The picture I am working on now is a circus story and naturally the camera must not stand stock still in one spot in such a gay place as a circus! It must gallop after the equestrienne; it must pick out the painted tears of the

Photo of George O'Brien COURTESY OF THE DARCY O'BRIEN ESTATE.

(TOP) Marguerite Churchill in Raoul Walsh's epic Western, *The Big Trail* (1930). (BOTTOM) Cast and crew of *The Big Trail* (1930), including Marguerite Churchill and John Wayne. PHOTO COURTESY OF THE DARCY O'BRIEN ESTATE.

clown and jump from him to a high box to show the face of the rich lady thinking about the clown. So I have had them build me a sort of traveling crane with a platform swung at one end for the camera. My staff his nicknamed it the 'Go-Devil.' The studios will all have Go-Devils, some day, to make the camera mobile."

George began working on John Ford's *Salute*, his first first all-talking picture. "That's where we took John Wayne, Ward Bond, all the guys from USC, and made actors out of them," George reminisced to Leonard Maltin. "*Salute* came out, and the same thing took place; various directors around the studio started to bid for me. So I was assured right away."

Hollywood studios had thoroughly raided New York theaters for every actor and actress who could deliver spoken dialogue effectively. Among the new recruits making strides in motion pictures was Marguerite Churchill. She had appeared on the Broadway stage in 1927 in *The House of Shadows* and *The Wild Man of Borneo*, and in 1928 appeared prominently in *Skidding*, a huge hit running for 472 performances. Marguerite was in New York playing the feminine lead in *The Wild Man of Borneo*, when Winifield Sheehan from Fox saw her and put her under contract. In 1929, the pretty, auburn-haired nineteen-year-old made her film debut in an early "talkie" called *The Diplomats*, and that same year appeared in four other films. In 1929, while George was still appearing on silent screens in *Masked Emotions*, Marguerite was winning good reviews for her work in another all-talking picture, *Pleasure Crazed*, a film about modern racketeers operating in high social circles and planning an ingeniously designed robbery. A reviewer in the *Zanesville Signal* wrote, "Marguerite Churchill and Kenneth MacKenna duplicate their former Broadway stage successes in their clever handling of the leading roles . . . in fact, we heartily recommend this feature as being an outstanding, all-talking screen entertainment."

In 1930, Fox kept Marguerite busy going quickly from one picture to the next. After eight pictures in a row, producers thought enough of her work to cast her in *The Big Trail*, one of their upcoming pictures to be directed by Raoul Walsh. A western epic, Fox hoped that *The Big Trail* would be to talking pictures what *The Covered Wagon* had been to silent films. The film was filled with splendid action, Indian attacks on a wagon train, and an unforgettable struggle fording the Colorado

River, all amplified with a wide-screen process called Fox Grandeur. Along for the ride was the fledgling film star, Marguerite Churchill.

As "Ruth Cameron," Marguerite had to undergo many hardships during the four months spent making this Fox Movietone triumph. For a girl who had never lived outside of the big city, it was doubly difficult for her to accustom herself to the primitive life necessitated by the 1,300-mile trip through the rugged country of seven States as the film was produced. She failed to make a single complaint during the four months it took to make the picture. In fact, cast members later recounted her enjoyment of every moment. When not called for work, she could often be found riding out on the desert, up in the mountains, or through the forest of whatever locale in which the company happened to be working. She liked outdoor life, and when she appeared on the Fox lot, George noticed her. For the first time in his life, a real romance sparked.

Chapter 8
FROM A FORD TO A STAGECOACH

By 1930, both Buck Jones and Tom Mix had left the Fox Studio without a Western star. The studio continued to pursue the proven audience for these films by budgeting up to $300 million for a series of high-class Westerns with four to six weeks allocated for the production of each. Sol Wurtzel, Fox's production head, brought the opportunity to George, who was less than enthusiastic. The idea of imitating Tom Mix's flamboyant style put him off.

"I told him Mix isn't on the lot anymore, and the first thing you'll want me to do is put arrows on my shirt and have little angels flying off my shoulders like he had," George told interviewer Joe Collura. "If I do a western, I want to play a working cowboy," he adamantly insisted.

Once Wurtzel agreed to George's terms, work began on *The Lone Star Ranger* (1930), the first in the series. Locations were highlighted for colorful backgrounds in picturesque California, Monument Valley, Utah, Arizona, Colorado, Montana, and Nevada. Making a talking picture outdoors proved to be more challenging than working inside a studio.

"Out on *The Lone Star Ranger*, it was rough on the crew bringing equipment to this entire location," George recalled. "We broke up the company into a skeleton crew of fifteen people. We loaded dry cell batteries onto burrows, also my horses, and horses we borrowed from the Indians. We all knew we were doing a pioneer job, the first in many ways . . . with the crew, staff, and all hands doing a history-making job. We had to carry the cable under our legs while the horse was going along; they were still inventing things," he explained. "On a long chase, they hid the microphones in the bushes, and Barney

Fergus, the sound man, would say, 'George, how close are you going to that bush? My main microphone is there' I'd say, 'All right, Barney, where's the other one?' and he'd say, 'The other one's over here.' Then, the director would say, 'Now George, I want that awful fast coming through there,' so I didn't want to be looking for microphones in the picture, and I came close one day. I didn't touch it, but I hit a rock or something, and the rock bounced, almost blew poor Barney's brains out. Then, they started covering the microphones with shammy, because the wind sounded like ocean waves."

There were other unusual challenges recording sound with film. "They hadn't perfected the microphone in those days," George clarified. "I have had a microphone shoved down under the blanket under a saddle. Then, we put the cable under my leg . . . now get this . . . on this horse. At any minute, this horse could take off and wreck everything. Then, I'd put my foot in the stirrup and pull my pants over so you didn't see it, and then one of the grips would walk alongside of me running out all this cable until we went to the end of it and I had to time my dialogue to get that movement in. Pioneering? Yes!"

The film industry's conversion to talking pictures beheaded the careers of many top stars. One by one, they began to fall like shooting stars from the sky. Emil Jannings, the Academy Award winning actor from Germany, retreated to his homeland convinced that there was no further work to be found in Hollywood. Norma Talmadge, at the pinnacle of her long stardom, could not overcome her Brooklyn accent and she retired after making only two sound films. Her sister, Constance, a perennially popular comedienne, simply quit, walking away from one of the most successful careers anyone had ever had in films and retreating to a comfortable retirement while still in the prime of her youth. She never made a talking picture. Ramon Novarro, the popular MGM star of *Ben-Hur*, had a marvelous singing voice, but his speech was rich with the roots of his upbringing. His Mexican dialect doomed him virtually overnight to ethnic roles. Greta Garbo, speaking with a thick, Swedish accent, was simply forbidden from making a sound film for most of 1929 while other MGM stars were well into making their transition to "talkies."

George's co-star in two pictures, Lou-Tellegen, was growing desperate and finding it difficult to obtain work in the changing industry, even though he spoke five languages and had a powerful speaking voice

(TOP) George O'Brien with Arthur Sutton, a young fan, while filming *Riders of the Purple Sage* (1931).

(MIDDLE) George O'Brien in *Riders of the Purple Sage* (1931).

(BOTTOM) George O'Brien, posing with Olympic swimmer, Stubby Krueger, Johnny Weismuller, and friend in the early 1930s.

honed through years of stage performances. In a few short months, he became a has-been carrying the cross of "Matinee Idol," and producers could not envision him as a character actor. They could not give him work in youthful roles and would not let him play older roles. Lawrence Windom, an independent director for Regal Productions, offered him a role in a low-budget film about bootlegging gangsters. He took on the part, but there was a catch.

"You're too old for the part, Lou," Windom told him. "You could play the part if you could do something to look about ten years younger. I can't take the time to do it with lights."

After discussing the dilemma with Eve, his wife, they decided he should have temporary plastic surgery. He put himself into the hands of a clever surgeon, and the unpleasant proceeding took about two weeks and involved injecting paraffin around the eyes. It was not guaranteed to last long, but it got him the part in *Enemies of the Law*.

Also having difficulty finding work was Alma Rubens, who had starred with George in *The Dancers*. Having appeared in approximately fifty silent feature films, she was briefly heard singing and playing a ukulele in a sound sequence in the 1929 film, *She Goes To War*. After this film, her career came to an abrupt end. The shadow of tragedy hung solemnly over her life. She had become addicted to heroin, and died in 1931.

George was one of the lucky actors that survived the transition to talking pictures. He wanted to portray a variety of he-man roles, including sailors, lumberjacks, and forest rangers, but they wanted him to make Westerns. He worked out a compromise, asking in return for good stories, casts, and locations, all of which he was given. He did not have to be an imitation of Tom Mix, even though his next films included remakes of three earlier Mix films, *A Holy Terror, Riders of the Purple Sage*, and *The Rainbow Trail*.

Rough Romance (1930) was refreshingly different. He played a lumberjack, and during the filming of the Fox Movietone all-talking production, he surprised the real lumberjacks, who were already acquainted with his skill as a boxer, swimmer, and equestrian. After a brief schooling in the wild forest, George climbed up a big tree and "topped it" in approved fashion, much to the astonishment of the real lumberjacks standing below.

George O'Brien on the Fox Studio lot in the early 1930s.

In 1931, Fox was suffering from the combined effects of the stock market crash, a Federal Trade Commission antitrust suit spurned from their acquisition of the Loews theater chain, and the voluntary

Marguerite Churchill, George O'Brien, and crewmembers filming the 1931 film, *Riders of the Purple Sage*. PHOTO COURTESY OF THE DARCY O'BRIEN ESTATE.

retirement of William Fox. In addition, theater attendance was dropping significantly. Their stock plunged, as the company posted a multi-million dollar loss for the second straight year. Film production slowed down drastically.

By comparison to many film actors, George found his career prospering. He began working with John Ford on *The Seas Beneath,* a submarine picture, portraying the commander of a crew in search of a dreaded German submarine. Marguerite Churchill, the lovely young actress then appearing in films, had originally been assigned the leading feminine role in *The Seas Beneath,* but had to forego the part to be the leading lady in *The Spider* opposite Warner Baxter and directed by Henry King. Her role in *The Seas Beneath* went to Marion Lessing, a recent addition to the roster of Fox players. The part called for a woman who could speak perfect German, and Miss Lessing had been an actress on the German stage.

John Ford was still earning a weekly salary on his current contract through October 1932. On the last day of shooting *The Sea Beneath,* and with no new projects scheduled, Ford talked George into accompanying him on a sailing trip to the Philippines. He and George left on a three-month adventure to the Far East on a Norwegian freighter, *Tai Yang.*

Once at sea, they endured one of the worst storms to hit the waters off Manila. Mountainous waves broke over the bridge, leaving the men little to do but stay below deck, read books, eat four meals a day, and sleep for twelve-hour marathons. Along the way, they passed a violently erupting volcano that deeply impressed Ford with its effect on the changing panorama of the sky. The long duration at sea left the director anxious to see a tree again, but he found the experience exhilarating. He wrote to his wife, telling her that he felt twelve years younger. After dozens of days at sea, the boat finally cruised into the Manila harbor. Awaiting his arrival were the local press, who made much of George's visit. Screen idols rarely slipped into their city, and George, always the gun-ho adventurer, could not wait to dock and begin visiting the sites.

"... I had forgotten I was a well-known movie personality," George wrote in a letter to Buck Rainey, "resulting in people turning out all over to greet me. I visited schools and colleges, played soccer with students, swam in races, played polo, wrestled, boxed, and danced the native dances at fiestas. At that time, I was the first motion picture actor to visit the Philippines. I must also mention that the U.S.N. Fleet was in the Philippine waters, preparing to get underway for a visit to Singapore, and many of my former shipmates did their best to encourage me to travel with them. There are some 10,000 islands in the Philippines, and most travel was by boat or canoe."

By comparison, Ford took the occasion to get drunk. For the next ten days, he was unable to leave his bed, even refusing to go out for dinners. George determined to continue with the planned itinerary in spite of Ford's stupor, and decided to go ahead without his friend. While Ford stayed in Manila in an alcoholic daze, George boarded the *SS Luzon* to visit exotic ports-of-call. He covered for the director's inability to join him on this leg of the trip by telling reporters that Ford was indisposed with fever, and for the next two weeks, enjoyed touring sites rarely visited by Americans.

"One day, having breakfast on the island of Zamboanga, Jack Ford and I decided perhaps we had better think about going home. However, we decided it would be a waste of our long voyage if we didn't visit Japan and Old China—which we did with gusto!"

On the return leg of the trip, Ford returned to sobriety, but was guardedly friendly, only seeming to be congenial. They continued together to Indonesia, met a sultan with twenty-three wives, and then journeyed on to Hong Kong. They visited the towns of Shanghai, Kyoto, Osaka, and Kobe, and then returned by boat to Hawaii. While there, the Honolulu newspapers again made a great fuss over the visiting star and virtually ignored the largely unknown film director. They completed the trip with a safe return to San Francisco, and while there, they met up with a police guard supplied by George's father.

"I visited there with my father, mother, and brother for a few days, and then departed for Hollywood, and upon my arrival at Fox Studio, discovered that my seventeen-day voyage to the Philippines had grown into six months!"

While on the trip, George was in Shanghai when a telegram came with bad news. He was shocked and saddened to learn of the unexpected death of F. W. Murnau. The director had completed work on his last film, *Tabu*, and planned to travel to New York by car. After an astrologer forewarned him he would lose his life on a car journey, Murnau changed plans and opted to drive from Los Angeles to San

John Ford and George O'Brien while on their 1931 trip to the Philippines.
PHOTO COURTESY OF THE DARCY O'BRIEN ESTATE.

Francisco, and there, catch a boat that would take him by sea via Panama. While driving from Los Angeles on March 10, 1931, the car in which he rode lost control and collided with another car. Murnau was thrown from the car, fractured his skull on a post, and died while on his way to a hospital.

Few came to bid farewell to the forty-two-year old Murnau as he lay in state in a funeral parlor on March 19. Among those attending were George O'Brien, Greta Garbo, William K. Howard, Thomas Mirande, Edgar Ulmer, Herman Bing, and five others. Bing rounded up funds to have the body embalmed and sent to Germany where a burial took place at the cemetery at Babelsberg.

On George's return from Murnau's funeral, he returned to work. He did not realize that John Ford seethed with resentment over the turn of events while they were on their trip together. The director viewed his abandonment as betrayal. For the next seventeen years, Ford ostracized George and would not work with him in another film.

"I had known him for nearly 10 years," George wrote in his diary, "yet after four months in which I was with him every second of every day, I think I knew less about him than ever before. He was the most private man I ever met, and even though I loved him, I guess the truth is that I never really understood him." Their friendship virtually ended.

George's original Fox contract expired, and they offered him a new contract. Another big change in his life came when a romance blossomed with Marguerite Churchill, the Broadway actress turned film star who previously had been bumped from the cast of *The Seas Beneath*. She continued to be in both films and stage plays. In 1932, Marguerite starred at the National Theater in *The Inside Story*. She originated the role of Paula Jordon in *Dinner at Eight*, the same role played by Madge Evans in the 1933 MGM film, appearing in 232 performances at the Music Box Theater in the original Broadway stage production of *Dinner at Eight*. George had seen her several times in the play and was crazy about her. He asked a friend to introduce the actress to him.

"A friend finally arranged for me to meet Marguerite one night at the Central Park Casino after the theater," George told Whitney Williams in *Picture-Play*. "They'd tipped her off, I guess, how I felt about her, and she knew who I was and what I did. She was as belligerent as could be.

"What have you got besides being a he-man to recommend you?" Marguerite asked.

"Well, I've never killed a deer," George told her, "and I hadn't either. I had one of them look at me once, with those sad, trusting eyes, just as I was about to pull the trigger, and I stopped right then and there. Never went hunting again. It's funny, but Marguerite really fell for it—she figured I couldn't be such a bad guy after all."

Fox executives asked George to convince Marguerite to play opposite him in his next film, *Riders of the Purple Sage*. "I didn't want her as leading lady, because I'd heard she had won a scholarship or a prize for acting in the Theatre Guild School, and out there we had at that time more prize winners who turned out to be anything but prizes than you could shake a stick at. Anyway, I went with the director to interview her at the office," he remembered.

"Well, when do we start?" asked Marguerite.

"Not so fast, please. When we start we go on location to Arizona, and there's plenty of action in this picture," he told her.

"What? Arizona in mid-August?" she asked, drawing back.

"That shouldn't bother an actress from the stage in New York," George challenged.

"But, Mr. O'Brien, I didn't play on the stage in New York in mid-August!"

Marguerite accepted the job, and George admired the way she neatly took the role into her own hands and made the best of the challenging locations. He also found they had many common interests. She liked music, and George had studied piano. They both loved the outdoors. There was enough common ground between the two of them to form a bond that quickly grew from friendship into a full-blown romance.

(TOP) George O'Brien with his father, Daniel O'Brien, ca. 1930s. (BOTTOM LEFT) Marguerite Churchill before she came to Hollywood in the 1930s, an ingénue fresh from the Broadway stage in New York. (BOTTON RIGHT) Marguerite after the Fox Studio revamped her for glamour portraits. PHOTOS COURTESY OF THE DARCY O'BRIEN ESTATE.

Claire Trevor and George O'Brien while filming *The Last Trail* (1933).

MARGUERITE AND MARRIAGE

Marguerite and George were married on July 15, 1933, at the Old Mission Santa Inés, the nineteenth of the twenty-one California Missions established by Franciscan priests from 1769 to 1823. Founded on September 17, 1804 by Father Estevan Tapis, the mission was named in honor of a fourth century Christian martyr. Old Mission Santa Inés was rich in tradition, legend, and history.

On their honeymoon, they traveled to Coronado, Agua Caliente, and then returned to Malibu for several weeks at the beach. When he returned to work, he immediately became so embroiled in details he completely forgot to phone Marguerite for a scheduled lunch. Several hours later, a telegram arrived to him with the message, "Mr. O'Brien, this is to verify reports you have left for Shanghai. Please advise." Signed, Marguerite.

Marriage did not change him much from his lifestyle as a single man living at Malibu the year around. He was accustomed to waking at dawn and taking a plunge in the ocean before exercising. Between pictures, he seldom stirred form his beach place, unless the idle period was unusually long. He and Marguerite moved to a hilltop house in Hollywood just twelve minutes from the studio, but a full forty-five minute drive from the nearest beach.

Once he was settled into married life, he went back to work on a series of Westerns for Fox. George and Marguerite completed their one starring film together, *Riders of the Purple Sage*, and in quick succession George made *The Rainbow Trail*, *The Gay Caballero*, *Mystery Ranch*, *The Golden West*, *Robbers Roost*, and *Smoke Lightning*. In each film, they tried to pair him with a different leading lady, using the O'Brien films as training for fledgling actresses such as Cecilia

Parker, Minna Gombell, Linda Watkins, Janet Chandler, Maureen O'Sullivan, and Nell O'Day. Claire Trevor was another new recruit from the legitimate stage trying her first venture in a motion picture with his next film, *Life in the Raw*.

Blond Claire Trevor, George's co-star in *Life in the Raw*, told a few white lies to get the job. She spent her first three weeks breathlessly galloping on a horse she had just learned to ride.

"Stage directors shy away from newcomers," Claire told a reporter for the *Zanesville Signal*. "They don't want to hire anyone who hasn't had stage experience. Not having any three years ago, except that little bit obtained in a dramatic school, I manufactured some experience, and talked myself into a job. I was tripped up, though, by one producer. He asked me in what shows I'd been, and I nonchalantly named one that had run a long time. He called his secretary to look in the files for my name. I didn't know that the show I mentioned was one he had produced. Anyway, I didn't get the job."

When a producer seeking players for his stock company in Ann Arbor, Michigan interviewed her, Claire had enough nerve to talk of herself as if she had been a star, when in reality, she had only been in a few shows. Her ruse worked, and at a summer theater there, she appeared in more than twenty plays, her principal experience before working in the movies.

When she got off the train, a script for *Life in the Raw* was handed to her. "Learn the first fourteen scenes," she was instructed. A car rushed her to the studio where gowns and things that had been previously ordered only by telegraph were fitted to her. Then, she posed for pictures. At four o'clock the next morning, she was driven by car to the outdoor location spot at Lone Pine near the Sierra Nevada Mountains. By noon, Claire was getting instructions from George on how to mount a horse and stay there. Claire was on safe ground with him. By 1933, he was getting used to breaking-in these pretty, young starlets recruited by Fox for appearances in these early talking pictures.

Just as his career and marriage were taking him to unexpected joys as an actor and as a man, tragedy struck. On October 12, 1933, Daniel, his beloved father, died of heart disease. On the morning of January 7, 1934, the *Nevada State Journal* reported, "Dan O'Brien Leaves Less Than $10,000," revealing the circumstances of his estate after his will was probated.

Chapter 9: Marguerite and Marriage

At this time, George's friend, Lou-Tellegen, was distraught and near the end of his wits. After suffering several operations for cancer, he was unable to find work in Hollywood, and he felt that he was losing his mind. He mailed the following message in a letter to his wife, dated October 24:

> "I have suffered more in one year that I have suffered my whole life, and if some miracle doesn't occur soon it will be the end of me. Love to you and Toodle-oo."

On the morning of October 29, 1934, Lou was in a distressingly depressed mood. A forgotten idol, Lou beheld a new day that offered no relief from his torture. He went into the bathroom to shave, and saw the face of a man who was years older and looked haunted by bitterness, despair, and pain. Lou carefully shaved, but in his melancholy, he decided he could not go on. In preparation for his last act, he placed a pillow on the cold, tile floor, then stood and faced the mirror. Near him was a pair of golden scissors. He seized them, and began plunging the sharply pointed scissors into his left side. He stabbed himself six times, and then with one final thrust, forced the tool with savage strength to where it found his heart. He staggered back from the sink, mortally wounded. Then, he wrapped his silk bathrobe about his bleeding body and lay down on the cold floor, his head positioned squarely on the pillow, his renowned profile displayed so that his body would be discovered at its most attractive angle. There he lay, while the life-stream in his body ebbed away. The next day, headlines around the world screamed, "Lou-Tellegen commits suicide."

With affection, Marguerite's pet name for George was "Toodles." Soon after their marriage, they planned to start a family. Brian, their first child was born on May 30, 1934, but he suffered pneumonia soon after his birth. George gave his blood for three transfusions, but to no avail. At only ten-days-old, little Brian died. The couple was devastated. Their second child, a daughter, Orin, was born in 1935, and their third child, a son Darcy O'Brien, followed.

Of his newfound happiness with Marguerite, George told Whitney Williams of *Picture-Play*, "I'm not one of those married men who go around saying, 'My wife doesn't understand me.' Once, soon after we

(TOP) George O'Brien in New York City in 1933 demonstrating horsemanship skills to city policemen. (BOTTOM) George O'Brien and his horse. PHOTO COURTESY OF THE DARCY O'BRIEN ESTATE.

were married, an old friend of my bachelor days showed up at the house in my absence. He didn't even know I was married. Marguerite told him she was the little woman. Well, my old pal had had a few drinks, just enough to make him expansive; and I got home a bit later to find him sobbing out to her the whole story of his life. Later, I asked her, with some trepidation, whether he had told her anything

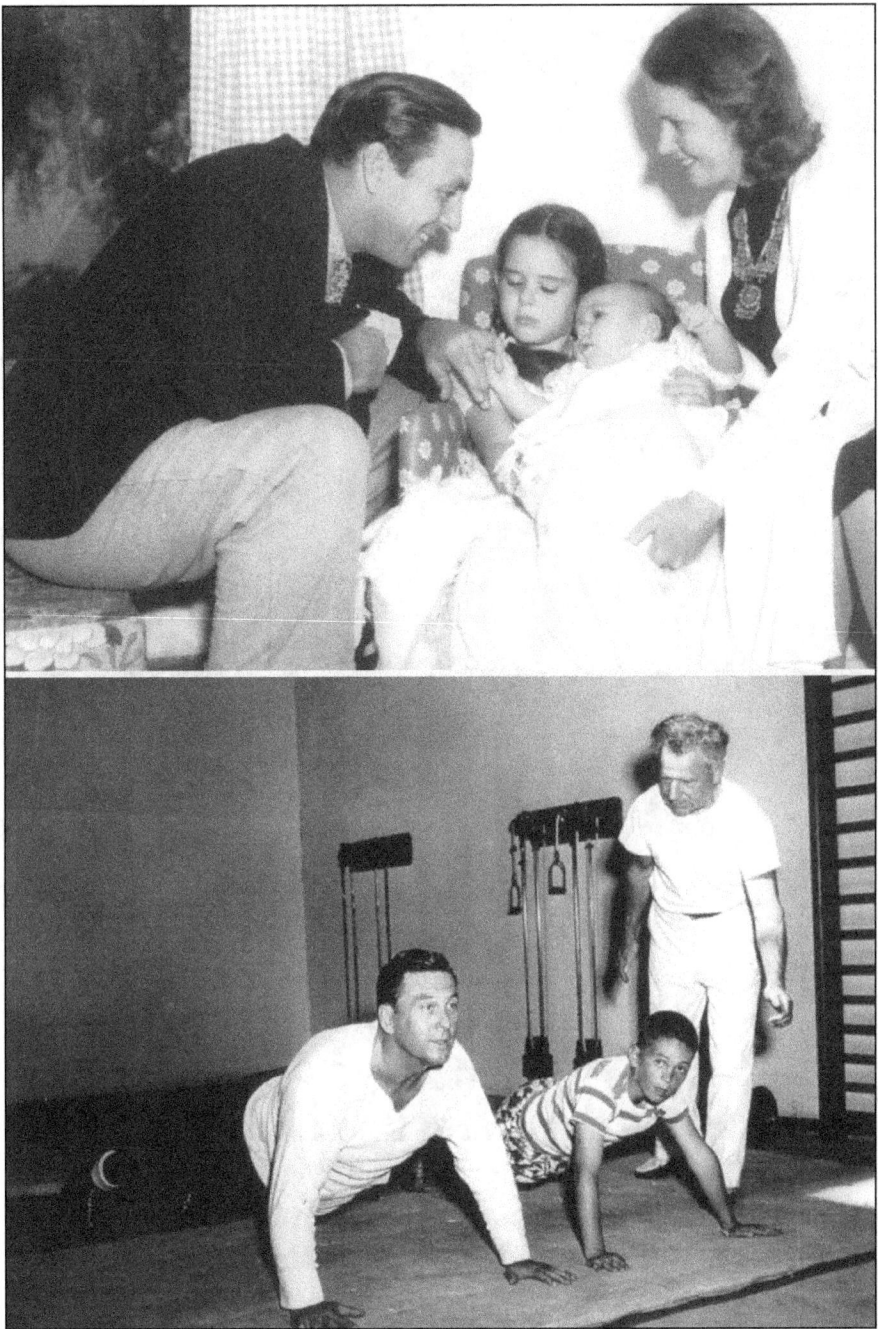

(TOP) George and Marguerite O'Brien with daughter, Orin, shortly after the birth of their son, Darcy. (BOTTOM) George O'Brien and son, Darcy, in the gym, ca. 1930s.
PHOTOS COURTESY OF THE DARCY O'BRIEN ESTATE.

Marguerite and George attending a motion picture premier in Hollywood in 1934.

about me. She smiled, and said, 'Enough to hang you nine times, Darling. But don't worry. I had your number before I ever married you.' So you can see why I don't go around saying my wife doesn't understand me. She's perfectly swell. She accepts me as I am and doesn't demand perfection—and that comes pretty close to being perfection in a woman, from a man's point of view, anyhow."

He and Marguerite loved to take trips together. They were both gypsies at heart, and liked to follow their noses and the open road without knowing what point of the compass they would next pick. Marguerite was excellent at horseback riding, and she enjoyed trout fishing. "I'm sorry for all the men who didn't marry my wife," George glowed in tribute. "But some men have all the luck, you know; and in my marriage, I figure I'm one of that group."

Paul Harrison wrote in the *Ironwood Daily Globe*, "Recently he began complaining that their establishment was too widely scattered, what with the home in Beverly Hills, a couple of houses at the beach, and a stable in Culver City. Also, their daughter, Orin, a three-year-old, hadn't a big enough place to play. So Miss Churchill scouted for a ranch and found a 380-acre place forty miles north of Los Angeles in the Trancas Canyon. George's only requirement was that he would be able to see the ocean from his house, and this place fills the bill."

Believing that Hollywood was the wrong place to bring up children and to make room for their growing family, Marguerite and George bought the ranch in the Malibu Mountains. At first, there was no electricity, and they were forced to use kerosene lamps. George installed the electrical lines himself, hitching up his white horse, Dobbin, and with some help, put up power poles and wired electricity in all the rooms.

The ranch was named "Casa Fiesta," and when the house was finished, George gave a great barbecue party to honor his wife. The roster of invited guests included Will Rogers, Ricardo Cortez, Douglas Fairbanks, Maureen O'Sullivan, Colleen Moore, Marian Nixon and her husband Eddie Hillman, Harold Lloyd, Robert Montgomery, Billie Dove, and many other friends. The O'Briens had "arrived," and George was at the crest of his burgeoning popularity, while the rest of the nation was in the depths of the crippling depression. The downturn in the nation's economy had a profound effect on the Fox Studio.

At that time, there was a change in the staff producing George's films. Fox studio was in financial trouble, and with Darryl F. Zanuck as head of production, a belt-tightening effort was in full swing. Zanuck divested the studio of its obligation to produce the profitable Western films in which he starred, and let his contract lapse, ending the long-running Western series.

After making his last two films for Fox, George signed with Major Zanft and Sol Lesser for a series of films to be made over a period of one year and to be released by 20th Century Fox. Lesser had proven successes with Buck Jones in a series of Western films. He set up offices using the name Atherton Productions. George went on to star in a new series of seven Western films. He was careful to retain the same high quality values that were the signature of his Fox productions, but with the Hays Office and the Legion of Decency compelling producers to conform to the letter of rules rigidly outlined in the Motion Picture Production code, excessive use of violence was forbidden. Gunplay was less emphasized, and humor was greatly increased. George was forced to inject more of his personality into the stories. Each film was made during a three-week to four-week schedule and used very few indoor sets.

"I'm making more money out of them than I've ever made before," he told a writer from *Silver Screen*. "Here's the kick. The papers are all signed and Fox will release them. If they hadn't made money on my pictures when I was under contract to them, do you suppose they would release my pictures when they don't have to? The first three stories have already been decided upon. One of them will be a late Zane Grey story, one by James Oliver Curwood, and one will be a Jack London story to be filmed in Canada. There will be no more 'hoss operas' so far as O'Brien is concerned. There will be action pictures, however. I mean, I may do some of London's sea stories and possibly a picture with a Bolder Dam background."

Through 1934 and 1935, George's pictures contained a fair amount of action and played up George's personable, easy manner. *Hard Rock Harrigan* (1935) took him into the world of construction tunneling, and *Whispering Smith Speaks*, another Western, was so successful that it became one of his most-loved pictures.

Evelyn Bostock, his leading lady in *Cowboy Millionaire*, had doubled for Gloria Swanson ten years earlier. Her petite beauty, sparkling brown eyes, and golden-brown hair were three of her many attributes that opened the door to her appearance on camera in motion pictures.

After making his next film, *The Frontier Marshal*, on location, George paused to ponder the direction his career had taken, and thought better of making more pictures in the Western theme.

He told S. R. Mook, a writer for *Silver Screen*, "You see, up until the time the talkies came in, I'd never made a Western picture. I'd made, among others, *Sunrise*, which Murnau directed, and I got some pretty swell notices for my work in that. But I've been in this business long enough to know that a *Sunrise* doesn't happen every day or even every two or three months, which was about as often as I made a new picture. I realized there'd be stretches when I'd be making pictures that would turn out to be run-of-the-mill program films."

He went on to explain, "One of the first pictures I made after *Sunrise* was *Salute*—a picture dealing with life at West Point and Annapolis. It should have been a swell picture, but the cast wasn't entirely right, so it turned out just fair. That gave me an idea of what to expect. Well, suddenly there sprang up a great demand for Westerns. Mr. Wurtzel said, 'You can ride. Why not make a few Westerns? It will develop a new public for you.' It was all right with me, so Sue Carol and I made *The Lone Star Ranger*, which was one of the most successful Westerns every produced. Naturally, the company wanted another one after that. And then another and another. First thing I knew, I was making nothing but Westerns. It was all right for a time. Every year I'd go into Mr. Wurtzel's office and say, 'Well, Sol, I'll make so and so many pictures this year and I want so and so much money for them.' And he'd say, 'All right, George,' and that would be that."

"But here's the rub: I like Westerns and I enjoy making them. But, at best, they're cheaply produced pictures and, as a rule, they're made in such a hurry you can't spend much time on details. They're designed principally for kids, so the stories don't have to be too plausible. Don't misunderstand me; we did the very best we could with them, but it was impossible to make as many as we made and still get *good* stories *every* time. And that's bad for any actor. Suddenly, it occurred to me that I was getting nowhere as an actor. I was doing the best I could with the parts offered me but one was pretty much like another. There was no chance to progress. Not by the highest stretch of imagination can Westerns be called 'Art'—not even if you spell it with a small 'a'— to begin with. I think there'll always be a market for Westerns. Every year a new bunch of kids grows old enough to go to picture shows, and kids are all alike. They always have been and they probably always will be. And just as long as kids are kids there'll be a market for

Westerns. Why, last summer, when I was on one of the smaller islands of the Hawaiians, I saw one of my old pictures advertised as 'coming in two months.' Can you imagine advertising a Western two months ahead of time if there was no market for it?"

Every week, he received hundreds of letters from hero-worshiping young boys of all ages, and took the time to answer each one. They came from a cross-section of adolescents in need of help, advice, and inspiration. Many letters came from mothers writing grateful appreciation for his positive influence on their sons. George did not drink or smoke, so they imitated him and refrained from using those vices. George was keenly aware of his responsibility to the legions of boys who wrote. Knowing his commitment to physical culture, many confided to him about their physical weakness. He steered them to their local Y.M.C.A. or suggested other practical, commonsense measures in the advice they received from him. Often, they would eagerly model their lives on anything they could find out about his eating, sleeping, or exercise habits.

As popular as George, his horse Mike appeared with him in many pictures. He often used two different horses, as nearly identical as possible. One was for showy, fast work, the other for scenes requiring more steadiness and intelligence than speed. Mike was a nine-year-old, trained by George since the horse was two years old.

"But we don't call them Westerns any more," he told writer Franc Dillon. "You know a Western used to be a picture in which the heroine wore a sunbonnet and the hero rode a horse. If the hero was called upon to act, he simply expanded his chest and followed it in a straight line across the stage. But that's the old-fashioned idea. We're making 'outdoor dramas' now. We buy the best stories available and hire actors who can act as well as ride a horse. In my last two pictures—*Thunder Mountain* and *Whispering Smith Speaks*—there aren't any horses. They're both railroad stories. We go wherever the script sends us for background. I went to England for exteriors for *Cowboy Millionaire* and recently, I've worked in Arizona and Mexico. There is more drama, to my way of thinking, in some of the wonderful scenery we have photographed for our pictures than there is in any film made in a studio. While Clark Gable sweats away under the hot lights, I'm outdoors on a horse having a swell time—doing the sort of thing I like to do."

In 1936, when his contract with Sol Lesser ended, George signed with producer George Hirliman's Condor Pictures for four independent films to be released through RKO. These films pleased his fans and were among the top moneymaking Westerns, second only behind those of Buck Jones. George A. Hirliman started working in the motion picture business at the age of fifteen in laboratory work. During the next twelve years, he was involved in many aspects of the technical side of the industry and owned his own laboratory complex. In 1927, he founded Exhibitor's Screen Services, which he then sold for a nice profit. During the next few years, he worked as a production executive, and by 1936, was with RKO as an associate producer.

George was earning $21,000 for each film, and by 1938, his popularity was such that his earnings increased to $25,000 a picture. He made sixteen films between 1936 and 1939, earning nearly a million dollars at a time when the average wage earner in America made $3,000-$5,000 annually.

About this new contract, George observed, "Not only am I privileged to name the director, writer and cast, and sit in on the story conferences—as I always have—but I am also privileged to make pictures on the outside—for major companies. That's stipulated in the contract. I can work for major companies but not for quickie outfits. At the moment, I am dickering with both Universal and MGM. The salary question is settled and as soon as they can show me a script that appeals to me, the papers will be signed. How's that for an outlook?"

His first film for Hirliman, *Daniel Boone* (1936), was a prestigue picture, often referred to as a "special" and rated as both his favorite film and one that has become a favorite for his fans. The film was made economically, but packs a powerful punch with the drama, especially the exciting climax in which Boonsboro Fort is besieged by Indians, nearly burned to the ground, and saved by nothing less than Divine intervention and a rainstorm.

In *Daniel Boone*, George refused to use any stunt double for the rough and tumble work. The film gave him plenty of opportunity to indulge in combat in scenes the script offered depicting him in the role of Indian fighter and trailblazer. George was especially proud of the work, and personally flew in a small plane to the film's premier in Kentucky at a theater near the site of the real-life hero's life. That day,

(TOP) Director David Howard and George O'Brien while filming *The Golden West* (1932).

(BOTTOM) A portrait of George O'Brien in *The Golden West* (1932).

George O'Brien in the late 1930s at the time of his series of films at RKO.

skies were whipped by a powerful thunderstorm, and the flight was rife with deathly hazard. The pilot steered the craft through the turbulent skies and barely managed to skid to a shaky landing on a rain-soaked runway. George emerged from the aircraft wearing the buckskin outfit he wore in the film. From the airport to the theater, he raced through the torrent. Rain soaked and dripping, he arrived at the premier looking as if he had fallen in a lake. Audience reception was

(TOP LEFT) George O'Brien demonstrating the physique and boxing prowess developed during his early years at the Columbia Park Boy's Club. (BOTTOM LEFT) Another example of the physical culture magazines of the 1930s featuring George O'Brien on the cover. (RIGHT) George O'Brien ca. 1935.

George O'Brien on the front cover of *Physical Culture*, April 1939.

brimming with pride, far better than the film fared when it faced its acid test with the New York critics at the Palace Theater on October 23, 1936.

According to the *New York Times*, the jaded mob in the theater that night kidded the film, applauded the pioneers, and hissed the Indians in mock-serious fashion. The picture did much better in the "sticks" where less discriminating audiences ate up the simplicity of the fanciful retelling of one chapter in Daniel Boone's life.

On July 8, 1936, Thomas Meighan, who helped George get his start in motion pictures, died at his estate, Grenwolde, near Great Neck, Long Island. The great star had been in declining health since the previous August, after an operation.

George's co-star in *The Painted Desert*, Lorraine Johnson, appeared for work properly wearing boots and packing a gun, exactly as the script called for her to appear. She created a comical stir on the set because the studio was forced to supply her with a nursemaid. The seventeen-year-old actress was not due to turn eighteen until October 13, 1938, and the law held that until the time she came of age, she was still a child to be guarded. The girl held a Winchester pistol at her hip when covering George in the action, but the law required a nursemaid to sit on the set and watch her intently. The blond was Betty Clopton, Lorraine's teacher, guardian, and protector while the green-eyed, 105-pound starlet was on the lot. She gave Lorraine her lessons during the day, saw that she stayed on schedule with her schooling according to the law, and kept the production from requiring her to put in no more than eight hours a day.

Lorraine, who moved to Long Beach, California, from Utah in 1932, had been given a screen test in 1937 after appearing in a Little Theater play, and had appeared with George in *Border G-Men*. She would again team with him in 1939 in *The Arizona Legion*, by that time, free of a nursemaid accompanying her every move while on the set or on a location.

In 1936, Marguerite appeared in seven films, and then she returned to Broadway in a play ironically titled *And Now, Goodbye*. The play opened in February 1937 at the John Golden Theater, ran for twenty-five performances, and then closed. With that, the curtain rang down on Marguerite Churchill's acting career. Other than inauspicious appearances in two television shows, she never appeared professionally again.

In 1938, RKO was seeking a sure-fire formula to improve their product and guarantee them a safe position in the competitive arena of film exhibition. According to Leo Spitz, head of production, plans were formulated for future operations on the basis of a method which

Hollywood had always contended would never work: they judged their next pictures solely on the merits of what previous films had done at the box office. As a result, the most turbulent shake-up in the studio's talent ranks of recent years occurred. Players of undoubted merit who had not recently been associated with profitable films were dropped, while those whose pictures had shown suitable returns were kept. Those actors who had managed, by virtue of their popularity, to turn admittedly undistinguished story material into money-making pictures were retained, while those who had failed to provoke enthusiasm except in high-class films were released from contract. For RKO, the test was not how many good pictures an actor had been in but how many bad ones he had managed to survive.

Irene Dunne, Cary Grant, Douglas Fairbanks, Jr. Richard Dix, Sally Eilers, and Chester Morris were stars consistently associated with profitable pictures, whether they were of A, B, C, or D stature. George was listed among the studio's best moneymakers.

George used his intelligence in gauging the interest of his audience, and made a sincere effort to invigorate the plots and characters of his films with authenticity. Starting with *Arizona Legion* (1939), he based his pictures on actual events. That film dealt with an actual episode from Arizona's history, the formation of the famous Arizona Legion, a law enforcement regiment along the lines of the Texas Rangers. George portrayed Thomas Rynning, and the scenario followed the restoration of law and order in Arizona with plenty of action to please the most excitement-loving schoolboy in an audience.

While Hollywood continued to grind out entertainment for the masses, conflicts rumbled in Europe. The rise of the Nazi's in Germany cast an ominous pal over politics. In America, plans were already begun to prepare for possible involvement. In 1939, John Ford began organizing a photographic unit for the US Navy to handle all propaganda, documentary, and reconnaissance photography. The Eleventh Naval District Motion Picture and Still Photographic Group consisted of 200 officers and enlisted men recruited from the studios. He planned to be an integral part in supporting the American military with his filmmaking skill.

By 1939, an entire decade had passed since the last silent films were made. A new generation of moviegoers had grown up knowing little about the old, forgotten stars of their parent's generation. Many silent stars disappeared, but Western stars found that encroaching age endeared them all the more to loyal fans. George's popularity remained high, but others fared worse.

Tom Mix survived by virtue of a regular radio show on which another actor appeared as him in Western dramas. The real Tom Mix took to performing circus-style Western extravaganzas in person under a tent. He had just returned from a successful tour of Europe, filled with enthusiasm for a fresh start with a contract for a new motion picture and a proposed tour of South America. He called Ruth, his daughter, at her ranch with the great news, and he planned to leave the following day for Hollywood.

After hanging up from the phone, he climbed into his green, custom-built Cord convertible to drive from New York to California. One week later, he again called her from Tucson, Arizona, and then resumed the journey. On a narrow ribbon of road about eighteen miles from Florence, Arizona, he suddenly came upon a partially constructed bridge with no warning sign of the obstruction. His car swerved and crashed into a gully at the bottom of the construction. Tom died on October 12, 1940.

The long-rumored production reorganization at Fox began the week of November 24, 1940. Because of their desperate need for profitable story properties, Charles Feldman of the Feldman-Blum Agency interested Fox in several package deals in which the studio acquired the story, script, stars, and director. These package deals removed a substantial share of production overhead, materially lowered the cost of films, and cut deep into executive personnel. The films were to be made with Fox money and probably on the Fox lot. All major participants were paid on a profit-sharing basis, with provision being made to include other personalities should Feldman wish to use them.

George's Westerns were remarkably profitable for RKO. Costing from $200,000 to $260,000 each, and filmed in three-week to four-week schedules, the films had a much greater attention to detail than the average programmer. As much as 47% of the studio's overhead was charged against his films before he started the first day of production. At that time, both Fox and RKO had their own theaters for immediate distribution of their product, and each city had their own distribution office. His films were sold before he made them, a great compliment to George and testament to the demand for his work. In

While at work, George O'Brien often insisted on the use of authentic firearms in his RKO films, an eye for detail often noted by reviewers as setting his films apart form the run-of-the-mill Western pictures.

spite of this, RKO made the decision to let him go after he completed the year's schedule of films in the series.

After making *Triple Justice* for RKO in 1940, George's contract ran out. In a cost-cutting measure, another up-and-coming Western star, Tim Holt, was promoted to a lower-salaried lead position, and George was ousted. Ever cheerful and wisely invested, George stepped aside, as Tim Holt filmed *Wagon Train* under a severely curtailed budget.

The abrupt change did not matter to George. Unknown to those at Fox, the war drums beating loudly over conflicts in Europe had caught his attention, and he was now focused in that direction. He had never lost his love for being a soldier, and with his Hollywood career temporariy halted, he reacted quickly when the US Navy contacted him.

George O'Brien in the late 1930s near the end of his long series of popular motion pictures.

Chapter 10
IN THE NAVY AGAIN

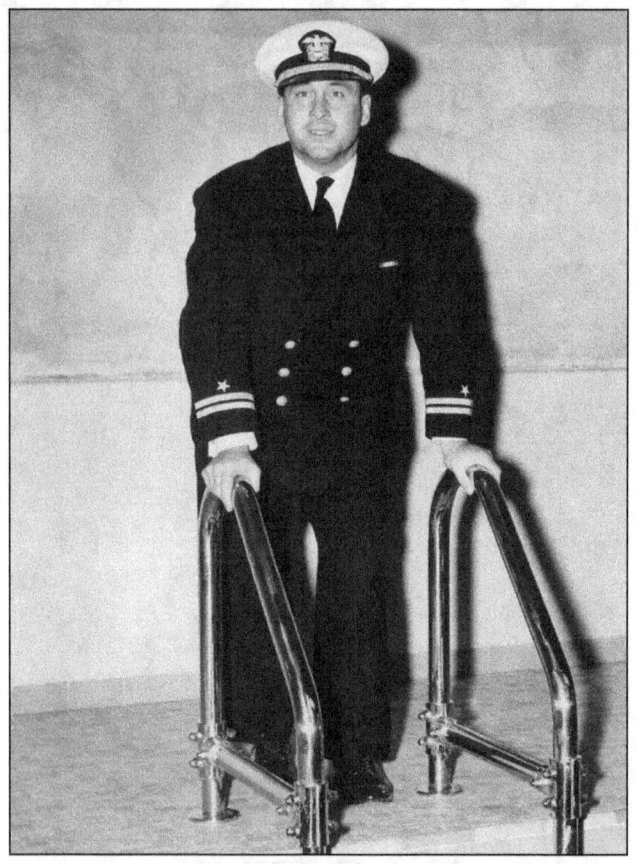

Lieutenant George O'Brien on April 28, 1942, entering the San Diego naval base three days after the attack on Pearl Harbor.

World War Two was in full operation and members of the US Navy approached George about reenlisting, George volunteered to enlist as soon as he learned of the formation of Ford's unit, but despite appeals by the director, the transfer was never approved.

"We figure your enlistment will help recruitment," military officials told him.

At the age of forty-one and the father of two children, George could have sat out the war. He could have pursued some kind of deal with any number of film studios. He was making good money in Hollywood, but he was at a rocky crossroad with his RKO contract ended and trouble with his marriage to Marguerite. He wanted to temporarily get away from the shaky marriage, thinking that living apart from her would heal their long-standing friction. He answered the call to arms.

In his second enlistment, George initially served as a recruit trainer in San Diego, and he had much to do with building the recreational and athletic program at that base. Because of his background in sports and his reputation as an athlete, George was put in charge of a $250,000 budget to implement programs in boxing, weight training, tennis, baseball, swimming, and other exercise regimes. He also took the example of his father's work with the San Francisco police and initiated a hand-to-hand combat routine as part of the navy's toughen-up program for new recruits.

On December 21, 1941, while George was involved with the war, his friend and frequent director, David Howard, died at the young age of forty-five. Howard cut his teeth in early Hollywood working on Spanish language film versions of pictures made in the early years of sound film production. He was a co-director for Nat Levine in a couple of Mascot cliffhangers, *Mystery Squadron* (1933), and *The Lost Jungle* (1934). His first film with George was *The Rainbow Trail* (1932), the sequel to *The Riders of the Purple Sage*. During nearly two decades, he and George collaborated on a total of twenty-five films, including George's last, *Triple Justice* (1940). When George turned his back on Hollywood and left films to return to the navy, Howard helmed the initial films in the Tim Holt series at RKO. His passing was one of deep sorrow for George, who lost a director who understood his particular abilities and a great friend, as well.

George's absence from the screen began to irk fans used to his regular appearances. Letters poured into the RKO mailroom in such volume that an RKO official contacted him at his navy base about the furor. He was compelled by a grateful sense of responsibility to those fans to compose a press release explaining what had happened to him. Mimeograph copies of the press release were promptly farmed out to major newspapers along with a new photo showing him wearing his navy blue uniform. The press release, dated April 28, 1942, read:

> "Lieutenant George O'Brien just three days after Pearl Harbor, big, broad-shouldered George O'Brien reported to the naval base at San Diego, Calif. In 48 hours he had terminated a picture career in Hollywood, closed his beautiful home, packed his wife and two youngsters into a station wagon and was off for active duty. Lieutenant George O'Brien is now director of Welfare and Athletics at the San Diego base. He enlisted at 16 as an ordinary sailor in the First World War. He was a champion boxer and wrestler in the Navy. Lieut. O'Brien is pictured here at the San Diego base."

George was the first to take the blame for his abrupt departure. In an interview with Lee O. Miller, he recalled his thoughts at the time, saying, "What could I do that wasn't already done? I suppose it was *I* who treated my studio shabbily, cutting off my career like that by enlisting in the navy, but at the time, I felt enlisting was the right thing to do, what with the situation abroad so sticky. I could offer neither my studio nor my fans anything beyond the press release I composed, and at the time I accepted whatever fate the future held for me."

According to his daughter, while George was away, Marguerite moved with their two children to New York where she opened a hat shop at Madison Avenue and 67th Streets. In a venture with her friend, Natalie Behrman Lieberman, the two women tried to earn additional family income during those difficult years while George was gone.

For six years while he was away, his brother managed his business affairs. George served in the navy and participated in fifteen island invasions in the Pacific Ocean. At the invasion of the Aleutians Islands, George was shot in his right knee. He was unconscious for five days, and woke up to find that he was suffering with double pneumonia, the result of over-exposure and exhaustion. He remained on sick leave throughout the winter and went back to daily workouts. During that time, he learned that Chester Bennett, who had directed George in *The Painted Lady* in 1924, was beheaded in Shanghai by the enemy.

George lost another of his oldest friends at this time. "Buck Jones was *all man*," he told Buck Rainey. "After his death in the Boston Fire, those of us who had worked with him felt a great loss. I was in the Aleutian Islands preparing for the invasion of Attu and Kiska Islands when I received the news. It broke my heart."

On the home front, one of his oldest film co-stars was embroiled in troubles of her own. On Tuesday, January 19, 1943, a San Francisco woman identified by Police Inspector Frank Lucey as Madge Bellamy, George's co-star in *The Iron Horse* and *Havoc* two decades earlier, was arrested. Officers said she fired three shots at Stanwood Murphy, lumberman, in the courtyard of a fashionable club on Nob Hill. Madge lost her mind with rage when she learned that Murphy, her boyfriend, had recently married another woman. She was booked at the San Francisco city prison on charges of assault with a deadly weapon. She gave her age to the police as thirty-five.

A few months after his illness, George returned to health and Los Angeles. The Admiralty felt he was the one man with the necessary stamina to train underwater crews in the Pacific, and for the next two years, he spent many months in the cold northern Pacific Ocean waters in guerilla warfare with the Japanese. In intense fighting, they held onto the little islands, battling Japanese fanaticism and eventually breaking their strangle hold on the land.

He was beach-master attached to Task Force 13 in bitter struggles at Saipan, Leyte, and other South Pacific death traps where the navy cleaned out the enemy. He was saddled with the nerve-wracking assignment of supervising the entry of troops and war equipment at the invasion sites. In this role, he was one of the first to enter Tokyo.

George emerged from World War Two with the rank of Commander, a Navy Commendation Medal, Presidential Citation for North Pacific duty, an American medal, and a South-Central Pacific campaign medal. His ribbons with four battle stars commended him for pre-Pearl Harbor duty. For many years, he stayed in the US Naval Reserve. Dysentery troubled him at the time of his discharge, and he was jumpy and irritable.

"You know what you need, George—a good vacation," his doctor advised. "Why don't you return to the kind of outdoor life you used to lead before you went into the navy? I know you love to swim, take sunbaths, and go down to the beach. Go back to this kind of life and your ailment will disappear." George took the doctor's advice and returned home to California.

George found many changes had taken place in Hollywood, especially in the making of Western films. During those years when he was at war, other stars that stayed behind took over his coveted position. A new generation of filmgoers had grown up never having seen him in the movies. He had difficulty finding work.

They were also earning much more than he had ever made.

Arlene Dahl had been on the Warner Bros. payroll for some time as a seven-year contract player, and she recalled in a 1975 interview, "... I sat around for about three or four months before Mr. Warner summoned me into his office, and said, 'I've got a part for you.'"

"I said, 'Great. What is it?'"

"He said, 'Well, it's called *My Wild Irish Rose*. You don't need to read the script, it's the lead. And Dennis Morgan is a star, and we're going to introduce you in this picture and make a star out of you.'"

"And I said, 'Well, that's marvelous!' I'd been sitting around dancing, and singing, taking all the lessons that contract players usually do. And that was my first film.'"

According to Erskin Johnson in an article appearing in the *Helena Independent Record*, there was consternation in the Warner studio casting office. They needed a barrel-chested muscle man to play the role of William Muldoon, known at the turn of the century as The Iron Duke, strongest man in American, for the movie, *My Wild Irish Rose*. Director, David Butler, getting desperate, said, "We need a man like George O'Brien."

"Yeah," said a casting office fellow sadly, "but George O'Brien is in the navy. As a matter of fact, I think he was killed up in the Aleutians."

An agent took the rumor of his death to George along with the news that director David Butler was looking for a "George O'Brien type." George had been back in Hollywood for six months and was anxious to re-start his stalled career. He was the same trim, youthful-looking man with the barrel chest, the slim hips, and the bulging biceps that his fans knew. He went all out to obtain the role.

"It's the art of living," George smiled. "I don't worry about things. You guys worry more than the fellows I spent five years with in the foxholes."

"What do you want to do, George?" they asked.

"Play good roles in good pictures," replied George.

For six months, there were no good roles. There were offers for pictures that did not excite him. George turned down a couple of action pictures, which when they were later made, turned out badly. He was better off not having been a part of them.

"I figured," he said, "it was time to cut out the heroics. I had been heroic on the screen for twenty years. I didn't have to work just because the rent was due. I told them I could always go back to wrestling or opening the door at my wife's millinery salon."

They arranged for a test, and director Butler said, "How long has it been since you read lines, George?"

"Five years," said George, and then he added sheepishly, "but I've been practicing at home."

Jack Warner saw the test, and said, "That's the guy."

My Wild Irish Rose presented a refreshingly robust George as a fitness-loving minstrel player in a musical tale of the life of Chauncey Olcott, who came out of Buffalo in the 1880s to win the hearts of Irishmen and others with his ballads of Old Erin. Although Dennis Morgan was the star of the film, George appeared in half a dozen scenes, and he showed a profound sense of humor, even going so far as to participate in one of the music sequences, contributing his fine-sounding, on-key voice to one of the songs.

After making a successful comeback, George was again out of work for many months. When Marguerite heard that John Ford was to make *Fort Apache*, a new Western, she called the director and begged him to give George a part. At first, Ford was reluctant to do so, but when Marguerite told him he would be taking great steps to "help keep a good Catholic marriage together," Ford relented.

Fort Apache brought George back to the screen. With a $15,000 salary, the director and star renewed their friendship. George was respectful of Ford to the point of worship. Always gregarious and charming, he gallantly appeared in a decidedly secondary part that offered him little to do. He looked great with his weight scaled-down to a figure remarkably similar to his physique of years before.

Ford sought to depict life on a frontier military outpost in the post-Civil War era with accurate details rich in national values and conflicts. Intense research went into the military and technical side of the story. In addition to the script, each character was profiled in a brief biography to prepare the actors for their interpretation.

George's role as Captain Samuel Collingwood was revealed to him in one of these biographies, rife with details of his life before and after the film's story. The convincing atmosphere of the fort erected at the Corrigan Ranch in Simi Valley, California, and also on RKO sound stages, reflected the unusually thorough research effort.

To add to the film's visual appeal, cast and crew assembled at Ford's favorite location in Monument Valley. Striking reproductions of Frederick Remington's beautiful paintings provided the inspiration for many camera set-ups. George O'Brien first brought the 96,000-acre Flagstaff vistas to Ford's attention. He had seen a set of photos of the area and was entranced with the permanent, seemingly implacable and sacred pillars spreading over its landscape painted with striking sandstone buttes and magnificent spires rising toward the sky. Fully 180 miles from the nearest railroad, the majesty and repose of the mountains provided a canvas against which he could stage the tale with epic grandeur. Their innate beauty became synonymous with Ford's films.

On October 12, 1947, the *Joplin Globe* reported the death of forty-five-year-old former silent screen star Olive Borden, with whom George had starred in *Fig Leaves* and *3 Bad Men*. She had been a top star, but the industry had forgotten her. She spent her final years in abject poverty living on charity, and in her last days, Olive descended into a nightmare of drug addiction. For her, death was a release. Her obituary in the *Coshocton Tribune*, October 2, 1947, read:

> "Former Film Star Dies in Poverty. Olive Borden, who rode high in the movieland firmament as a $1,500 a week star 20 years ago, died in poverty yesterday. At 40, she had lost the fickle favor of the movie-going public and the studios, her health and wealth were gone, but was not entirely forgotten—her mother was at her deathbed. Death came in the Sunshine mission for women in the heart of Los Angeles' downtown skid

row. Her mother, Mrs. Sybil Borden, is manager of the mission's commissary. Olive, who had lived and worked there since 1945, succumbed to heart and lung ailments. Only the day before, Olive brushed back her dark hair and told an interviewer: 'The whole world has fallen in on me. But the doctors will make we well.' Miss Borden, starting as a Mack Sennett bathing beauty, starred in the 1920s with the late Tom Mix, Lew Cody, John Boles, George O'Brien, and others."

After three decades of work in motion pictures, George finally made his stage debut. Press announcements on January 1949 revealed the impending production of a revival of the stage play, *What Price Glory?*, for the benefit of the Purple Heart Association. John Ford, was set to direct the play and a spectacular cast was assembled with George O'Brien, Ward Bond, Pat O'Brien, John Wayne, Gregory Peck, Alan Hale Sr., Robert Armstrong, and Oliver Hardy in a rare appearance without Stan Laurel. Wallace Ford, Charles Kemper, Henry O'Neill, Jimmy Lydon, Larry Blake, Ed Begley, and Forrest Tucker played other roles. Maureen O'Hara was the only woman in the cast.

Most of the actors worked at various film studios, and their schedules were coordinated so the actors could freely rehearse at night. A location was selected that was convenient to all, the former mansion once owned by Antonio Moreno, a magnificent Mediterranean villa on a six-acre estate mounted on the crest of a hill. Christened "Crestmount," it was originally a lonely estate nestled among the hills looming over Los Angeles. In time, it became a packed subdivision known as Moreno Highlands. After his only marriage ended in divorce, Moreno sold the property to a charitable organization, and it later became the site of the Masquers Club. The *What Price Glory?* cast gathered in the home to rehearse.

Progress went smoothly despite the logistical nightmare of such a production. Only John Ford could have gotten the project off the ground. The actors donated their time and effort and they took no salary. Sets were also designed and built for free. Western Costume generously donated costumes for the entire cast.

Ford accepted the challenge of directing the play despite his inexperience with theater. Initial progress did not go well, so Ralph Murphy was called in to stage the show more appropriately.

"Ford never once interfered with Murphy," recalled Harry Carey, Jr., who later recalled that John Ford "sat out in the audience and never said a word, but he was at every rehearsal. He loved the stage, and he was fascinated with it."

However, one night when Murphy was absent, Ford stepped in at the rehearsal and took delight in unmercifully picking on every aspect of Ward Bond's performance, a common occurrence during their long relationship. A first dress rehearsal was given, and then the final dress rehearsal was held Feb. 21, 1949, at the Masquers Club before an audience of 450 invited guests, including many paraplegic veterans and Secretary of the Navy John Sullivan. Before the performance, James Stewart—a decorated veteran himself—explained how the play's proceeds would be used to help veterans.

Harrison Carroll, a reviewer for the *Bradford Era*, wrote on March 22: "Ward Bond, as Captain Flagg, stole the show in John Ford's stage production of *What Price Glory?* Charles Kemper is another who played to the hilt. The others all were good."

Hedda Hopper wrote, "Secretary of the Navy John Sullivan attended the dress rehearsal of *What Price Glory?* at the Masquers Club. He was invited by John Ford. No one can resist Mr. Ford. No one, I might ad, resisted Mr. Sullivan. Ward Bond, who was on the stage before, gave an inspired performance as Capt. Flagg, but it was the spirit of the performers, the distinguished audience of paraplegics in wheel chairs, and Hollywood's finest people that made the evening memorable. The play can't be shown in Los Angeles because the theaters object to the cuss words, but it is sold out in San Francisco, Oakland, and Pasadena."

The following night, *What Price Glory?* opened in Long Beach, and then began a six-city tour of one-night stands in San Jose, Oakland, San Francisco, Pasadena, and finally at a final performance in Los Angeles at Grauman's Chinese Theater.

In the *Los Angeles Times* article by Michael F. Blake, cast member Harry Carey, Jr., reported, "The audience would just applaud when Ward Bond and Pat O'Brien came on stage. When John Wayne made an entrance, they'd just gasp. With Greg Peck, it was like Frank

Sinatra: he was such a heartthrob, the girls would just start squealing when he came on stage." The audience became wild with enthusiasm when the entire cast came out in a line to take their final bows. Critics were respectful, and some mentioned the show would be a natural success on Broadway.

The huge success of the play earned more than $82,000, but shortly after the final performance at Grauman's Chinese Theater, all the money mysteriously disappeared. "The guy who handled all the money for the production ran off with all the receipts," Carey said. "People asked Jack if they should go after the fella and Jack said, "No, he'll be looking over his shoulder the rest of his life.'" Later, Ford made up for the stolen receipts by dipping into his personal savings. There had been discussions about taking the play to New York or Washington, D.C. for a week, but nothing came of it. Ford lost interest after the Los Angeles performance, and the play disbanded. Thousands of dollars were ultimately gleaned from the performances and transferred to the Purple Heart Association, and everyone involved had a good time.

On April 4, 1949, twelve nations from Western Europe and North America signed the North Atlantic Treaty in Washington, D.C. agreeing "an armed attack against one or more of them in Europe or North America shall be considered an attack against them all." Initially, there were no preparations to carry out the mission, and there was no command structure to direct the overall defense of Western Europe. In 1948, after the outbreak of the Korean War in June, all this changed.

An integrated command structure was created to increase the defense of the twelve nations, and an overall commander for NATO forces was selected. General Dwight D. Eisenhower, who had led Allied forces in Europe during World War Two, was appointed for the task on December 19, 1950. He arrived in Europe the following January and set to work devising a structure for his new command, Allied Command Europe (ACE), and new headquarters, Supreme Headquarters Allied Powers Europe (SHAPE). Always ready to serve his country, George again put his career in films behind him, walking away to again serve his country.

"I was slowly but surely rebuilding my second career in films when the trouble in Korea started," he observed. "Maybe it was my inner sense of patriotism or loyalty, I don't exactly know, but whatever it was forced me to again abort my career in films and resume the life of an officer in the navy." Much to his wife's consternation, George left her and his two children, and in 1955, he returned to San Diego for active naval duty in the Korean conflict. He served in the US Naval Intelligence and operated behind Red lines in North Korea on top-secret activities.

Chapter 11
SUNSET ON THE TRAIL

By the early 1950s, the first retrospectives of old films were emerging. A new generation looked at movies from the 1920s and 1930s with curious interest, while older generations looked back on them with nostalgia. In the summer of 1953, The Brown Derby Restaurant in Hollywood inaugurated a "Western Wall of Fame." George was invited to observe the unveiling of charcoal portraits by artist, Nick Volpe. He posed for photographs next to the permanent exhibit of original artworks, which included renditions of George, Bronco Billy Anderson, William Farnum, William S. Hart, Buck Jones, Hoot Gibson, Tom Mix, Harry Carey, Sr., Ken Maynard, Tim McCoy, Will Rogers, Johnny Mack Brown, Leo Carrillo, Randolph Scott, Joel McCrea, Gary Cooper, John Wayne, Roy Rogers, Gene Autry, William Boyd, and George Montgomery.

In March 1957, producer Robert Youngston purchased the negative rights to the film, *Noah's Ark*. It was re-released in association with Hal Roach Studios and Associated Artists in a truncated version that was edited down from the original two hours to seventy minutes. All the careful dialogue scenes were removed, and a new soundtrack score with sound effects and a vulgar narration were added. A new generation of moviegoers saw the film for the first time, but what they saw bore little resemblance to the magnificent film that was originally released in 1928.

George served in the US Navy for the several years. In 1958 when Kumoi, Korea was bombed, George was there along with others. In April and May 1958, he traveled to Taiwan and Korea with John Ford to produce two orientation films for the US Navy Defense

Department. The films were constructed to help servicemen, civilians, and their dependents adjust to their new posts in those countries.

Korea: Battleground for Liberty, and *Taiwan—Island of Freedom*, were both commissioned by the Office of Armed Forces Information and Education to counteract Communist propaganda about American imperialism. These documentaries were designed to coordinate better relations between Americans and friendly Asian countries. As project officer, George was delegated to accompany Ford and Frank Capra, another veteran of films and the military, on a location scouting trip. With them was Joe Longo, a World War Two veteran, who volunteered to work on the film. While there, George suffered an odd mishap that resulted in some peculiar photographs of him.

"He lost the sight in one eye, due to an insect burrowing into his eye during one of his visits to Cambodia, and he had a corneal replacement, I believe, in San Francisco," recalled Orin O'Brien in a letter to this author. She and her brother, Darcy, and his wife, Ruth Ellen Berke, visited the hospital every day to feed him and visit. At that time, eye surgery required a recovery time of six weeks. While flat on his back, George endured the difficulty with sandbags placed on each side of his head to keep him from moving.

On April 20, 1959, Ford and O'Brien arrived at a press conference in Taipei sporting identical eye patches that caused some people to look at the pair with great curiosity. For the next ten days, they shot location scenes with a 16mm camera manned by cameramen from the Lookout Mountain Air Force Laboratory. From there, they journeyed to Seoul, Pusan, and filmed along the demilitarized zone separating North and South Korea. When one actor failed to arrive, George substituted on-camera talking with Heran Moon, a Korean model and actress. Work was completed after they returned to Los Angeles for additional scenes shot with young actors briefing American airmen in the particulars of life and work in Asian communities.

In June 1959, the *Newport Daily News* reported that he was one of ninety-three Naval Officers attending the Naval War College's annual Global Strategy Discussions. He was involved with a special project with the Department of the Defense in connection with President Eisenhower's People to People Program. George served as Project Officer for a series of government-sponsored orientation films on eight Asian countries to be shown to American military

During the Eisenhower administration, the U. S. Navy released this candid photo depicting Captain George O'Brien examining old and rare books at the Mahan Library at the Naval War College where he was on two weeks of Naval Reserve duty. The eye patch covered an infected eye. Those in attendance were startled to see him arrive at the event with John Ford, who also wore an eye patch.

personnel and their families. The customs, traditions, and customs of the Asian nations were portrayed in an attempt to help Americans abroad dispel their reputation for rudeness and incompatibility.

After the Korean War ended, George earned a Department of Defense special citation and Special Projects medal for duties rendered in eight Southeast Asian countries from 1957 to 1961 in Taiwan, Japan, Korea, Okinawa, Philippines, Vietnam, Cambodia, and Thailand.

While his military career kept him occupied, his personal life deteriorated. His wife left him when she was no longer content to be relegated to a position second to his military work.

"My biggest sorrow and disappointment came when my wife Margie filed for divorce. I'd married Margie prior to World War Two and she had stuck with me during the long, lonely years of absence, so, when the Korea mess happened and I again returned to duty, she couldn't take it. Nor, she said, could the kids take it. So, she divorced me and kept Orin and Darcy. We're still good friends today . . . ."

For a time, he was involved with a partnership producing TV films including *Assignment Underwater*, a project on navy underwater demolition teams called "frogmen." On September 8, 1957, television lured George before the cameras when he appeared in an episode of the Heinz Studio 57 anthology series in a filmed, half-hour drama called *Typhoon*.

In February 1961, George made a surprise appearance as himself in an episode of the popular television show, *This Is Your Life*, hosted by Ralph Edwards. In the episode paying homage to Richard Arlen, George burst onto the stage in front of the live audience and shared good-natured anecdotes about his and Arlen's early years in pictures.

During the early years of the conflict with Vietnam, George briefly returned to active military duty as a naval attaché to the NATO conferences in France, Italy, Turkey, Greece, and England. He left service for inactive duty in 1963 with the rank of captain, having three times been recommended for the rank of Admiral. His major duty stations included Adak, Attu, Dutch Harbor, Kodiak, Great Sitkins Island, Manila, Leyte, Saigon, Phnom Penh, plus flagships, destroyers, APA Attack ships, LST, LCT, and other amphibious invasion craft. His NATO stations in Europe were France, Italy, Turkey, Greece, and England.

With his military career behind him, George again sought involvement with Hollywood filmmaking. In 1963, John Ford was planning production on his next film, *Cheyenne Autumn*. Based on a book first published in 1953 by Mari Sandoz, the story had been shopped around Hollywood for some time with little success. With Ford at the helm, the Indians in the picture were cast with several famous Mexican and Italian actors, including Sal Mineo, silent stars Gilbert Roland and Dolores del Rio, Victor Jory, and Ricardo Montalban.

At the age of sixty-nine, George was as vigorous as in his sagebrush days, and he was eager to work in films again. "But there's no pressure. Thank God I saved my money," he said. George joined Richard Widmark, Carroll Baker, Edward G. Robinson, and James Stewart, and spectacular location filming began.

Technicolor representative were on hand to supervise the particular lighting requirements, and the performers went through their paces. This was his first appearance in a wide-screen, Technicolor epic. The cinematography by William Clothier was splendid, and the end result was one of the best-photographed pictures of Ford's career. The Academy of Motion Picture Arts and Sciences nominated Clothier's work for an Oscar.

Around this time, George's younger brother, Daniel, passed away. He had spent his whole life as a lawyer in San Francisco, and after the death of their father, he personally handled George's financial affairs.

Orin O'Brien recalled George meeting her in 1969 when she came out to Los Angeles on tour with the New York Philharmonic. He offered to take her and some friends from the orchestra to dinner. When she told him that she did not want to hurt anyone's feelings and did not know whom to invite, George decided to bring the whole orchestra to an outdoor feast at his home in Santa Monica. Her colleagues were bused from their Hollywood hotel out to his house, and spent the afternoon eating and telling stories. John Ford dropped in for a surprise visit, which entertained the movie fans in the group.

At this time of multiple television networks and wide screen films, the second and third generations of children of some silent film stars were now busy in Hollywood. John Barrymore's son was appearing in a number of foreign films; John Wayne's son, Patrick, was making his first on-screen appearances; and on Saturday, March 14, 1964, Hickman Hill, the 19-year old grandson of Tom Mix made his acting debut in a small role on CBS Television in an episode of *Gunsmoke* with James Arness. The old men of Hollywood were rapidly being replaced with a new breed of actors, the same age as their fathers and grandfathers were when they first began working in films.

The following year, John Ford was in the middle of making the film, *Young Cassidy*. He was sixty-nine years old, and he was looking pale. Wearing dark glasses, he flew from Dublin to London in a private plane to receive treatment for a throat infection. "He is very low," said assistant director, Jay Quested to the London press. "At first we thought it was his cigars, but that was not so. He has been seen by doctors here, but his own doctor, who flew here over the weekend, decided it would be best for him to return home for treatment ... we don't know how long Mr. Ford will be away. He may be back very soon."

While vacationing in Hawaii in 1968 with his daughter, George was reunited with Dorothy Mackaill, then living in the tropical state. It was the first time they had seen each other since she co-starred with him in *The Man Who Came Back*.

In 1973, the NBC network sent George to Europe and the Orient producing and directing a TV special, *Windjammer*. Although he kept his hand in film work, it was not the central focus of his life. His work in silent films seemed like forgotten, ancient history to him. Just as he was unaware of his swelling popularity after his initial success in *The Iron Horse*, he was unaware of the mushrooming interest in classic films of the 1920s and 1930s. He seldom looked back, and he spent little time recalling his earlier success.

When pressed to discuss his past glories, interviewers found he was not one to live in the past. "My father taught me to live in the present, and I've been doing just that," he told Buck Rainey. "After four years in Vietnam, plus the other wars I have come back from, I feel my life is at present all down hill and shady, which is an old cowboy saying when everything is smooth, cool, and happy."

His film career was coming to an end, and when he was asked which film was his favorite, he said, "I guess I'd have to say *The Iron Horse*, because it was a success, and it could have been an awful flop,

George O'Brien at age 53, in the summer of 1953, at the Brown Derby Restaurant in Hollywood for the inauguration of their "Western Wall of Fame."

and Ford and I would still be trying to make a living someplace. So it did two things: it gave me my opportunity and it gave Ford his opportunity, because up until that time, he'd been making 'Harry Careys.' So you see how things happen. If Ford and the Fox Company had not been happy with one of the fifty-eight tests they made, I'd probably be off sailing a ship someplace. Then, I would also say something that wasn't George O'Brien: the characterization in *Sunrise*, because I like to think

George O'Brien in the 1970s.

that everybody sees what I saw in *Sunrise*, a chance to prove that I could concentrate on something besides my ever-lovin' personality."

John Ford also still thought highly of *The Iron Horse*. In a 1971 interview with Vernon Scott, he said, "Someday maybe I'd like to write a story on the making of *The Iron Horse*. It was done in the snow under magnificent conditions. It's still a damn good picture and that's forty-five years ago." At the time, he was working on a CBS television special, *The American West of John Ford*. "I don't like interviews. Never have. But I'm doing this for my grandson, Daniel Sergeant Ford. Daniel is just back from Vietnam where he was decorated seven times, including the Silver Star, and he was wounded several times," Ford said. "So the least I can do is help him out."

In the 1960s and 1970s, Hollywood's past achievements found favor with a new generation of film aficionados. Festivals sprang up on the East and West coasts, and many tried without success to lure George as a guest at a retrospective of his work. Initially, he had little interest.

"I'd just as soon be remembered as an old navy man than a movie star," George said to Ed Hulce, director of the 1979 Cinecon Film Festival, a yearly convention of film collectors. That particular year, the Museum of Modern Art was having a screening of an original, 35mm nitrate print of *Sunrise*, and with that event attracting him to New York, Hulce convinced him to visit the Cinecon Film Festival. Once George agreed, Hulce went to work locating a number of rare films for the occasion.

At the Cinecon Festival, Hulce arranged screenings of George's silent films, *Noah's Ark, 3 Bad Men, The Dancers,* and *The Blue Eagle*, and his sound films, *When a Man's a Man,* and *The Marshal of Mesa City*.

Hulce sat next to George during the screening of *Sunrise*, and at the end of the film, Hulce wiped tears from his eyes. In part, he was exhausted from the effort spent organizing the festival, but he was also touched by *Sunrise*. As they left, George turned to him in the car and said, "Thank you for your tears."

"Cinecon never had a guest who was more accessible than George O'Brien," recalled Hulce. "He didn't just pop up at the MOMA screening or the banquet; he wandered around the convention every day, signing hundreds of autographs, and conversing with attendees for hours. Whenever I wanted to find him, I had only to walk through the convention area and see where a crowd had gathered; invariably, he was in the middle of it. The evening he arrived in New York, I picked him up at the airport and drove him to the hotel, going over our schedule. As he was then eighty years old, and I fully expected that the cross-country flight had exhausted him. But he was eager to get acquainted, and after a shower and a nap, he was ready for a late dinner. I wanted to take him to a fancy restaurant. He shot that idea down and asked, 'Where can we get a good hamburger and some fresh apple pie?' My kind of guy. Several committee members accompanied us, and we stayed out until 3 o'clock in the morning while George regaled us with stories and answered dozens of questions. He described himself as 'a man of few thousand words,' and proved it time and again. He had a way of answering questions in a circuitous manner, often going far off the subject for minutes or even hours at a time before coming back to the original query. It became apparent to me that George had no illusions about who he was and how his film career had progressed. You might think that somebody who had starred in such classic films as *The Iron Horse, 3 Bad Men*, and *Sunrise*—and who had worked for Ford, Hawks, Murnau, Walsh—would have been bitter that he wound up top-lining B-Westerns, but that wasn't the case. Not by a long shot. George loved doing Westerns, and he retained many fond memories of them."

As a result of having enjoyed himself so much at Cinecon, the following year he accepted an invitation to appear at the Memphis Western Film Festival, joining another convention guest, Cecilia Parker, who had been the female lead in two of his best Fox Westerns: *The Rainbow Trail* and *Mystery Ranch*, and a later film, *Hollywood Cowboy*. That convention reunited the two for the first time in over forty years. The next day, at a screening of *Thunder Mountain*, one of the films he made in partnership with Sol Lesser, George sat next to Ed Hulce, and delivered a running commentary on the film. He was trying to do this in a sotto voice, and half the viewers in the room had their heads cocked in their direction to listen.

On August 31, 1973, John Ford died of cancer. George visited him just days before he passed away. He had a chance to say goodbye to the man who had been such a dynamic force in forming his early success in motion pictures.

In 1980, Janet Gaynor, George's costar in *The Johnstown Flood*, *The Blue Eagle*, and *Sunrise*, was attracted to the quirky romance between a lunatic youth and an antiestablishment senior citizen in the film *Harold and Maude*, a unique and startling, low-budget film hit in the early 1970s that garnered a cult following with legions of admirers who flocked to midnight screenings of the picture. Colin Higgins had shaped the tale into a musical with lyrics by David Amram. Janet came out of retirement to star in a Broadway production of the same story. On January 19, the curtain went up for twenty-one previews at the Martin Beck Theater, and it opened on February 7, 1980. Four days later it closed, a resounding failure, and Janet went back into retirement.

George knew he had also come to the end of the trail. He moved to Tulsa, arriving at his son's house in a five-ton truck loaded with his personal possessions. He was not a guest in their small home for long. Because their space was limited, he chose to move into a cottage at the Franciscan Villa in Broken Arrow, Oklahoma. On June 6, 1981, his first night at the new home, George charmed all the women in the residence at a dinner. The next day, he suffered a heart attack and a stroke, and then he was confined to a bed for the last few years of his life. While there, his health gradually declined.

George died on September 4, 1985, in the Franciscan Villa at Broken Arrow, Oklahoma. From the *New Orleans Times Picayune*, reporters wrote on September 5, 1985:

> "Broken Arrow, Okla. Actor George O'Brien, a veteran of 75 films, including the Westerns, *Fort Apache* and *The Iron Horse*, died Wednesday in a convalescent home after a long illness. He was 86. O'Brien, whose Hollywood career spanned 42 years, had lived in the nursing home since a stroke left him partially paralyzed in 1979. One of his most acclaimed roles was in the silent film, *Sunrise*, which also starred Janet Gaynor. O'Brien worked with some of the biggest names in Hollywood during the 1920s and 1930s, including Mary Astor, Wallace Beery, Douglas Fairbanks, Jr., William Powell, and Myrna Loy. After a rosary in Broken Arrow, O'Brien will

be buried at sea by the US Navy in San Diego."

Because of George O'Brien's life-long love of the sea, he was buried by the US Navy just off the coast of San Diego. He was an original, a good man, and a man's man in Hollywood.

The End

Filmography

JUST TONY (1922)
FOX
PRODUCER: WILLIAM FOX
DIRECTOR: LYNN F. REYNOLDS.
SCENARIO: based on a novel, *Alcatraz*, by Max Brand
CAST: Tom Mix, Tony, Claire Adams, J. P. Lockney, Duke R. Lee, Frank Campeau, Walt Robins
SYNOPSIS: The story follows a wild horse named "Tony" and the efforts of a cowpuncher to rescue the horse and save the heroine from a gang of outlaws.

"This picture is unique in that it has the only absolutely natural actor on the screen," wrote the reviewer for *Variety*. "He is Tom Mix's horse, 'Tony,' and for delineation of horse character, is a wonder. The subtitles constantly impute to the animal emotion and motives that are human, and then by some sort of legerdemain, manage to make the animal express them. The acting is excellent. Mix is always a likable player in his familiar roles, and Claire Adams makes an attractive heroine both for beauty and grace of subdued acting."

"Tom Mix is a likable fellow and an excellent horseman," wrote a reviewer for the *New York Times*, "and his horse is a splendid animal. Dissolving subtitles, subtitles that ought to dissolve before they ever appear, and a lot of sentimental tosh about animals are among the other annoying things in the film."

A reviewer in the *Lima News* wrote, "Tony, Tom Mix's wonder horse, is the featured performer in the newest Mix Production. Remarkable feats by exceptional horses. Besides the attraction supplied by his own performance, Tony proves a necessary factory in the romance between the friendly cowboy who rescues him and cowgirl who befriends the man."

George O'Brien worked as an assistant cameraman on this film, and may have played an unaccredited role as an extra.

WHITE HANDS (1922)
GRAF PRODUCTIONS
DIRECTOR: LAMBERT HILLYER
PRODUCER: MAX GRAF
SCENARIO: Lambert Hillyer, based on a story by C. Gardner Sullivan
CAST: Hobart Bosworth, Robert McKim, Freeman Wood, Al Kaufman, Muriel Frances Dana, Elinor Fair. George O'Brien played a small role as a sailor.
SYNOPSIS: In Africa, Hurricane Hardy, a seaman, rescues a lost party of explorers and falls in love with the heroine.

"This is a typical C. Gardner Sullivan tale," wrote a reviewer in *Variety*, "and although laid in the African desert country, has all the thrills that were in his Klondike tales screened several years ago. Sullivan seems to have the screen angle first and foremost, and his manner of working out a tale of this kind cannot be improved on. The real star of the picture, however, is Baby Muriel Frances Dana. She is better than Jackie Coogan, although in this picture she has not as much to do as he had in *The Kid*. Made on the Ince lot at Culver City, the picture does not look to represent more than a $50,000 outlay, but it has all the flash of a production that would have cost more than double that under ordinary circumstances."

A reviewer in the *Lima News* wrote,

An advertisement for the Tom Mix film, *Just Tony*, as it appeared in the *Lima News*, February 1, 1929.

Hobart Bosworth, writer, director, and actor, kept George O'Brien from abandoning his hopes of a film career by offering him a role in his film *White Hands* (1922).

"Whenever you see the name of Hobart Bosworth in a cast, you know that the picture is a sea-going one with bare-fisted fights and everything. *White Hands* may briefly be described as an average program picture, completely dominated by the rugged personality of Mr. Bosworth."

George O'Brien played an unaccredited extra role in this film.

(LEFT) A newspaper advertisement for *Moran of the Lady Letty*, as it appeared in the *Coshocton Tribune* April 9, 1922. (RIGHT) Dorothy Dalton and Rudolph Valentino in a scene from *Moran of the Lady Letty* (1922), one of the first motion pictures to feature George O'Brien prominently.

MORAN OF THE LADY LETTY (1922)
FAMOUS PLAYERS-LASKY
DIRECTOR: GEORGE MELFORD
ADAPTATION: Monte M. Katterjohn, based on a novel by Frank Norris
CAST: Dorothy Dalton, Rudolph Valentino, Charles Brinley, Walter Long, Emil Jorgenson, Maude Wayne, Cecil Holland, George Kuwa, Charles K. French.
SYNOPSIS: Ramon Laredo, a society idler who is sought after by debutantes, is drugged, kidnapped, and spirited onto a pirate ship where he and Moran, daughter of the skipper of the Lady Letty, save their ship from thieves and end up in a clinch at the fadeout.

According to a review in *Variety*, "It works as an interesting melodrama of the sea with a wealth of action, and has its dramatic punch in a man-to-man battle all over the deck of a three-masted sailing vessel and into the lofty rigging, ending with the hurling of the villain from the lofty main trunk into the sea. The marine scenes are splendid photographically, and all the settings on board ship are tremendously realistic."

The *New York Times* reviewer wrote, ". . . You just can't take the story of this film seriously, and it takes itself too seriously to permit you to accept it as frank melodrama. But you can enjoy its ships and sailors and sea. Practically all of its action is on the waterfront or the open ocean. It is soaked in salt. Dorothy Dalton fits into the action, too, when she keeps out of the close-ups and does not show her artificial Broadway make-up. Rudolf Valentino, as the hero, of course, is not so well-suited to the sea. He fits better into the romantic and melodramatic excesses of the story. He doesn't impress one as the kind of youth who would be attracted by Moran."

A review in the *Manitoba Free Press* wrote, ". . . it is no less colorful than *The Sheik*, and the salt tang of the sea is in every scene. The big punches come in the battles with mutinous sailors."

George O'Brien played an unaccredited role as a sailor in several scenes, and performed the stunt at the climax of the film when one character takes a sixty-foot dive from the ship's mast into the sea.

THE GHOST BREAKER (1922)
FAMOUS PLAYERS-LASKY PARAMOUNT
DIRECTOR: ALFRED E. GREEN
SCREENPLAY: WALTER DELEON
ADAPTATION: Jack Cunningham from the play by Paul Dickey and Charles W. Goddard
CAST: Wallace Reid, Lila Lee, Walter Heirs, Arthur Carewe, J. Farrell MacDonald, Frances Raymond, Snitz Edwards, Richard Arlen, Mervyn LeRoy, George O'Brien. Arlen, LeRoy, and George O'Brien played unaccredited roles as one of three sheet-covered ghosts.
SYNOPSIS: In Spain, Duke D'Alva and Marla Theresa search for buried treasure in an old castle, but an conspiring cousin resorts to spiritual manifestations to scare her away."

"It could have been a great deal better than it is," wrote a reviewer in the *New York Times*, "and this is disturbing to anyone's enjoyment of a comedy. The Dickey-Goddard play offered almost boundless opportunities for fun and thrills on the screen, and they have been taken advantage of only halfway and half-heartedly."

"This is one of those usual Wallace Reid starring pictures," began a review in *Variety*, "fairly well done, with considerable comedy element that prevents the picture from falling into the classification of

Three photos with Wallace Reid in *The Ghost Breaker* (1922) that appeared in *Film Fun*, November 1922. Before his untimely death, "Wally" was the third most-loved actor in the movies, just behind Mary Pickford and Charlie Chaplin.

ordinary. To the Reid fans, the feature will prove pleasing; to others, it will be but mildly entertaining. As a box office attraction, the draw depends whether or not the exhibitor's average audience is strong for the star. There is nothing in the production that will pull additional business. If it wasn't for the work of Walter Hiers, who plays a blackface valet to the star, there wouldn't be anything to the story. His work in this picture polls all the laughs that there are. It looks as though Reid had made up his mind that he was going to do as little work in this picture as possible, and possibly conspired with the script writer and the director to help out. Things of this sort are about as sure a road to oblivion, as far as the screen is concerned, as being involved in some unsavory scandal."

Though he was credited in the small role, George O'Brien appears unrecognizable as one of the sheet-covered ghosts in scenes inside the castle.

THE NE'ER-DO-WELL (1923)
FAMOUS PLAYERS-LASKY PARAMOUNT
PRODUCER: ADOLPH ZUKOR
DIRECTOR: ALFRED E. GREEN
SCREENPLAY: Louis Stevens, based on a novel by Rex Beach
CAST: Thomas Meighan, Lila Lee, Gertrude Astor, John Miltern, Gus Weinberg, Sid Smith, George O'Brien, Jules Cowles, Laurance Wheat, Cyril Ring
SYNOPSIS: Kirk Anthony, played by Thomas Meighan, the idle son of a New York millionaire and a reckless hero, is celebrating victory and the center of attention involving an incident at a wild party when a friend of Kirk's father slips dope into his drink and he is shanghaied for Panama. Kirk gets caught up in South American political and romantic intrigue, and eventually, returns home.

"The picture is bound to make good if only on the strength of Meighan's presence at the head of the cast," said a 1923 review in *Variety*. "That one best bet of Famous Players has a following loyal enough to support him in almost anything that will pass muster. This production is only so-so."

A *New York Times* reviewer wrote, "There are interesting and amusing moments, but owning to the treatment of Rex Beach's story, it does not reach any great heights as a picture. It begins very well, but tapers off toward the end, and a dozing spell at that point does not cause one to lose anything. Meighan, who is always a manly actor, ought to be told to eliminate some of the gestures with his right hand."

Thomas Meighan, star of *The Ne'er-Do-Well* (1923).

Although George O'Brien is listed in the credits in both the *New York Times* and *Variety* reviews, his role was not noted in the analyses of the films when reviewed.

Advertising poster for *Woman Proof* starring Thomas Meighan, a 1923 film featuring George O'Brien in a small role.

WOMAN PROOF (1923)
FAMOUS PLAYERS-LASKY PARAMOUNT
PRODUCER: ADOLPH ZUKOR
DIRECTOR: ALFRED E. GREEN
SCREENPLAY: Tom Geraghty, based on a story by George Ade
LENGTH: 70 MINUTES
CAST: Thomas Meighan, Lila Lee, John Sainpolis, Louise Dresser, Robert Agnew, Mary Astor, Edgar Norton, Charles A. Sellon, George O'Brien, Vera Reynolds, Hardee Kirkland, Martha Mattox, William Gonder, Mike Donlin.
SYNOPSIS: Comedic complications follow when Thomas Rockwood stands to inherit a million dollars if he marries by June 30, or the money will go to a home for the aged.

"Good deal better picture to watch than read or write about," wrote a reviewer in Variety. "Probably one of the surest sure things Famous Players-Lasky has put out this fall. The direction is splendid in its taste and settings, and a splendid cast has been assembled to do the star and author justice. There is an extraordinary capable cast, with Lila Lee as leading woman and Louise Dresser playing gracefully a Grande Dame part. Charles A. Sellen and George O'Brien make two comedy characters worthy of Mark Twain."

". . . one of those photoplays brimful of chuckles and laughter," wrote a reviewer for the *New York Times*. "The narrative itself is not especially novel or sparkling, but the way in which it has been handled by Ade as the author, Green as the director, and Meighan as the principal player renders it well worthy of the trio. The acting in this film is especially good."

Although George O'Brien is listed in the credits as a featured player, his work earned no mention in the New York Times review.

Shadows of Paris (1924)
Famous Players-Lasky Paramount
Director: Herbert Brenon
Screenplay: Eve Unsell
Adaptation: Fred Jackson from the French play, *Mon Homme*s by André Ricard and Francis Carco
Cast: Pola Negri, Charles De Roche, Huntley Gordon, Adolphe Menjou, Gareth Hughes, Vera Reynolds, Rose Dione, Rosita Marstini, Edward Kipling, Maurice Cannon, Frank Nelson, George O'Brien.
Synopsis: Pola Negri essays the role of the Claire, the queen of crooks known as "The Blackbird," a brazen girl of an underworld band. She masquerades first as a war widow, and later as a Polish Countess, only to learn that the man she once loved is nothing but a common, low-life thief.

"The picturized version of the French play, *Mon Homme*, gives Pola Negri a far better opportunity to display her histrionic talent than any of her other productions made in Hollywood," wrote a reviewer in *Variety*. "She seems to revel in the contrasting notes of the life of a character . . . and is really quite effective both as the brazen girl of an Apache den and the mistress of an Avenue Marigny mansion.

Although George O'Brien is listed in the credits as a featured player, his work earned no mention in reviews.

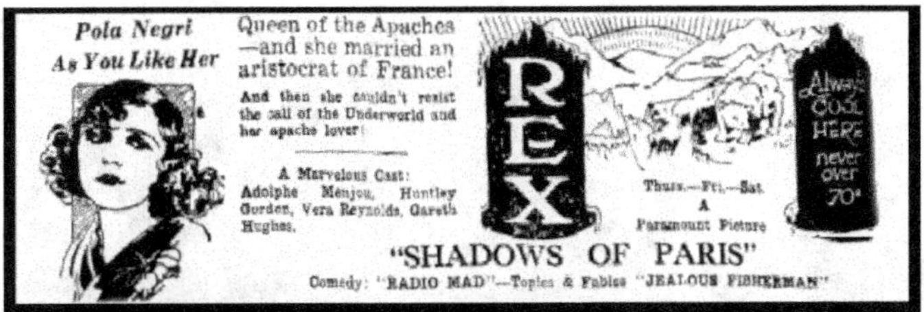

(TOP) Newspaper advertisement for *Shadows of Paris* (1924) as it appeared in the *Sheboygan Press* August 21, 1924. (BOTTOM) Pola Negri, star of *Shadows of Paris* (1924).

(LEFT) A newspaper advertisement for *The Sea Hawk* (1924) as it appeared in the *Lima News* September 21, 1924. (TOP) Milton Sills, star of *The Sea Hawk* (1924).

THE SEA HAWK (1924)
FRANK LLOYD PRODUCTIONS AND ASSOCIATED FIRST NATIONAL
DIRECTOR: FRANK LLOYD
SCREENPLAY: J. G. Hawks, based on a novel by Rafel Sabatini
LENGTH: 129 MINUTES
CAST: Milton Sills, Enid Bennett, Lloyd Hughes, Wallace Beery, Mark MacDermott, Wallace MacDonald, Bert Woodruff, Claire Du Brey, Lionel Belmore, Albert Prisco, Frank Currier, William Collier, Jr., Medea Radzina, Fred De Silva, Kathleen Key, Hector V. Sarno, Robert Bolder, George E. Romain, Christina Montt, Nancy Zann, Louis Morrison, Kate Price, Al Jennings, Bert Woodruff, Walter Wilkinson, Andrew Johnston, Henry Barrows, Edwards Davis, Claire Du Brey, Robert Spencer, Theodore Lorch. George O'Brien appeared in an unaccredited role as a galley slave.
SYNOPSIS: In old England, two brothers, Lionel and Oliver Tressillian, enjoy life as elite members of the aristocracy until Oliver is abducted and sold into slavery to the Moors. After three years chained to oars, he becomes their greatest warrior, capturing prize after prize until his new name, "The Sea Hawk," is feared around the world.

Variety raved about *The Sea Hawk*. "Just about every so often a picture comes along that has a real kid in it, a kick that makes a couple of hours of time pass while you are viewing the picture at a speed that makes it seem less than the usual seventy minutes it takes to see the average production. Its handling is a work of art that will go down in screen history as a really great picture."

"An ambitious production," expressed the *New York Times* reviewer, "the setting of which must have cost the proverbial king's ransom. There are several stretches in this picture, which make an indelible impression upon a viewer. This is far and away the best sea story that has ever been brought to the screen, and we doubt if anybody who sees the scenes of the galley slaves will forget them. Frank Lloyd, who started picture work as an extra himself, is to be congratulated on this film masterpiece of the sea."

George O'Brien appeares as an unaccredited extra in the slave galley scenes.

THE IRON HORSE (1924)
FOX
PRODUCER: WILLIAM FOX
DIRECTOR: JOHN FORD
SCREENPLAY: Charles Kenyon, based on a story by John Russell
LENGTH: 130 MINUTES
CAST: George O'Brien, Madge Bellamy, Charles Edward Bull, Will Walling, Gladys Hulette, Fred Kohler, Cyril Chadwick, J. Farrell MacDonald, James Marcus, Francis Powers, James Welch, Charles O'Malley, Colin Chase, Jack O'Brien, Walter Rogers, George Waggner, John Padjan, Charles Newton, Delbert Mann, Chief Big Tree, Chief White Spear, Edward Piel, James Gordon, Winston Miller, Peggy Cartwright, Thomas Durant, Stanhope Wheatcroft, Frances Teague, Dan Borzage.
SYNOPSIS: An epic of the building of America's first trans-continental railroad, the story follows David Brandon and his son Davy, searching for the railroad passage through the site of a spectacular mountain passage and crossing paths with the owner of a large ranch, who conspires to kill Davy. The east and west lines meet in a spectacular climax building to the driving of the golden spike connecting the two lines.

A studio advertising poster for *The Iron Horse* (1924).

"John Ford, who directed, put his story over on the screen with a lot of punch," wrote the reviewer in *Variety*. "His handling of the trio of ex-soldiers of the civil War who as the three musketeers of America battled through the building of the great Union Pacific

Two scenes from *The Iron Horse* (1924) with Madge Bellamy, George O'Brien, and Cyril Chadwick.

railroad is exceedingly clever. They lend the touch of comedy in this picture much the same as did Ernest Torrence and Tully Marshall in *The Covered Wagon*. Francis Powers, J. Farrell MacDonald, and James Welch enact the roles and Ford touched them with just a bit of pathos in the end that made them stand out as real humans and not as out-and-out buffoons just created for laughs. The love interest is carried on by George O'Brien and Madge Bellamy, as Davy Brandon and Miriam Marsh, with Fred Kohler and Cyril Chadwick as Deroux, and Peter Jesson, the heavies. O'Brien gave a corking performance as the youthful scout and lover, and Miss Bellamy shone as his beloved. Kohler's characterization of Deroux was a piece of classic work. But it isn't the roles that make this a great big picture; it is the combination of the playing, the direction, and the general theme, together with its big scenes that bring *The Iron Horse* into the classification of great motion pictures. George O'Brien, who impersonates the heroic Davy Brandon, is quite good in most of his acting. The producers have permitted him to have too much of the show at certain junctures, especially where he heaves his many chest. In the fights with Cyril Chadwick, who plays Peter Jesson, he is capable, although at times too theatric. He seems to remember that he is to give one a good view of his biceps, which appear to be frequently strained for effect."

THE MAN WHO CAME BACK (1924)
FOX
PRODUCER: WILLIAM FOX
DIRECTOR: EMMETT J. FLYNN
SCREENPLAY: Edmund Goulding, based on a play by Jules Eckert and a novel by John Fleming Wilson
LENGTH: 104 MINUTES
CAST: George O'Brien, Dorothy Mackaill, Ralph Lewis, Cyril Chadwick, Emily Fitzroy, Harvy Clark, Edward Piel, David Kirby, James Gordon, Walter Wilkinson, Brother Miller.
SYNOPSIS: George O'Brien plays a young wastrel addicted to drugs and drink. He and a cabaret singer, played by Dorothy Mackaill, fall under the seductive spell of the vices and nearly lose their lives to the curses.

(TOP) A newspaper advertisement for *The Man Who Came Back* (1924) as it appeared in the *Bridgeport Telegram* March 13, 1924. (BOTTOM) George O'Brien and Dorothy Mackaill in *The Man Who Came Back* (1924).

"It is interesting, although there are a couple of spots where the picture could stand a little cutting," observed a reviewer in *Variety*. "George O'Brien, who is co-featured, will register strongly on the strength of his work in this film, and it is a safe bet that he is going to be a favorite with women fans. This boy is there. He has looks, can troupe, and sells his winning personality for all it's worth. The picture itself is sure-fire at the box office, and it should not only make money for Fox, but for exhibitors."

"Ardent enthusiasts of lurid melodrama, saturated with tears, sighs, drink and drugs, may be interested in *The Man Who Came Back*," wrote a reviewer in the *New York Times*. "George O'Brien is capable as young Potter, and Cyril Chadwick is good in his interpretation of the supposed villain. The settings of this film and the photography are of high standard, and when quickened up, it will be a production with an appeal to those who favor this sort of melodrama."

THE PAINTED LADY (1924)
FOX
PRODUCER: WILLIAM FOX
DIRECTOR: CHESTER BENNETT
SCREENPLAY: Thomas Dixon, Jr., based on a story by Larry Evans
LENGTH: 84 MINUTES
CAST: George O'Brien, Dorothy Mackaill, Harry T. Morey, Lucille Hutton, John Miljan, Lucille Ricksen, Margaret McWade, Frank Elliott, Lucien Littlefield.
SYNOPSIS: A woman of easy virtue find redemption after meeting Luther Smith, played by George O'Brien, on a South Sea Island cruise.

A reviewer in the *Nevada State Journal* wrote, "One wonders if Larry Evans, who originally wrote the story for the *Saturday Evening Post*, ever imaged his 'Painted lady' would move so glowingly in the flesh. Chester Bennett, the director, has made the presentation strongly dramatic and beautiful with the strange lure of the tropics. He has portrayed the stark terror that it holds for those unaccustomed to its thick, threatening nights; has made the tale creepingly real. George O'Brien, playing the lead, is particularly well-fitted to the character of the sea-going lad who follows his love over the seven seas, who pursues to the end of the world the man he rightfully hates,

A newspaper advertisement for *The Painted Lady* (1924) as it appeared in newspapers around the country.

who fights to the last ditch for those things that he holds priceless. O'Brien is a human hero in a most convincing film story. No lily-white hands in this fellow's acting. He's good stuff and six feet high. The climax has crashing power, and will linger in the minds of those who see the photoplay."

(LEFT) A newspaper advertisement for *The Roughneck* (1926) as it appeared in newspapers around the country. (RIGHT) George O'Brien in the boxing ring in *The Roughneck* (1926).

THE ROUGHNECK AKA THORNS OF PASSION (1926)
FOX
PRODUCER: WILLIAM FOX
DIRECTOR: JACK CONWAY
SCREENPLAY: Charles Kenyon, based on a story by Robert W. Service
LENGTH: 87 MINUTES
CAST: George O'Brien, Billie Dove, Harry T. Morey, Cleo Madison, Charles A. Sellon, Maryon Ave, Anne Cornwall, Harvey Clark, Edna Eichor, Buddy Smith.
SYNOPSIS: Jerry Delaney, a boxer who thinks he has killed another boxer in a bout in San Francisco, escapes to an island where he discovers that his long-lost mother has taken refuge with a brute.

"This is a corking box office picture of the program variety, a combination of San Francisco and South Sea island tales that carries a couple of fight wallops and likewise a flash of the undressed stuff among the island maidens. All great for the box office," exclaimed a reviewer in *Variety*. "George O'Brien, the hero, pulls the only new thing that has been seen in a screen scrap in a long while. Early in the fight, his arm is injured, and he fights through to the finish with one hand. It is effective."

"The film version of Robert W. Service's *The Roughneck* is a boy's idea of adventure with plenty of scenes of George O'Brien's biceps and ankles," reviewed the *New York Times*. "After observing all that

Mr. O'Brien experiences as Jerry Delaney, one concludes that he needs his deep chest and brawny arms. Mr. O'Brien goes to no particular pains to conceal that he has the strength of an ox and the ankles of Mercury. He has an artistic waistline, a physiognomy suited to adventurous roles in melodramatic pictures, and dark hair with the suggestion of a curl. Mr. O'Brien appears to have a weakness for displaying his figure, but otherwise his performance is good. This is an extravagant story which is only likely to appeal to the youthful mind."

A reviewer for the *Bridgeport Telegram* wrote, "*The Roughneck* lives up to the description. George O'Brien gives a superb piece of acting, and his physical prowess and pleasing personality add much to the interpretation."

THE DANCERS (1924)
FOX
PRODUCER: WILLIAM FOX
DIRECTOR: EMMETT J. FLYNN
SCREENPLAY: Edmund Goulding, based on a play by Hubert Parsons
LENGTH: 74 MINUTES
CAST: George O'Brien, Alma Rubens, Templar Saxe, Madge Bellamy, Joan Standing, Alice Hollister, Freemon Wood, Walter McGrail, Noble Johnson, Tippy Grey.
SYNOPSIS: Tony, the son of English nobility, leaves his fiancé, travels to South America, becomes successful operating a cabaret, and falls in love with Maxine, a dancing girl.

"While *The Dancers* has some entertaining stretches, it winds up as an unconvincing and disappointing story," wrote a reviewer in the *New York Times*. "Certainly, better acting in the part of the heroine and real subtlety in the direction might have made it a strong photoplay. George O'Brien, who has been seen recently in several of William Fox's productions, has a decidedly prepossessing appearance, and in this current effort, he displays more knowledge of pantomime before the camera than he has done before. Mr. Flynn's close-ups outdo anything we have seen. There are in this film two of the largest heads ever thrown on the screen. Madge Bellamy evidently found the role of Una too much for her. She attempts to express hysterics or scream through the scenes with her mouth wide open. In her quiescent periods, she is attractive, but she loses this good point

The Dancers, as advertised in the *Bridgeport Telegram* January 23, 1925, page 8.

George O'Brien in *The Dancers* (1924).

when she tries to go beyond her ordinary screen efforts. By far the best performance in this picture is that of Alma Rubens, who seems to be ahead of everybody in her appreciation of what the situations demand. With a curl of hair over her right eye, she makes a bewitching Argentinean dancer."

"One thing not to be overlooked, however, and that is the performance of two of the principal women," wrote a reviewer in *Variety*. "Madge Bellamy, first and foremost. In *The Dancers*, she is giving a performance that is going to make her as far as the screen is concerned if anything ever will. And atop of that, is the performance of Alma Rubens gives, as the little dancer of the Central American café. She is there 100 percent. Of the men, George O'Brien stands out like a house afire as the hero."

HAVOC (1925)
FOX
PRODUCER: WILLIAM FOX
DIRECTOR: ROWLAND V. LEE
SCREENPLAY: Edmund Goulding, based on a story by Henry Wall
CAST: George O'Brien, Madge Bellamy, Walter McGrail, Eulalie Jensen, Margaret Livingston, David Butler, Edythe Chapman, Leslie Fenton, Harvey Clark, Wade Boteler, Cyril Chapman, Captain E. H. Calvert, Bertram Grassby.
SYNOPSIS: Dick Chappel enlists in the military in World War One, falls in love with Violet Deering, who shifts her affections between him and Captain "Roddy" Dunton, life-long friends. After Roddy ends up blinded in battle, Dick marrys the girl.

A reviewer for *Photoplay Magazine* said of *Havoc*, "One of those war plays showing London society in a shell-shocked condition. If soldiers in the trenches were really so concerned with love affairs, it's a wonder they got any fighting done. The war scenes are long and gloomy and only illuminated by the smile of George O'Brien. Artificial treatment spoils a well-meaning story."

A reviewer for the *Helena Independent* wrote, "There is no question about the quality of *Havoc*, the William Fox photoplay which opened last night at the Bethell. It is a powerful and convincing adaptation of the stage play. Director Lee has shown a cross section of war madness and havoc. George O'Brien, as Dick Chappell, gives by far the greatest

(LEFT) George O'Brien and Madge Bellamy in *Havoc* (1925). (RIGHT) A newspaper advertisement for *Havoc* as it appeared in the *Newark Advocate* June 16, 1927.

characterization of his career. Walter McGrail and Leslie Fenton both get from their excellent roles every bit that is in them."

THE FIGHTING HEART ALSO KNOWN AS ONCE TO EVERY MAN (1925)
FOX
PRODUCER: WILLIAM FOX
DIRECTOR: JOHN FORD
SCREENPLAY: Lillie Hayward, based on the novel *Once to Every Man* by Larry Evans
CAST: George O'Brien, Billie Dove, Victor McLaglen, J. Farrell MacDonald, Diana Miller, Bert Woodruff, Francis Ford, Hazel Howell, Edward Piel, James Marcus.
SYNOPSIS: George appears as Denny Bolton, a young man dealing with his grandfather's destructive drinking habit, and the gradual ruin of the family farm. He becomes a boxer, defeats McLaglen in a championship bout, shines as a New York celebrity, and then wins Billie Dove's affection.

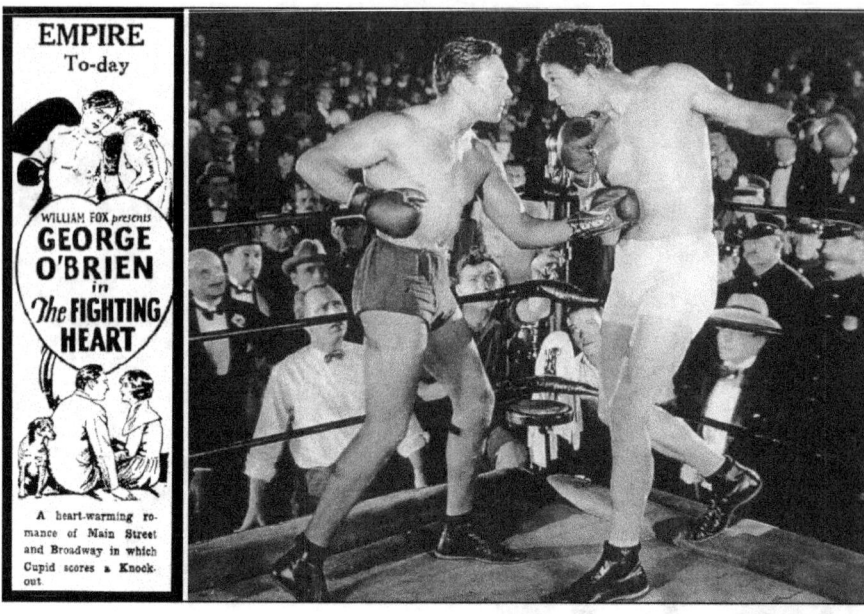

(LEFT) A newspaper ad for *The Fighting Heart* (1925) as it appeared in the *Frederick Post* October 11, 1926. (RIGHT) George O'Brien in the ring with Victor McLaglen in *The Fighting Heart* (1925).

Photoplay Magazine, in their review of *The Fighting Heart*, wrote: "What an amusing hour it will be for the boys and grown-ups who like their two-fisted heroes! This is an ideal vehicle for the athletic George O'Brien. The plot deals largely with the prize-ring, a prize-fighter whose ambition swept him to Broadway—love brought him back to Main Street. O'Brien stages three of the most thrilling fights ever screened."

A reviewer for the *Bridgeport Telegram*, wrote, "George O'Brien, star of *The Iron Horse*, is coming to Poli's Vaudeville Theater Sunday night in what is probably the best picture of the season. Billie Dove and an all-star cast make this heart-warming romance of Main Street and Broadway the nearest thing to the ideal motion picture than has yet come this way."

A reviewer for the *Mansfield News* wrote that the film "... contains some boxing and fighting that brings you right up to the edge of your seat in excitement. George O'Brien plays the part of the country boy whose ancestors were habitual drunkards. Being turned down by the villagers and even the girl he loves, he leaves for New York where he rises almost to the top in the pugilistic world. He is matched with the champion, but his nightlife takes its toll, and he is knocked out. Before he leaves, he gets into a fight on the street with the champion and knocks him cold. When he returns to the old village, he finds his girl still waiting for him. Billie Dove plays the lead opposite O'Brien."

THANK YOU (1925)
Fox
PRODUCER: JOHN GOLDEN
DIRECTOR: JOHN FORD
SCREENPLAY: Frances Marion, from a play by Winchell Smith and Tom Cushing
LENGTH: 75 MINUTES
CAST: George O'Brien, Jacqueline Logan, Alec B. Francis, J. Farrell MacDonald, George Fawcett, Cyril Chadwick, Edith Bostwick, Marion Harlan, Vivian Ogden, James Neill, Billy Rinaldi, Aileen Manning, Maurice Murphy, Robert Milasch, Ida Moore, Frankie Bailey.
SYNOPSIS: Kenneth Jamieson, the devil-may-care son of a wealthy man, is sent to live on a chicken ranch in the town of Dedham, falls for Diane, renounces his wicked ways, and settles down as a decent member of the town.

"*Thank You*, as a play, was a corking comedy drama," wrote a reviewer in *Variety*. "It may not have been a tremendous box office wallop, but it went along for a number of months in New York and got some money. As a screen entertainment, it has lost much of the value it had on the stage, and the only place that the blame can be laid is at the doorsteps of the adaptor and the director. It is well-played, particularly in the roles handled by Alec Francis, Jacqueline Logan, J. Farrell MacDonald, George O'Brien, and Vivian Ogden. The cast looks as though a try was being made for an all-star aggregation on the Fox lot when they went after this one."

"The photography is far too sugary and the titles by no means gems of wit," wrote Mordaunt Hall in the *New York Times*. "When the churchwomen are meeting to do needlework, one read: 'The sewing circle spends a ripping hour.' George O'Brien, the hero of *The Iron Horse*, officiates in a similar capacity in this picture. This subject was directed by John Ford, who turned out *The Iron Horse*, in which he

(TOP) A newspaper advertisement for *Thank You* (1925) as it appeared in the *Inwood Daily Globe* March 15, 1926. (BOTTOM) Alec B. Francis and George O'Brien in *Thank You* (1925).

took full advantage of a big opportunity; but in this picture, he has evidently not found much inspiration."

(TOP) *The Johnstown Flood*, as advertised in the *Appleton Post Crescent*, March 16,1927, page 7. (BOTTOM LEFT) George O'Brien in *The Johnstown Flood*. (BOTTOM RIGHT) Janet Gaynor, at the time of the making of *The Johnstown Flood* (1926).

THE JOHNSTOWN FLOOD (1926)
FOX
PRODUCER: WILLIAM FOX
DIRECTOR: IRVING CUMMINGS
SCREENPLAY: Edfrid Bingham and Robert Lord, based on a story by Edfrid Bingham and Robert Lord
65 MINUTES.

CAST: George O'Brien, Florence Gilbert, Janet Gaynor, Paul Panzer, Anders Randolf, Paul Nicholson, George Harris, Max Davidson, Walter Perry, Sid Jordan.

SYNOPSIS: Tom O'Day, a young construction engineer, warns the owner of a lumber camp of the impending danger in his over-loaded dam. When the dam begins to crack, Anna Burger, daughter of a workman, gallops on a horse through the valley, warning people. The menacing flood sweeps trees in its path, devastation engulfs the community, and the girl drowns.

"Primarily, this is a thrill picture, with the *Johnstown Flood* well reproduced, as the outstanding punch," revealed *Variety*, in a 1926 review. "The picture is good throughout. George O'Brien is good, but Janet Gaynor, a newcomer and a corker, wins the lion's share of everything. In production, this film rates highly, for the flood scenes look on the level in most places and it is virtually impossible to spot the points where miniature stuff was used. That in itself makes a hit with the audience, and when caught, it was apparently liked by everyone."

A reviewer for the *Bridgeport Telegram* wrote, "One of the most powerful films ever brought to Bridgeport, gripping its audience with surprising tenseness. An intensely dramatic story. It is a tremendously impressive film spectacle, full of thrilling action, as well as an appealing romance."

RUSTLIN' FOR CUPID (1926)
FOX
PRODUCER: WILLIAM FOX
DIRECTOR: IRVING CUMMINGS
SCREENPLAY: L. G. Rigby
64 MINUTES
CAST: George O'Brien, Anita Stewart, Russell Simpson, Edithe Yorke, Frank McGlynn, Jr., Herbert Prior, Sid Jordan

SYNOPSIS: Bradley Blatchford exposes cattle thieves and reunites with his girl.

"*Rustlin' for Cupid* is another of the celluloid ways a charming school marm falls in love with a young man who later proves to be a second Tom Mix in handling a cow pony," reported *Variety*. "George O'Brien is every inch the hero—looks manly, fights and rides well,

(LEFT) A newspaper advertisement for *Rustlin' for Cupid* (1926) as it appeared in the *Frederick Post* January 25, 1925. (RIGHT) George O'Brien with Anita Stewart in *Rustlin' for Cupid* (1926).

and handles his melodramatic climaxes A1. The picture is corking in photographic values, and some scenes are very well directed."

FIG LEAVES (1926)
FOX
PRODUCER: WILLIAM FOX WITH WINFIELD R. SHEEHAN
DIRECTOR: HOWARD HAWKS
SCREENPLAY: Hope Loring and Louis D. Lighton from a story by Howard Hawks.
LENGTH: 68 MINUTES
CAST: George O'Brien, Olive Borden, Phyllis Haver, André de Beranger, Heinie Conklin, William Austin, Eulalie Jensen.
SYNOPSIS: A comedy in which Adam and Eve and their modern counterparts, Eve and Adam Smith, struggle with The Serpent in his various disguises.

"Picture of paramount feminine interest," said a review in *Variety*, "and high general interest as well, both for subject matter and handling. The story is a novel comedy in treatment, expensively and beautifully mounted. It has subdued horseplay for those who like their laughs rough, and it has certain subtleties that the discriminating will appreciate. Olive Borden makes a pretty heroine, and in the fashion show episode, she is ravishing. Those big, dark, soulful eyes ought to

(TOP LEFT) A newspaper advertisement for *Fig Leaves*, as it appeared in the *Appleton Post Crescent* June 3, 1927. (TOP RIGHT) George O'Brien and Olive Borden in a scene from the prehistoric sequence of *Fig Leaves* (1926). (BOTTOM) A studio portrait of George O'Brien and Olive Borden in costumes worn for *Fig Leaves*.

carry her far in the picture field."

A reviewer wrote in the *Sheboygan Press*, "It is a beautiful film of women who claim to have 'Nothing to Wear.' The colored scenes showing the fashion revue are the finest ever seen on the screen. The picture has been made on a lavish scale, and will impress those who see it."

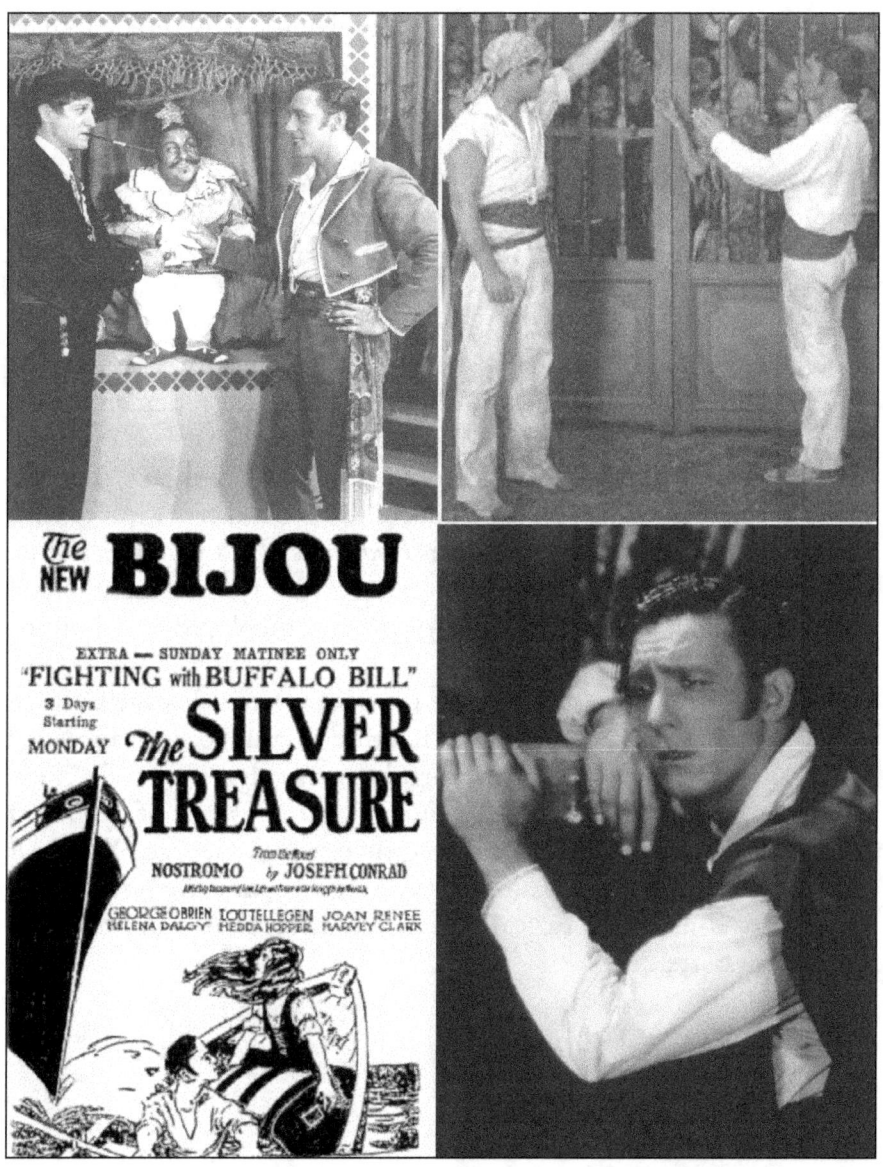

Scenes from *The Silver Treasure* (1926). (TOP LEFT) Lou-Tellegen and George O'Brien. (BOTTOM LEFT) A newspaper advertisement from the *Appleton Post Crescent* November 6, 1926.

THE SILVER TREASURE (1926)
FOX
PRODUCER: WILLIAM FOX
DIRECTOR: ROWLAND V. LEE
SCREENPLAY: Robert N. Lee, based on a novel by Joseph Conrad

CAST: George O'Brien, Jack Rollins, Helena D'Algy, Joan Renee, Lou-Tellegen, Hedda Hopper, Evelyn Selbie, Otto Matieson, Stewart Rome, Daniel Makarenko, Fred Becker, Harvey Clark, Gilbert Clayton, Sidney De Grey, George Kuwa.

SYNOPSIS: Nostromo, an adventurer in a mythical Sough American republic of Costaguana, protect a cargo of silver ingots, but when his ship sinks, he must struggle with bandits in order to save the day and get the girl.

"Action in every reel of this film, lots of it, while the backgrounds are elaborate and filled with thousands of supers," reported the reviewer for *Variety*. "O'Brien, in the lead, does nice acting and fancy fighting, while the others, all of them thoroughly capable, round out an impressive cast. Lee's direction is noteworthy in that the comedy touches are not forced. Indeed, the general attention to cast, direction, and detail in *The Silver Treasure* should give the picture large commendation among exhibitors of every type, because it is a good, serviceable, 'cloak and sword' romance and played to the hilt by O'Brien."

A reviewer for the *Appleton Post Crescent* wrote, "George O'Brien and Lou-Tellegen are seen in enchanting picture of romance and action in South America. For colorful drama, high-powered action, and beautiful scenic effects, *The Silver Treasure* is one of the finest pictures that have reached the screen this season. George O'Brien is seen in the leading role and, as the spirited romantic, two-fisted Nostromo, chief of the cargadores, he has a role that could not have suited him better."

3 BAD MEN (1926)
FOX
PRODUCER: WILLIAM FOX
DIRECTOR: JOHN FORD
SCREENPLAY: John Stone, based on a novel, *Over the Border*, by Herman Whitaker
LENGTH: 75 MINUTES
CAST: George O'Brien, Olive Borden, J. Farrell MacDonald, Phyllis Haver, Lou-Tellegen, Tom Santschi, Frank Campeau, George Harris, Jay Hunt, Priscilla Bonner, Otis Harlan, Walter Perry, Grace Gordon, Alec B. Francis, George Irving, Vester Pegg, Bud Osborne

George O'Brien and Olive Borden in *3 Bad Men* (1926).

SYNOPSIS: Dan O'Malley, an expelled West Point cadet, joins a group of settlers in the Dakotas in the 1870s. On the trail, they run afoul of Layne Hunter, a villain played by the famous actor, Lou-Tellegen, who stalks through the tale brandishing a whip, and lashing it like the tail of a panther. A thrilling land-rush sustains an unequalled climax of action, as horses, wagons, men on bicycles, and settlers on foot race to stake their claims.

Variety raved about the film: "This feature falls just short of being a terrific knockout. But as an out-and-out Western thriller, it is a wow from beginning to end. There are scenes in it as effective as the wagon train in *The Covered Wagon*, and the thousands in the mad race across country when the government lands are opened to the public is bigger than anything of its kind that has been shown in a picture. There is almost as much thrilling stuff as in the *Ben-Hur* chariot race. This is a super Western and every bit as big as *The Iron Horse* was."

A reviewer for the *Sheboygan Press* wrote, "It is a massive production dealing with the early days of the West, the gold rush, and the land rush. It is a big picture made on a big scale. The cast numbered over two thousand. It is gripping, exciting, and thrilling. Anyone who enjoys an outdoor picture should not miss seeing *3 Bad Men*."

THE BLUE EAGLE (1926)
FOX
PRODUCER: WILLIAM FOX
DIRECTOR: JOHN FORD
SCREENPLAY: L. G. Rigby, based on *The Lord's Referee*, by Gerald Beaumont
CAST: George O'Brien, Janet Gaynor, Margaret Livingston, William Russell, Robert Edeson, David Butler, Philip Ford, Ralph Sipperly, Jerry Madden, Harry Tenbrook, Lew Short.
SYNOPSIS: George Darcy, a stalwart and lovable stoker, competes during World War One for the affection of adorable Janet Gaynor. The two men meet in the pugilist ring for a rip-roaring, no-holds-barred boxing match.

A review in *Picture Show*, commented, "Spectacular comedy-drama of the amusing antagonism of two naval stokers. George O'Brien works hard as the hero, and strenuous supporting parts are played by Robert Edeson and Janet Gaynor."

Unlike many of George's silent films, *The Blue Eagle* has been preserved by the combined efforts of several organizations in a fascinating rescue effort involving a nitrate print loaned to the Academy of Motion Picture Arts and Sciences for its tribute to O'Brien. After the event, the Academy gave the print to the American Film Institute. It was copied into a 16mm preservation print at a commercial lab in March 1970. On further examination, some of the nitrate fragments

The Blue Eagle (1926) as advertised in the *Appleton Post Crescent* February 21, 1927, page 6.

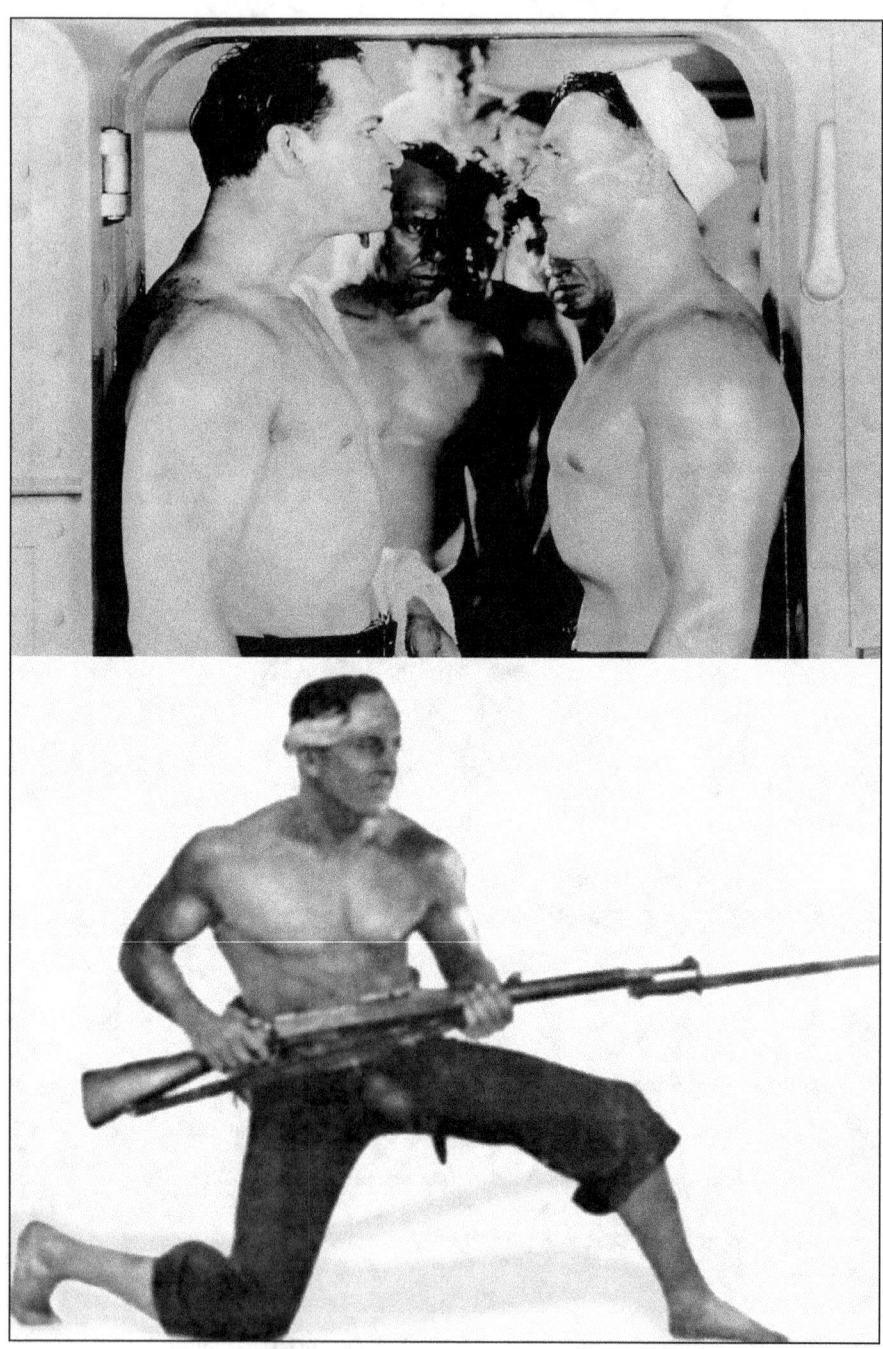

George O'Brien in two scenes from John Ford's *The Blue Eagle* (1926).

were mislabeled during the AFI's preservation. Both the Library's and the AFI's 16mm prints had been resequenced, but the original negatives were left as found.

In 1970, when the preservation was completed, the AFI stored the nitrate print at the Library. In 1976, after the Library established its own preservation lab, the surviving nitrate was again preserved in 35mm. In the interim, it was painfully discovered that more of the nitrate had decomposed, leaving the surviving original footage even shorter than before.

In 1995, the Louis B. Mayer Foundation was attempting to restore all Janet Gaynor films. The AFI records indicated that in addition to the Library of Congress print, both the Cinémathèque Royale de Belgique and the Narodni Filmovy Archiv in Prague both had copies of *The Blue Eagle*. The Prague print had two of the seven reels, but more than half of the footage was unique, including the missing Janet Gaynor footage. However, the Czechs had rearranged scenes and changed the story. All the title inserts were in Czech.

The Library edited all available prints and titles into a newly compiled version as complete as possible. Most of the last four and a half reels are exactly as they were when the film first left the Fox Studios.

IS ZAT SO? (1927)
FOX
PRODUCER: WILLIAM FOX
DIRECTOR: ALFRED E. GREEN
SCREENPLAY: Philip Klein, based on a play by James Gleason and Richard Taber
LENGTH: 60 MINUTES
CAST: George O'Brien, Edmund Lowe, Douglas Fairbanks, Jr., Kathryn Perry, Doris Lloyd, Richard Maitland, Cyril Chadwick, Dione Ellis, Phillip De Lacy, Jack Herrick.
SYNOPSIS: Ed "Chick" Cowan, a streetcar motorman, is snapped up by a down-and-out boxing manager, who ruthlessly exploits the dumb prizefighter and abuses his sister.

"Nobody means anything in the film outside of George O'Brien and Edmund Lowe, as the dumb prizefighter and manager respectively," wrote a reviewer in *Variety*. "O'Brien makes the fight stuff convince, and handles himself well with or without the gloves."

George O'Brien in *Is Zat So?* (1926).

"This production has been shrewdly directed by Alfred E. Green, who has adhered fairly close to the original story," thought the reviewer from the *New York Times*. "Mr. O'Brien, a wonderful physical specimen, is remarkably successful in making Chick appear almost devoid of the powers of reasoning, but when he is in the ring, he is a marvel at speed."

Virginia Valli and George O'Brien in *Paid to Love* (1927).

PAID TO LOVE (1927)

FOX
PRODUCER: WILLIAM FOX
DIRECTOR: HOWARD HAWKS
SCREENPLAY: William M. Conselman and Seton I. Miller, adaptation by Benjamin Glazer, based on a story by Henry Carr
LENGTH: 80 MINUTES
CAST: George O'Brien, Virginia Valli, William Powell, J. Farrell MacDonald, Thomas Jefferson, Merta Sterling, Hank Mann.
SYNOPSIS: A Crown Prince, who is more interested in cars than women, is vamped by a cabaret singer.

"The only thing serious about *Paid to Love* is the problem-suggesting title," wrote a reviewer in the *New York Times*. "There isn't any problem, however. Comedy is plentifully supplied."

"Virginia Valli plays the super-heroine role flawlessly," surmised a reviewer in *Variety*. "George O'Brien is almost believable as the picturesque crown prince, and the scenic settings of the story are exquisite beyond telling. The regal atmosphere is conveyed remarkably

George O'Brien as the prince of a mythical kingdom in Howard Hawk's *Paid to Love* (1927).

well. Some of the shots of deluxe seashore scenes are in their pictorial beauty, such, for instance, as a view of rain-swept countryside at dusk with a gnarled Cyprus tree as the only landmark. The acting matches the settings in its quiet suavity."

Two scenes from F. W. Murnau's *Sunrise* (1927.) (TOP) George O'Brien and Margaret Livingston. (BOTTOM) George O'Brien and Janet Gaynor.

Portrait of George O'Brien as "The Man" in *Sunrise* (1927).

SUNRISE: A SONG OF TWO HUMANS (1927)
FOX
PRODUCER: WILLIAM FOX
DIRECTOR: F. W. MURNAU
ASSISTANT DIRECTOR: HERMAN BING
SCENARIO: Carl Mayer
EDITING AND TITLES: Katherine Hilliker and H. H. Caldwell
PHOTOGRAPHY: Charles Rosher and Karl Strauss
LENGTH: 90 MINUTES

Three scenes from F. W. Murnau's *Sunrise* (1927).

CAST: George O'Brien, Janet Gaynor, Margaret Livingston, J. Farrell MacDonald, Bodil Rosing, Jane Winton, Ralph Sipperly, Arthur Housman, Eddie Boland, Sidney Bracey, Gibson Gowland, Sally Eilers, Gino Corrado, Eddie Arnold, Barry Norton, Robert Kortman.

SYNOPSIS: Ansas, a young, happily married farmer, is infatuated by a temptress from the big city to drown his wife, but a twist of fate intervenes and prevents the tragedy from taking place.

The *New York Times* thought the eloquent presentation was a distinguished contribution to the screen, realizing the promise Murnau offered with his earlier films. "What Murnau has tried to do is to crystallize in dramatic symbolism those conflicts, adjustments, compromises and complexities of man-and-woman mating experiences that ultimately grow into an endearing union," the reviewer pointed out. "The dramatic action of this humble hero and workaday heroine is spaced between one drawing and another, but in that scant interval, there is packed an emotional lifetime. Many elements enter into the success of this ambitious effort. Murnau reveals a remarkable resourcefulness of effects: the playing of George O'Brien and Janet Gaynor and their associates is generally convincing and the story unfolds in settings inexpressibly lovely and appropriate."

Another *New York Times* article from 1927 said, "The principals in this gripping subject are George O'Brien and Janet Gaynor, who both give inspired performances. It is a slowly told tale, and sometimes Mr. O'Brien appears to be just a little lethargic in his movements, but this is explained by the nature of the character he is portraying—a susceptible, thick-headed country lout, a man who never gives a thought to his appearance and who is utterly ignorant of anything approaching social amenities."

In another review some weeks later, a *New York Times* reviewer wrote, "Isn't this a rare film? Real movie stuff, with seduction, crime, suspense, rumpus, action, storm. Even with jokes. Even with humor. And still everything is wonderfully linked up in the story of two souls."

A *Vossische Zeitung* reviewer found the film disappointingly bitter. "This Murnau film leaves one cold," he wrote. "In places it fairly drips with sentiment, but one so quickly notes the intention to move the spectator that one is not moved. Murnau, the director of *Faust* and of *The Least of Men*, has great ability but little imagination. The only thing that it occurs to him to do is to have the two leading figures of *Sunrise*, the man and the woman, cry when they are unhappy and laugh when they are happy. The thousand nuances between weeping and laughing, however, all of them genuine mental happenings, are not once hinted at by Murnau."

Photoplay Magazine, in their review of *Sunrise*, wrote, "The sort of picture that fools high-brows into hollering 'Art!' Swell trick photography and fancy effects, but, boiled down, no story interest and only stilted, mannered acting."

In 2003, the National Film and Television Archive recalled materials from surviving prints and completed fully restoring *Sunrise*. Combining the best technologies available, the film was preserved along with the original soundtrack.

EAST SIDE, WEST SIDE (1927)
FOX
PRODUCER: WILLIAM FOX
DIRECTOR: ALLAN DWAN
SCREENPLAY: Allan Dwan, based on the novel by Felix Riesenberg
LENGTH: 60 MINUTES
CAST: George O'Brien, Virginia Valli, J. Farrell MacDonald, Dore Davidson, June Collyer, Sonia Nodalsky, John Miltern, Holmes Herbert, Frank Dodge, Don Wolheim, John Dooley, John Kearney, Edward Garvey, Frank Allsworth, William Fredericks, Jean Armour, Gordon McRae, Harold Levett.
SYNOPSIS: A Jewish boy surviving a shipwreck is taken in by an East Side family, becomes a professional boxer, and finds love with a lowly saloon girl.

"Not strong enough to stand up alone in the first runs for a full week," *Variety* warned exhibitors. "Picture has been directed with an apparent indifference or worse. The story is jumpy, incoherent, and at no time interesting. This is the impression given by the screen treatment. Miss Valli hardly gives the impression, on the screen, that she could torment anyone sufficiently to cause what happened. Miss Collyer, in the first few side shots, looks too mature for comfort. A good-sized laugh where O'Brien has punched his ring opponent into insensibility when the latter is suddenly transported to another world, attired in a green velveteen coat and Robin Hood hat surrounded by a group

Two scenes from Allan Dwan's *East Side, West Side*. (TOP) George O'Brien with Virginia Valli. (BOTTOM) George O'Brien with Holmes Herbert.

of dancing nymphs. Then, he is carried out of the ring."

Mordaunt Hall, a *New York Times* reviewer, disagreed with *Variety*, saying that the film ". . . is indubitably the best picture Allan Dwan has fashioned since he produced *Big Brother*. He has succeeded in eliciting really fine performances from both George O'Brien and Virginia Valli. Two of the outstanding sequences in this picture are the sinking of a transatlantic steamship, which is inspired by the Titanic disaster, and a cave-in in a subway in course of construction. Miss Valli is amazingly good as Becka. Mr. O'Brien, the male lead in F. W. Murnau's *Sunrise*, also gives an intelligent portrayal."

A reviewer for the *Wisconsin Rapids Daily Tribune* wrote, "With George O'Brien in the leading role, Allan Dwan has directed a marvelous picture. He has done the finest work of his career."

SHARP SHOOTERS (1928) ALSO RELEASED IN THE U.K. AS THREE NAVAL RASCALS

FOX
PRODUCER: WILLIAM FOX
DIRECTOR: JOHN G. BLYSTONE
SCREENPLAY: Marion Orth, based on a story by Randall H. Faye
LENGTH: 60 MINUTES
CAST: George O'Brien, Lois Moran, William Demarest, Noah Young, Tom Dugan, Gwen Lee, Joseph Swickard
SYNOPSIS: Sailors on leave in a Mediterranean port fight and "sharp shoot" for every girl in port."

The *New York Times* reviewer wrote, "Sailors with a weakness for hoisting their trousers when fists are about to fly parade through *Sharp Shooters*. George O'Brien, who gives a sterling performance in *Sunrise*, in the good-natured but not always plausible affair, figures as a happy-go-lucky member of Uncle Sam's navy, but the story is not much more than a jumble of mildly entertaining scenes in which suspense is unnecessary."

"This version of gob life on land packs a heft wallop," declared a reviewer in *Variety*. "Story is familiar, but the gagging in business and titles is smart and fast. Laughs are numerous. As a whole, one of the best programmers turned out by Fox this season. A couple of hot scenes stand little chance with out-of-town censors."

A scene from *Sharp Shooters* (1928).

HONOR BOUND (1928)
FOX
PRODUCER: WILLIAM FOX
DIRECTOR: ALFRED E. GREEN
SCREENPLAY: C. Graham Baker, with adaptation by Philip Klein, and based on a novel by Jack Bethea
LENGTH: 60 MINUTES
CAST: George O'Brien, Estelle Taylor, Leila Hyams, Tom Santschi, Frank Cooley, Sam De Grasse, Al Hart, Harry Gripp, George Irving.
SYNOPSIS: A handsome young man falls prey to a lustful, married woman, until a wild automobile ride and an accident lead him to fall in love with a nurse.

"A slow-moving, uninteresting story without color that allows of little for anyone or anything," wrote a reviewer in *Variety*. "The names of George O'Brien and Estelle Taylor are poignant enough to stand off

George O'Brien in *Honor Bound* (1928).

the dullness. Miss Taylor is excellent in the picture, carrying the burden of the real playing, but Mr. O'Brien as that self-same mistreated one, isn't so nifty here, in appearance or work. It's not the sort of a picture for this extremely well built and attractive young man, and it's an error to have him hide that."

The *New York Times*' reviewer thought, "It is a drama with well-sustained suspense. Mr. O'Brien gives a fairly competent portrayal. Estelle Taylor is capital as Evelyn. Tom Santschi is convincing as the mine owner, and Sam DeGrasse is splendid as the foreman."

NOAH'S ARK (1928)
WARNER BROS.
DIRECTOR: MICHAEL CURTIZ
SCENARIO: Anthony Coldeway, from a story by Darryl Zanuck
CAST: Dolores Costello, George O'Brien, Guinn Williams, Conrad Nagel, Louise Fazenda, Noah Beery, Myrna Loy, Paul McAllister, Nigel De Brulier, Anders Randolf, Armand Kaliz, William V. Mong,

A magazine advertisement for *Noah's Ark* (1928) as it appeared in many magazines around the country.

Malcolm Waite, Noble Johnson, Otto Hoffman, Joe Bonomo.
SYNOPSIS: Two parallel stories combined the Biblical tale of the great Flood young, modern lovers drowning in the hardships of World War One.

George O'Brien in Michael Curtiz' *Noah's Ark* (1928).

George O'Brien and Dolores Costello in Michael Curtiz' *Noah's Ark* (1928).

Two scenes from Michael Curtiz' *Noah's Ark* (1928).

Variety praised the film: "Warner Bros. have turned out more spectacle and thrill than any producer has ever achieved in 14,000 feet of film or less dealing with a subject applicable to this type of production. They have in it touches reminiscent of *The Ten Commandments, The King of Kings, Wings,* and *The Big Parade*. Better than $1,500,000 is reported to have been spent on this film, and from what is shown on the screen, looks as though the Jack Warner staff did not do any cheating. They show everything conceivable under the sun—mobs, mobs, mobs, and mobs; Niagras of water, trains wrecks, war aplenty, crashes, deluges, and everything that goes to give the picture fan a thrill. They have turned out the biggest and best edited—that is, from the standpoint of cramming in instances and stressing on them plentifully—the picture of the industry."

The review in *Variety* examined the use of synchronized sound in the film: "Talk did not enter into the picture until after the first thirty-five minutes. It started with a love scene between O'Brien and Miss Costello, and then brought in talk by Beery, McAllister, and Williams. The talk really can be left out of this one. The Costello voice is just not for the talkers and hurts the impression made by her silent acting. Her silent acting is great. O'Brien is surprising on the talk. He has a pleasing voice, clear diction, and enunciation. Part is possibly his best so far as acting is concerned. Beery is great as the Russian spy and as the King. McAllister. The Vitaphone musical synchronization provided by Louis Silvera is most fitting and well played by the symphony orchestra."

The *New York Times* reviewer wrote, "Sounds not only issued form the screen but also from various sections of the theater. The latter sequences of this film, in which there are only a few snatches of Vitaphoned voices, are imposing, for they depict King Nephilim and his hosts in jangling coverings, but the long stretches concerned with the World War, introduced as the deluge of blood, are somewhat wearisome. Miss Costello, who is lovely in many sequences, is heard through the medium of the Vitaphone. Her voice is quite charming, but her lines are frequently inept. Mr. O'Brien has his turn at talking, and while there is no reflection on his voice, what he has to say would have been far more eloquent in simple pantomime. This dialogue is little more than audible spoken-titles, which are all very well in text, but when these utterances are heard, they frequently border on the ridiculous."

Earl Fox and Lois Moran with George O'Brien in *Blindfold* (1928).

BLINDFOLD (1928)
FOX
PRODUCER: WILLIAM FOX
DIRECTOR: CHARLES KLEIN
SCREENPLAY: Ewart Adamson, with adaptation by Robert Horwood, from *Fog*, a story by Charles Francis Coe
LENGTH: 65 MINUTES
CAST: Lois Moran, George O'Brien, Maria Alba, Earle Foxe, Don Terry, Fritz Feld, Andy Clyde, Crauford Kent, Robert E. Homans, John Kelly, Phillips Smalley.
SYNOPSIS: A policeman out for blood rallies fellow officers to avenge the murder of one of their own.

    Variety said the film suffered from "long stretches of inactivity, in one of those regulation amnesia and ridiculously improbable crime cop and girl stories."

    A reviewer for the *Lima News* wrote, "A satisfactory plot and a good cast blend harmoniously to make an entertaining motion picture. A feature of the picture is the skillful camera manipulation of Charles

Klein, the new German director, recently brought to Hollywood. *Blindfold* is his first American picture. Instead of depending on facial display and subtitles for an interpretation of mental action, the camera reveals in graphic manner what takes place in the mind of the heroine, who incidentally has a compelling double role. For the first time in his screen career, George O'Brien plays the role of a cop. He cuts a figure both human and illuminating."

Sheet music for the theme song from *True Heaven* (1929).

TRUE HEAVEN (1929)
FOX
PRODUCER: WILLIAM FOX WITH KENNETH HAWKS
DIRECTOR: JAMES TINLING
SCREENPLAY: Dwight Cummins, based on a story, *Judith*, by Charles Edward Montague
LENGTH: 53 MINUTES

George O'Brien in *True Heaven* (1929).

CAST: George O'Brien, Lois Moran, Phillips Smalley, Oscar Apfel, Duke Martin, André Cheron, Donald MacKenzie, Hedwig Reicher, Will Stanton.
SYNOPSIS: An unexpected romance between a British Secret Service man and a German agent leads to a disastrous spying mission, a firing squad, and a surprising, last moment turn of events.

A reviewer in *Screenbook* wrote, "Just as they have Chief Spy O'Brien lined up before a firing squad, the Armistice bells tinkle over the fields of Flanders and everything ends happily ever after. If you have a sense of humor you may get some irreverent giggles out of this picture."

"Another war picture," wrote a reviewer in *Variety*, "unrelieved by any new twist or combination of circumstances. Based principally on the love interest but suffers from the war surroundings and doesn't figure for any matinee business. Sound effects seem to have been attached after the picture was made and mostly ineffective, with the exception of the synchronized score. O'Brien and Lois Moran, kept to the foreground throughout, photograph well in most scenes."

"*True Heaven* is handsomely photographed and sometimes competently directed," wrote a reviewer in the *New York Times*, "but it is invariably weak during the dramatic junctures. George O'Brien is perceived as a British officer, in which role he is excellent."

MASKED EMOTIONS (1929)
FOX
PRODUCER: WILLIAM FOX
DIRECTOR: DAVID BUTLER AND KENNETH HAWKS
SCREENPLAY: Harry Brand and Benjamin Markson, based on a story, *A Son of Anak*, by Ben Ames Williams
LENGTH: 60 MINUTES
CAST: George O'Brien, Nora Lane, J. Farrell MacDonald, David Sharpe, James Gordon, Edward Peil, Sr., Frank Hagney.
SYNOPSIS: Two brothers unwittingly find themselves in the middle of intrigue with Oriental smugglers, pirates, and a slave ship operating along the California coast.

"For twenty minutes, George does nothing but flex his muscles and extend that chest astern the catboat," complained a *Variety* reviewer. "Excepting title being a complete misnomer, *Masked*

George O'Brien and J. Farrell MacDonald in *Masked Emotions* (1929).

Emotions is a good program entertainment of the George O'Brien physical culture and hero variety. There's plenty of kick in it all for the O'Brien fans."

A reviewer for the *Lima News* wrote, "Chinese opium smugglers, an attempted murder, revenge, and undiscovered love are the elements of the plot."

SALUTE (1929)
FOX
PRODUCER: WILLIAM FOX
DIRECTOR: JOHN FORD AND DAVID BUTLER
SCREENPLAY: John Stone, based on a story by Tristram Tupper and John Stone
CAST: George O'Brien, Helen Chandler, Joyce Compton, Ward Bond, William Janney, Stepin Fetchit, Frank Albertson, David Butler, Clifford Dempsey, Lumsden Hare. John Wayne, Rex Bell, John Breeden, Jack Pennick, Harry Tenbrook, and Lee Tracy played unaccredited small roles in the film.

Scenes from John Ford's *Salute* (1929.) (TOP LEFT) Ward Bond and John Wayne are to the immediate left of George O'Brien in one of their earliest screen appearances.
PHOTOS COURTESY OF THE DARCY O'BRIEN ESTATE.

SYNOPSIS: West Point Cadets are profiled in documentary-like realism, as first class midshipmen rival each other for the attentions of a girl.

A reviewer in *Variety* wrote, "The characters are subordinated in interest to the backgrounds in which they move. There is more intrinsic kick to some of the pictures of the navy cadets in drill on their parade grounds, the pictorial splendors of real settings taken in the grounds of the Naval Academy, and in the breathless atmosphere of the great American football classic itself, than in any fictitious literary maneuvering of hero and heroine."

A reviewer for the *Bee Register* wrote, "An intimate glimpse of life at the United States Naval Academy at Annapolis, as lived by the 1,800 young Americans in training there, is given in *Salute*, the all-talking Fox Movietone West Point-Annapolis football romance which comes today and tomorrow to the Rialto Theater. George O'Brien, who portrays the role of an All-American West Point halfback, is shown competing in a swimming meet in the Annapolis gymnasium plunge. Plebes taking the oath of allegiance to the United States; Their living quarters, mess hall, drills, and football practice; their departure on annual summer cruise; a prom; a seventy-piece band; and the annual Army-Navy football game are all part of *Salute*."

The *New York Times* said, "George O'Brien does tolerably well in his speech and acting."

This pseudo-documentary was George O'Brien's first all-talking picture.

THE LONE STAR RANGER (1930)
FOX
PRODUCER: WILLIAM FOX WITH J. K. MCGUINESS
DIRECTOR: A. F. ERICKSON
SCREENPLAY: Seton I. Miller, with Dialogue by John Hunter Booth and S. I. Miller, based on a Zane Grey novel of the same name.
LENGTH: 64 MINUTES
CAST: George O'Brien, Sue Carol, Warren Hymer, Walter McGrail, Russell Simpson, Elizabeth Patterson, Dick Alexander, William Steele, Bob Fleming, Caroline Rankin, Lee Shumway, Richard Alexander, Joel Franz, Colin Chase, Oliver Eckhardt, Billy Butts, Ralph LeFever, Roy Stewart, Warren Hymer, Joe Rickson, Delmar Watson. Hank Bell, Ward Bond, Willie Fung, Jack Keckley, Jack Perrin, and Lon Poff played unaccredited small roles in the film.

Sue Carol and George O'Brien in *The Lone Star Ranger* (1930).

SYNOPSIS: Buck Duane, a reformed outlaw turned ranger, fights ruthless cattle bandits in an effort to win a pardon and a girl.

An article in *Picture Show* heralded the making of the film, saying it "... seems to be a hardy perennial so far as Fox is concerned. Both Tom Mix and William Farnum have played the role of its hero. Now, the Zane Grey character falls to George O'Brien. This time, however, the picture is to be made as a Movietone, so that the engaging young O'Brien will have one advantage over his predecessors."

Variety lamented the sound quality of this early talking picture: "Poor recording on dialog and a marked slowness in getting started are all that keeps this talking Western from stacking up as material for the better class first runs. If the picture has to be satisfied with bookings in houses of lesser importance, it will certainly stand up okay. Beautiful scenically, color would have enhanced heaps. Entire production was photographed in the Rainbow Arch country of Utah, a desert and mountain region ... George O'Brien makes an impressive Buck Duane."

Two scenes from *Rough Romance* (1930). (Bottom with Antonio Moreno.)

ROUGH ROMANCE (1930)
FOX
PRODUCER: WILLIAM FOX
DIRECTOR: A. F. ERICKSON
SCREENPLAY: Elliott Lester, based on a novelette, *The Girl Who Wasn't Wanted*, by Kenneth B. Clarke, and dialogue by Donald Davis
LENGTH: 57 MINUTES

CAST: George O'Brien, Antonio Moreno, Helen Chandler, Roy Stewart, John Wayne, Eddie Borden, Frank Lanning, Harry Cording, David Hartford, Noel Francis. John Wayne appears in an unaccredited role as a lumberjack.

SYNOPSIS: Billy West, a lumberjack in the North woods, faces a life and death struggle after witnessing a murder committed by two fur thieves.

The reviewer from *Variety* lamented the fact that the film was written by a man, adapted by a man, directed by a man, and had a male star. He felt the film would fail with women audiences. "Here is what Hollywood calls a 'major production.' It has a moderately expensive cast, a wealth of accessories was produced on distant location in marvelous scenic settings, and was made with all the painstaking technical skill of which Hollywood is capable. And it isn't worth much at the box office. If it were, it wouldn't go into pre-release at the Hippodrome . . . it's just a routine sentimental tale of the type that used to be called 'kitchen fiction,' all hokey, artificial romance. What gets this reviewer's goat is that this junk was made into a really magnificent technical melodramatic film, as far as its stage effects and its settings were concerned. And also that it must have cost a barrel of money."

A reviewer for the *Nevada State Journal* wrote, "Some of the high spots of *Rough Romance* include a thrilling race between two teams of malamute sled dogs, a rough and tumble free-for-all battle between the loggers and trappers at a logging town 'jamboree,' and a hair-raising gun battle between O'Brien and Moreno."

According to a reviewer in the *New York Times*, "Those responsible for the production of *Rough Romance* have not bothered to introduce any new ideas. The result is a nitrogenous collection of odd bits of familiar material warped into a merely passable picture."

THE LAST OF THE DUANES (1930)
FOX
PRODUCER: WILLIAM FOX
DIRECTOR: ALFRED WERKER
SCREENPLAY: Ernest Pascal, from a story by Zane Grey
LENGTH: 62 MINUTES
CAST: George O'Brien, Myrna Loy, Lucille Brown, Nat Pendleton,

Two scenes from *The Last of the Duanes* (1930). (TOP) with Lucille Brown, and (BOTTOM) with Myrna Loy.

Walter McGrail, James Mason, Lloyd Ingraham, James Bradbury, Jr., Willard Robertson, Blanche Frederici, Frank Campeau, Jim Mason, Lloyd Ingraham, Clara Blandick

SYNOPSIS: The renowned story by Zane Grey follows Buck Duane as he returns home and learns that his father has been shot in the back.

"Better that Westerns never found a voice, if the stupid dialog which prevails throughout this one preoccupies the lines that may substitute for the old, lurid subtitles," warned Variety. "Hazy memories of the silent version are that it was far more favorable and a better picture than this reincarnation. This talker is sloppily edited."

The *New York Times* reviewer wrote, "It is a narrative with hard riding, fast shooting, and fine scenes of winding roads, mountains, and valleys. This edition is considerably more believable than was the silent version, in which William Farnum impersonated the redoubtable Buck Duane."

THE SEAS BENEATH (1931)
FOX
PRODUCER: WILLIAM FOX
DIRECTOR: JOHN FORD
SCREENPLAY: Dudley Nichols, from a story by James Parker, Jr., with dialogue by William Collier, Sr. and Kurt von Fuerberg
LENGTH: 98 MINUTES
CAST: George O'Brien, Marion Lessing, Mona Maris, Warren Hymer, William Collier, Sr., Larry Kent, John Loder, Steve Pendleton, Walter C. Kelly, Walter McGrail, and Henry Victor. Many actors took parts in the film as unaccredited extras, including Philip Ahlm, Al Bennett, Earl Wayland Bowman, Bill Brand, William Collier, Sr., Leonard Davidson, Joseph Depew, Francis Ford, Robert Ford, Hans Fuerberg, Al Generaux, Bob Gillette, George Golden, Ben Hall, George Harris, Bob Kyle, Jack Martin, Harry Mount, Jack Murphy, Maurice Murphy, Bob Nelson, Edward Piel, Jr., Nat Pendleton, Terrance Ray, Harry Schultz, Ferdinand Schumann-Heink, Marvin Shechter, Robert Shepherd, Harry Strang, Anton Tell, George Templeton, Harry Tenbrook, T. J. F. von Fuerberg, Frank Walton, Harry Weil, Hans Winterhalder
SYNOPSIS: A decoy ship for the US Navy lures enemy submarines to their destruction.

"Naval picture that will fall short in most of its deluxe spots, but should have a better chance in lesser houses," wrote a reviewer in *Variety*. "What little punch it carries rests in the baiting of a German

Marion Lessing with George O'Brien in *The Seas Beneath* (1931).

submarine into a trap and the sinking of it by an American sub. Drama in the story is mortally wounded by over-footage. No reason for this film to run an hour and a half, leave alone eight minutes past that extreme deadline, and entire sequences can come out . . . a love theme has been inserted, with George O'Brien as the American officer, a cinch part for O'Brien, who may lack flapper appeal, but who is more authentic in these parts than the pretty boys."

The *Variety* reviewer added, "Ford, apparently taking his *Men Without Women* as a guide post, has diluted the tenseness of the danger periods with comedy so that there's actually no wallop anywhere. And the picture never quite gets away from telegraphing the inference that there's to be no disaster, and that no one is going to get hurt. The various stretches of padding are ruinous."

"It is not a picture to be taken very seriously, so far as war activities are concerned, for no mystery ship could ever have survived long in such circumstances. All its action is theatric in the extreme. George O'Brien does quite well. Dramatic tension is extreme, and George performed well in this great example of entertainment served up in the indubitable style of John Ford."

George O'Brien in *Fair Warning* (1931).

FAIR WARNING (1931)
FOX
PRODUCER: WILLIAM FOX
DIRECTOR: ALFRED L. WERKER
SCREENPLAY: Ernest L. Pascal, based on a novel, *The Untamed*, by Max Brand
LENGTH: 62 MINUTES.
CAST: George O'Brien, Louise Huntington, Mitchell Harris, George Brent, Willard Robertson, Nat Pendleton, John Sheehan, Ernie Adams, Erwin Connelly, Alphonz Ethier

A studio advertising poster for *Fair Warning* (1931).

SYNOPSIS: "Whistling Dan," a boy lost in the desert, grows up with a rancher and his daughter, Kate. When he interferes with a robbery, desperados kidnap and imprison Kate's father. Dan trails the outlaw gang, kills all of them except their leader, and takes him to a no-holds barred brawl climaxing with Dan strangling him. With revenge accomplished, Jim and Kate reunite for a life of happiness together.

"This remake of a silent, made by Fox about ten years ago, released under the original title of the novel by max Brand, now shapes up as a lively Westerner for the grinds," stated *Variety*, in its 1931 review. "Crammed full of action, it employs talk only where necessary, with chases, fisticuffs, and gunplay taking up most of the footage. It's a cinch to please the kid trade in most of the neighborhoods."

A reviewer for the *Lima News* wrote about the virile story of Western romance and excitement: "George O'Brien, who portrays the leading male role, has never been seen and heard to better advantage and he has a new leading woman in Louise Huntington, who is as charming as she is talented. O'Brien enacts the role of an untamed youth, who fights his way to romance, and when it comes, he is afraid of it."

A HOLY TERROR (1931)
FOX
PRODUCER: WILLIAM FOX WITH EDMUND GRAINGER
DIRECTOR: IRVING CUMMINGS
SCREENPLAY: Ralph Brock, based on the novel, *Trailin'*, by Max Brand, with adaptation and dialogue by Alfred A. Cohn, Myron C. Fagan, and Ralph Block
LENGTH 52 MINUTES
CAST: George O'Brien, Sally Eilers, Humphrey Bogart, Rita La Roy, James Kirkwood, Stanley Fields, Robert Warwick, Richard Tucker, and Earle Pinegree. Actors appearing in unaccredited roles include George Chandler, John Elliott, Julien Rivero, Slim Whitaker, and Jay Wilson.
SYNOPSIS: Tony Bard, a polo-playing playboy, follows a twisting trail of intrigue that leads to the discovery of the truth about a murder.

"Where, not so long ago, the hero would have met the heroine struggling with the ropes that tied her to the railroad track, he now introduces himself by smashing his airplane into the room in which she is taking a shower," wrote a reviewer in the *New York Times*. "Perhaps this is progress; perhaps it is a salute to an age that has all but forgotten its remote tradition. Picture is not for those whose memories cannot forget the earlier days."

Variety wrote in its review, "Hybrid Western starting out in New York like a gangster item and finishing in Wyoming as a horse opera.

Three scenes with Sally Eilers and George O'Brien in *A Holy Terror* (1931).

It is cut along conventional Western lines, with hero from east looking for ranch owner he believes shot his father. Everything that could have been given story, that including dialog, has been provided. George O'Brien looks heavier than ever, but good. His voice has improved a lot since early talker days."

Riders of the Purple Sage (1931)
Fox
Producer: William Fox
Director: Hamilton MacFadden
Screenplay: Philip Klein, John F. Goodrich, and Barry Connors, based on a novel by Zane Grey
Length: 58 minutes
Cast: George O'Brien, Marguerite Churchill, Noah Beery, James Todd, Yvonne Pelletier, Stanley Fields, Frank McGlynn, Jr., Lester Dorr, and Shirley Nail. Actors appearing in unaccredited small roles include Joe Brown, Dick Hunter, Cliff Lyons, Frank Meredith, Herman Nowlin, Vinegar Roan, and Delmar Watson.
Synopsis: Jim Lassiter, an outcast saving a rancher from murderous outlaws, barely survives an avalanche, battles an evil judge, and prevails in a dramatic gunfight

"It is well-pictured," described a review in the *New York Times*, "and although it is not photographed on the wide film known as 'Grandeur,' it is being shown in magnified form on a screen that fills the proscenium arch. This causes the open-air scenes to be most impressive. It is gratifying to observe the improvement in this production over the silent editions. Here the players look as though they belonged to the times, which is more than can be said for most of those who figured in the mute versions of this narrative. The stalwart Mr. O'Brien is thoroughly in his element, both as a rider and an actor."

"Here the story gets dialog for the first time, and that seems one of its troubles," described a reviewer for *Variety*. "Every so often the conversation becomes a little formal and stilted for Arizona in the middle of the nineteenth century. But George Schneiderman's lens ability plus a tot named Shirley Nails go a long way to overcome the inept talk. The photography, incidentally, is probably the main reason the Roxy decided upon the big screen. Any number of times during the screening it's obvious that Schneiderman's glass and the wide angle projection lens are tossing bouquets at each other as there are many instances in which one enhances the other. O'Brien interprets Lassiter as of the familiar strong and silent type. It's a likeable performance by the featured player, whose dexterity with a gun is noteworthy here. Marguerite Churchill is often in the embarrassing

Marguerite Churchill and George O'Brien in *Riders of the Purple Sage* (1931).

predicament of long and theatric speeches which won't help her impression in the better houses."

In *Riders of the Purple Sage* (1931), (TOP) Marguerite Churchill and George O'Brien, and (BOTTOM) George, Marguerite, and Frank McGlynn, Jr.

A reviewer for the *Nevada State Journal* wrote, "The dramatic story of a man's single-handed fight to protect the life and interests of a beautiful girl. It presents also the most ambitious and costly exterior setting ever built by a Hollywood motion picture company miles away from the home studio. This setting is a complete ranch house of the period of 1870, with barns, granaries, corrals, carriage sheds, and stockades. This ranch house is destroyed by fire in one of the most amazing scenes ever brought to the screen. George O'Brien and his fellow players, during filming of the picture, made their homes in a camp that was a miniature city under canvas. All sorts of natural forces and hazards were encountered and combated by Director Hamilton MacFadden and his staff. Almost daily, thunder storms peculiar to this region made work difficult, and the extreme heat of mid-day made it necessary to start the cameras shortly after dawn, continue shooting until noon, and then call a rest under 3 p.m., when the company was re-assembled to work until seven at night."

This version of the famous Zane Grey story was filmed at least twice before in silent versions starring William Farnum and Tom Mix.

THE RAINBOW TRAIL (1932)
FOX
DIRECTOR: DAVID HOWARD
SCREENPLAY: Philip Klein and Barry Connors, based on a story by Zane Grey
LENGTH: 62 MINUTES
CAST: George O'Brien, Minna Gombell, Cecilia Parker, Roscoe Ates, James Kirkwood, Ruth Donnelly, Robert Frazer, Niles Welch, William L. Thorne, J. M. Kerrigan, W. L. Thorne, Landers Stevens, and Hamilton Hearn. Actors appearing in unaccredited small roles include George Montgomery, Alice Ward, Laska Winters, Edward Burns, George Burton, Sy Clegg, Iron Eyes Cody, Dick Hunter, Johnny Luther, Cliff Lyons, Frank McGrath, Herman Nowlin, Little Pine, Vinegar Roan, Clint Sharp
SYNOPSES: A ranger defying a gang of desperadoes searches for a lost trio in an impossible gulch, battles the sinister, masked leader of an outlaw gang, and searches for a gold mine mine belonging to Fay Larkin.

A studio advertising poster for *The Rainbow Trail* (1932).

Variety's reviewer wrote that this version was an "... above average production," and noted the enthralling outdoor photography. "O'Brien gives a good interpretation of the super-heroic hero of this cast full of villainous and angelic contrasts. For every square person in the cast there are fifty dastards, but the good people cop the decision. In the lead role, O'Brien probably resembles Farnum more than Mix. The latter made *Rainbow Trail* a fast-moving chase film. O'Brien is more suggestive of power than action. He's the best-built guy in Hollywood, and his thin jersey shirt always shows it."

Two scenes from *The Rainbow Trail* (1932), top with Cecilia Parker.

A reviewer for the *Zanesville Signal* wrote, "Disregarding its sterling qualities, from an entertainment point of view, *The Rainbow Trial* is sufficiently interesting from an educational standpoint to warrant its success. It is filmed in the Grand Canyon of the Colorado, affording many excellent views of this wonder of nature. George O'Brien, in the leading role, has a part that is made-to-order for him. *The Rainbow Trail* is much better than the average Western picture. It will keep you in suspense."

The *New York Times* reviewer said, "In the audible screen transcription of Zane Grey's Western thriller, *The Rainbow Trail*, there are a few shootings, a stabbing, and plenty of fast riding. A note of cheer is struck in this film by the presence of J. M. Kerrigan, who, although he is not assigned to an important part, at least, gives his usual splendid performance."

THE GAY CABALLERO (1932)
FOX
PRODUCER: WILLIAM FOX
DIRECTOR: ALFRED E. WERKER
SCREENPLAY: Philip Klein and Barry Connors from a novel by Tom Gill
LENGTH: 60 MINUTES
CAST: George O'Brien, Victor McLaglen, Conchita Montenegro, Linda Watkins, C. Henry Gordon, Weldon Heyburn, Willard Robertson, Wesley Giraud, Martin Garralaga, Juan Torena. Actors appearing in unaccredited small roles include Cecilia Parker, Al Earnest Garcia, and Wesley Giraud.
SYNOPSIS: Ted Radcliffe, an ex-gridiron athlete from an Eastern college, returns home to the family ranch to discover the family fortune has dwindled to nothing due to the ruthless activities of a crafty Mexican cattle baron.

"Possibilities never were sweet for Westerns for Broadway," noted the reviewer from *Variety*. "When they are no better than *The Gay Caballero*, which in adaptation, direction, and continuity does not evidence much care, their chances are not very good elsewhere. The fight in a cantina between O'Brien and his Mexican rival is one of the most action-filled in a long time, with O'Brien falling back on some wrestling tricks. Nearly everyone drew thankless roles and dialog in

George O'Brien at the time of the making of *The Gay Caballero* (1932.)

this feature, but Linda Watkins as El Coyote's girl friend got the poorest break of all."

The *New York Times* reviewer wrote, "Although the story is so lacking in suspense that it becomes rather wearying, there are some noteworthy scenes in *The Gay Caballero*. Mr. O'Brien gives an excellent account of himself in the wrestling match."

A studio lobby card for *Mystery Ranch* (1932).

THE MYSTERY RANCH (1932)
FOX
PRODUCER: WILLIAM FOX WITH WALTER MAYO
DIRECTOR: DAVID HOWARD
SCREENPLAY: Alfred A. Cohn, based on *The Killer*, a novel by Stewart Edward White
LENGTH: 55 MINUTES
CAST: George O'Brien, Cecilia Parker, Charles B. Middleton, Charles Stevens, Roy Stewart, Forrester Harvey, Virginia Herdman, Noble Johnson, Russell Powell, Betty Francisco. Steve Clemente and Frank Rice appear in unaccredited small roles.
SYNOPSIS: As Bob Sanborn, George crosses with a cruel ranch owner, Henry Steele, who cuts out a man's tongue because he talks too much, and plays the piano as he gives his orders, casually striking melodious notes on the keyboard as he outwits his rivals until the inevitable happy ending.

"A naïve melodrama of the great Southwest in which the producers appear to be spoofing the cowboy yarns of other days," wrote

Mordaunt Hall in the *New York Times*. "It has the majestic scenery of what looks like the Grand Canyon, and dialogue that might belong to any old thriller ... this ingenious affair, told with tongue in the cheek or not, has some of the most beautiful glimpses that have ever been seen on the screen. The photography is so good that is seems almost stereoscopic. But that is, alas, all that there is to praise."

Variety's reviewer thought the film was ". . . conventional Western hokum, which the Winter Garden first-nighters turned into a rollicking affair by hissing the villain and applauding the to-the-rescue Texas Rangers, or anything heroic which George O'Brien did. Picture starts slowly but soon picks up to a better pace, and finished strong with less than an hour's running time. Costs little, obviously, and as such, with a Broadway week for ballyhoo, it should show up nicely on the tally sheet."

THE GOLDEN WEST (1932)
FOX
PRODUCER: WILLIAM FOX WITH EDMUND GRAINGER
DIRECTOR: David Howard
SCREENPLAY: Gordon Rigby, based on a story by Zane Grey
CAST: George O'Brien, Janet Chandler, Marion Burns, Arthur Pierson, Onslow Stevens, Bert Hanlon, Emmett Corrigan. Actors appearing in unaccredited roles include Julia Swayne Gordon, Edward Brady, Fred Church, Steve Clemente, Iron Eyes Cody, Edmund Breese, Sam West, Ben Hall, Hattie McDaniel, Sam McDaniel, Russ Powell, George Reed, Charles Stevens, Stanley Blystone, George Regas, Dorothy Ward, Sam Adams, Edward Dillon, Chief Big Tree, and John War Eagle.
SYNOPSIS: George plays a dual role as a father killed by Indians and his son who is raised by the tribe to become a savage attacking the white settlers.

A reviewer for the *Monessen Daily Independent* wrote, "The color and romance of the South in pre-rebellion days and the adventure and excitement of the far West in the days when the red man ruled the plains, are blended in Zane Grey's *The Golden West*, the Fox picture with George O'Brien. In the first part of the picture, he is a frontiersman, striving to save his family from the scalp-relishing redskins. Twenty years later, he also doubles as an Indian brave, Mazano, exposing the

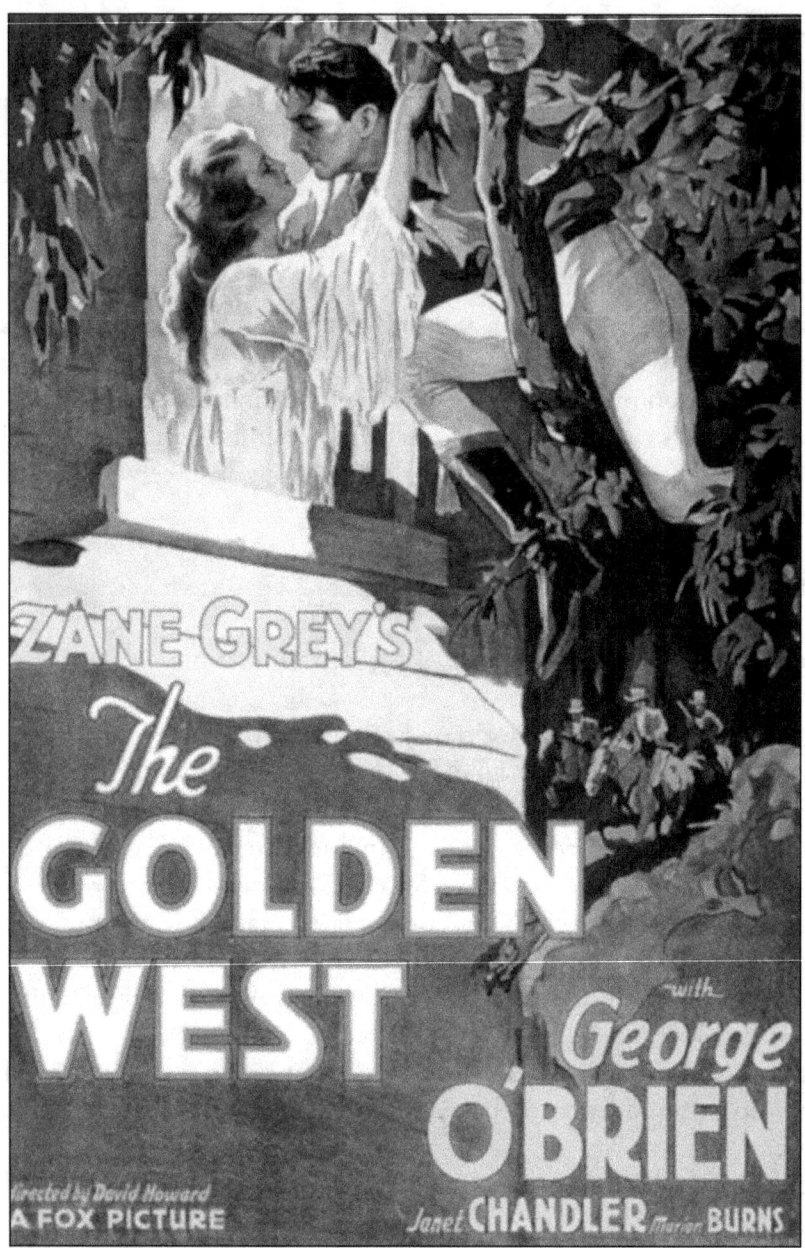

A studio poster for *The Golden West* (1932).

perfection of his torso with the shamelessness of Gunga Din. It has the vitality of action, coupled with the majestic beauty of sun-drenched plain and forest."

Three scenes with George O'Brien and Marion Burns in *The Golden West* (1932).

Studio advertising poster for *Robbers' Roost* (1933).

ROBBER'S ROOST (1932)
FOX
PRODUCER: SOL LESSER
DIRECTOR: DAVID HOWARD AND LOUIS KING
SCREENPLAY: Dudley Nichols, based on a story by Zane Grey
LENGTH: 64 MINUTES
CAST: George O'Brien, Maureen O'Sullivan, Walter McGrail, Maude Eburne, Reginald Owen, William Pawley, Clifford Santley, and Robert Greig. Actors appearing in unaccredited roles include Frank Cordell, Gilbert Holmes, Dick Hunter, Doris Lloyd, Frank McGrath, Bill Nestrell, Ted Oliver, Frank Rice, Vinegar Roan, Clint Sharp, and Fred Toones.

George O'Brien with Maureen O'Sullivan in *Robbers' Roost* (1933).

SYNOPSIS: An Arizona ranch hand named exposes the cattle-rustling activities of a ranch foreman.

"Strictly for the youngsters," claimed the reviewer in *Variety*. "While containing plenty of action, the adapter and director have emphasized only the familiar bromides of the plains. O'Brien and Miss Sullivan ring amateurishly."

A reviewer in the *Illustrated Daily News* wrote, "It has been a long time since the writer has seen a star do such thrilling stunts as George leaping from mountain peak to mountain peak in a fashion that would make a Catalina goat seem jumpless. From a photographic standpoint, it is almost a poem of beauty in certain sequences, thanks to the craftsmanship of George Schneiderman, a cameraman of exceptional artistic ability. Good old George—O'Brien is swell. He always is in this type of stuff."

A reviewer writing in *Film Daily* said, "Grown up Western has unusually strong love interest and plenty of thrills and action. George O'Brien handles his romantic scenes with almost as much skill as he does with his horse and gun. O'Brien stages a sensational rescue with some unusual stunt stuff that packs a punch."

SMOKE LIGHTNING (1933)
FOX
PRODUCER: SOL LESSER
DIRECTOR: DAVID HOWARD
SCREENPLAY: Gordon Rigby and Sidney Mitchell, based on *Canyon Walls*, a novel by Zane Grey
CAST: George O'Brien, Nell O'Day, Betsy King Ross, Frank Atkinson, E. Allen Warren, Douglas Dumbrille, and Arthur Hoyt. Actors appearing in unaccredited roles include George Burton, Betsy King Ross, Virginia Sale, Morgan Wallace, Fred Wilson, and Harry Semels.
SYNOPSIS: Smoke Mason, a roving cowpuncher, battles wits with a local sheriff, who covets an orphan girl's ranch.

A reviewer for the *Newark Advocate* wrote, "Maintaining a swift pace from the very beginning, George O'Brien's latest Fox picture, *Smoke Lightning*, proved highly entertaining to the audience at the Auditorium Theater."

A reviewer for the *Monessen Daily Independent* wrote, "George O'Brien demonstrates that a cowboy's life in the modern West can

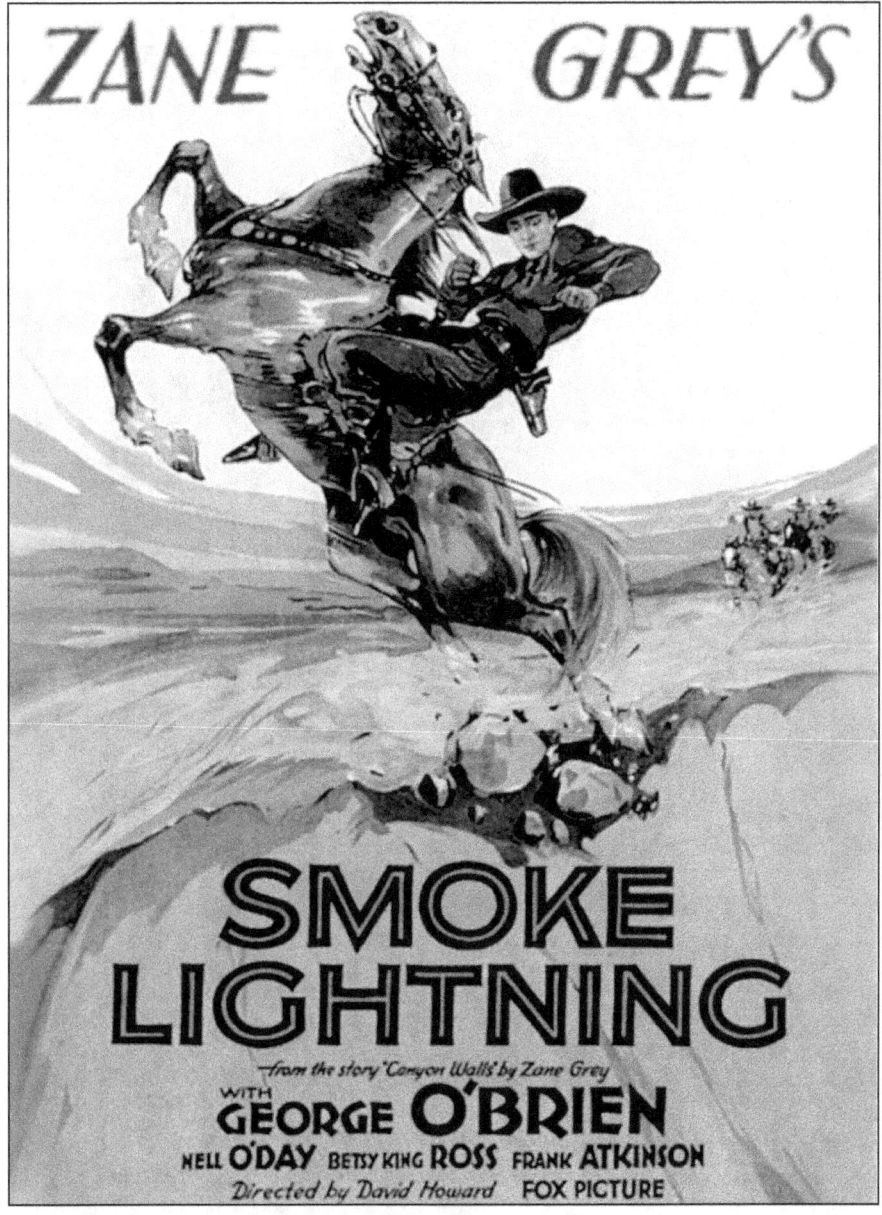

Studio advertising poster for *Smoke Lightning* (1933).

be a thrilling one bristling with gunfights, a jail-break, a poker game that ruins one of the players, a gripping duel across the car roofs of a racing train, and some of the most brilliant riding ever shown on the screen."

Two scenes with George O'Brien and Greta Nissen in *Life in the Raw* (1933).

LIFE IN THE RAW (1933)
FOX
PRODUCER: SOL LESSER
DIRECTOR: LEWIS KING
SCREENPLAY: Stuart Anthony, based on a novel by Zane Grey
LENGTH: 60 MINUTES
CAST: George O'Brien, Claire Trevor, Greta Nissen, Francis Ford, Warner P. Richmond, Steve Pendleton, Alan Edwards, and Nigel De Brulier. Actors appearing in unaccredited roles include Si Jenks, LeRoy Mason, Sam McDaniel, Paul Panzer, Stanley Price
SYNOPSIS: Jim Barry and a girl escape bad-guys and hold up in a cave where romance blossoms.

"Interest nicely sustained," said a review in *Variety*, "in this adaptation which lifts it to the upper bracket in its class. Based on a not very original theme but adroitly handled, so it builds. George O'Brien plays with proper dash and gets help from Claire Trevor. An excellent example of what a Western can be and very seldom is."

A reviewer for the *Delta Herald Times* wrote, "There is romance, adventure, danger, acts of undaunted heroism, all set against the dynamic background of the West. It is reported as a story of humans whose emotions are laid bare by the unrelenting pressure of arid wastes."

THE LAST TRAIL (1933)
FOX
PRODUCER: SOL LESSER
DIRECTOR: JAMES TINLING
SCREENPLAY: Stuart Anthony, based on a novel by Zane Grey
LENGTH: 59 MINUTES.
CAST: George O'Brien, Claire Trevor, J. Carol Naish, El Brendel, Matt McHugh, Lucille La Verne, Edward J. LeSaint, Ruth Warren, George Reed, and Luis Alberni. LeRoy Mason appears in an unaccredited small role.
SYNOPSIS: From a novel by Zane Grey, this updated comedy/Western pits O'Brien against racketeers trying to muscle in on his family's ranch.

"Western story, but better than average," reported *Variety*. "Based on a Zane Grey yarn with much material added. Nothing new, though shrewdly assembled and makes fast moving entertainment. O'Brien heads the cast well, getting good support from Miss Trevor."

George O'Brien with Ruth Gillette in *Frontier Marshal* (1934).

FRONTIER MARSHAL (1934)
FOX
PRODUCER: SOL LESSER
DIRECTOR: LEWIS SEILER
SCREENPLAY: William Conselman and Stuart Anthony, based on a novel, *Wyatt Earp Frontier Marshal*, by Stuart N. Lake
CAST: George O'Brien, Irene Bentley, George E. Stone, Alan Edwards, Ruth Gillette, Berton Churchill, Frank Conroy, Ward Bond. Actors appearing in unaccredited roles include Edward LeSaint, Jerry Foster, and Russell Simpson.
SYNOPSIS: Michael Wyatt, a stalwart Wyatt Earp type, enters Tombstone to serve as the new marshal, and proves himself to be a crafty sleuth and crackerjack marshal when he rids the town of the outlaws.

According to the *New York Times*, "They are a hard-riding, quick-shooting lot in *Frontier Marshal*. A frank melodrama, it does not bother about plausibility, and one gathers that it was produced with the adapter and the director having their tongues in their cheeks."

A studio advertising poster for *Frontier Marshal* (1934).

"Mae West sows her Wild West oats in this picture, or more correctly, Ruth Gillette, a ringer for the come-up lady who nearly steals the picture form George O'Brien in two or three spots," reviewed *Variety*. "She's the billowy box of the dancehall in Tombstone, and puts considerable punch in an otherwise vigorous picture that might have been much better with a more skillful tailoring job. As is, it's entertainment, and good enough to stand alone in the second division. O'Brien is his usual he-man self."

Mary Brian and George O'Brien in *Ever Since Eve* (1934).

EVER SINCE EVE (1934)
FOX
PRODUCER: SOL LESSER
DIRECTOR: GEORGE MARSHALL
SCREENPLAY: Henry Johnson and Stuart Anthony, from a play, *The Heir to the Hoorah*, by Paul Armstrong.
LENGTH: 75 MINUTES
CAST: George O'Brien, Mary Brian, Herbert Mundin, Betty Blythe, Russell Simpson, Roger Imhof, George Meeker. Actors appearing in

unaccredited roles include Wally Albright, Helene Chadwick, Billy Franey, Eula Guy, Jeanne Hart, John Lester Johnson, Mary Mersch, Gloria Roy, Yorke Sherwood, Fred Toones, James Wang, and Larry Wheat.

SYNOPSIS: Neil Rogers, a good-looking country lad who owns a substantial share of a Western gold mine meets a wild gold digger, who falls in love with him.

Mordaunt Hall, reviewer for the *New York Times*, wrote: "There is enough wholesome humor in *Ever Since Eve* to atone for its antiquated plot. Mr. O'Brien does well enough in his part, and Miss Brian is pleasing in hers. Betty Blythe, once the vampire of old silent films, here assumes the role of a respectable society woman, and she plays it competently."

"Very light and ordinary lesser run program material is a laudatory commentary for a theme which would experiment with George O'Brien largely in the drawing room," explained *Variety's* review. "There's nothing wrong with O'Brien. He does his work in business clothes almost as well as in cowboy and seaman's togs. There's a definite something about the part in which he is cast in *Eve*, a title which is the very antithesis of the action, that doesn't give him the chance to prove his capability for miscellaneous characterizations. He's clean-cut; perhaps a little too much so. He's virile, because he has a chance to ride a horse, and yet inconsistent. He doesn't seem to handle a woman, or men with whom she flirts, in the manner expected by the type of audience that would patronize such a picture. He's too nice."

THE DUDE RANGER (1934)
FOX
PRODUCER: SOL LESSER
DIRECTOR: EDWARD F. CLINE
SCREENPLAY: Barry Barringer, based on a story by Zane Grey
LENGTH: 63 MINUTES
CAST: George O'Brien, Irene Hervey, LeRoy Mason, Henry Hall, Sid Saylor, James Mason, Sid Jordan, Alma Chester, Lloyd Ingraham. Actors appearing in unaccredited roles include Silver Tip Baker, Hank Bell, Earl Dwire, John Ince, Si Jenks, Jack Kirk, Murdock MacQuarrie, Lafe McKee, Vester Pegg, and Dick Rush.

Irene Hervey with George O'Brien in *The Dude Ranger* (1934).

SYNOPSIS: A cowboy inherits his uncle's ranch in Arizona, battles cattle thieves, and finishes off the bad guys in a blaze of six-shooters on the edge of a cliff.

"*The Dude Ranger*, which brings the cactus and sagebrush drama back to Broadway, provides an hour of elegant hoss," wrote Andre Sennwald in the *New York Times*. "Having the proper respect for Westerns, the sponsors have endowed their work with the kind of photography it deserves. The Dude is played with bronzed and modest splendor by George O'Brien, who can take care of himself on or off a bronco. O'Brien acts in his usual easy manner, and is given the customary opportunity to display his riding ability."

George O'Brien with Dorothy Wilson in *When a Man's a Man* (1935).

WHEN A MAN'S A MAN (1935)
FOX
PRODUCER: SOL LESSER
DIRECTOR: EDWARD F. CLINE
SCREENPLAY: Agnes Christine Johnson and Frank Mitchell Dazey, based on the novel by Harold Bell Wright
LENGTH: 68 MINUTES
CAST: George O'Brien, Dorothy Wilson, Paul Kelly, Harry Woods, Jimmy Butler, Richard Carlisle, Edgar Norton, Clarence Wilson. Actors appearing in unaccredited roles include Stanley Blystone, Ken Cooper, Lester Dorr, Frank Ellis, Sid Jordon, Rose Plummer, Fred Toones, and Slim Whitaker
SYNOPSIS: Kitty Baldwin, a lovely cowgirl, struggles against all odds to retain her only water hole, until an Eastern tenderfoot figures out a way to draw water underneath the ground from the other side of the fence.

"Twas danged fortunate, stranger, that tenderfoot George O'Brien reached the Bar-Triangle Ranch when he did, for that old varmint, Harry Woods, had fenced off the water hole, and the cattle owned by Dorothy Wilson and her paw, Richard Carle, were purty far agone," wrote a reviewer in the *The New York Times*. "But the tenderfoot outsmarted them, he did, and showed he was a man's man after all. Mr. O'Brien's the broth of the boy to do it. So, here's a salute and a 'welcome, stranger!' for the latest of the horse operas. Long may they ride!"

Variety informed exhibitors: "Harold Bell Wright's name and the star, George O'Brien, who has a following, are about all this Western has to recommend it anywhere. Since Wright wrote the story, his plot has been worked to death, and in bringing it to the screen again, the producers have made no effort to freshen it up. Even the kids will give most of the picture a laugh. It's that commonplace and juvenile."

COWBOY MILLIONAIRE (1935)
FOX
PRODUCER: SOL LESSER WITH JOHN ZANFT
DIRECTOR: EDWARD F. CLINE
SCREENPLAY: George Waggner and Daniel Jarrett
LENGTH: 65 MINUTES
CAST: George O'Brien, Evalyn Bostock, Edgar Kennedy, Alden Chase, Maude Allen, Daniel Jarrett, Lloyd Ingraham, Dean Benton, Thomas A. Curran.
SYNOPSIS: The chief cowboy of a dude ranch works on a gold mine and woos a young Englishwoman.

"This new George O'Brien opera ought to please his followers," thought the reviewer in *Variety*. "Picture ranks above the usual type of Western comedy drama. Film packs some good laughs and enough punch to make it worthy as dual material anywhere."

A reviewer for the *Hammond Times* wrote, "Fast, furious action! Ultra-modern settings! A new kind of zippy Western feature that will keep you thrilled, keep you howling with joy, and hold you in delightful romantic suspense. George O'Brien slips with ease from drawing room to saddle in a bang-up picture that has everything. It's sure-fire pleasure."

George O'Brien in 1935 when he made *Cowboy Millionaire*.

George O'Brien with Irene Hervey in *Hard Rock Harrigan* (1935).

HARD ROCK HARRIGAN (1935)
FOX
PRODUCER: SOL LESSER
DIRECTOR: DAVID HOWARD
SCREENPLAY: Raymond L. Schrock and Daniel Jarett, based on a novel by Charles Furthman
LENGTH: 60 MINUTES
CAST: George O'Brien, Irene Hervey, Fred Kohler, Dean Benton, and David Clyde. Actors appearing in unaccredited roles include Frank Rice, Victor Potel, Olin Francis, William Gould, George Humbert, Edward Keane, Lee Shumway, Glenn Strange, Jack Kirk, Lee Phelps, Curley Dresden.
SYNOPSIS: As "Hard Rock Harrigan," a husky toiler in the mines, George O'Brien joins an outfit of workers trying to bore a giant tunnel through hills and mountains to provide water for their lowland city and its surrounding country.

According to a reviewer in *Variety*, "One of those stern pictures of he-men, it gives George O'Brien an opportunity to get away from a saddle in a melodramatic story. He fits, and the film seems suitable second feature. Some excellent shots showing workers digging underground, and after a draggy start, David Howard speeds up the direction."

Andre Sennwald from the *New York Times* wrote, "Not being a glutton for punishment, this column was forced to quit *Hard Rock Harrigan* after forty minutes. It would, therefore, be incautious, on the basis of such a brief acquaintance with George O'Brien's new work, to say that it is the most aggressively mediocre entertainment of the season. To submit it on Broadway is to be unfair both to the picture and to Broadway audiences."

THUNDER MOUNTAIN (1935)
20TH CENTURY FOX
PRODUCER: SOL LESSER
DIRECTOR: DAVID HOWARD
SCREENPLAY: Daniel Jarrett and Don Swift, based on a novel of the same name by Zane Grey
LENGTH: 60 MINUTES
CAST: George O'Brien, Barbara Fritchie, Frances Grant, Morgan Wallace, George F. "Gabby" Hayes, Edward J. LeSaint, Dean Benton,

Barbara Fritchie with George O'Brien in *Thunder Mountain* (1935).

William N. Bailey, and Sid Jordan. Actors appearing in unaccredited roles include Lloyd Ingraham, Lafe McKee, Hal Price, Carl Stockdale, and Arthur Thalasso.

SYNOPSIS: O'Brien appears as Kal Emerson, a prospector staking a claim to a gold mine, in the era when mining towns mushroomed overnight.

"In turning out *Thunder Mountain*, Sol Lesser bridges some rather wide gaps in the action and, in some cases, does it so that the gap is a bit startling, though not seriously injuring the continuity," wrote a reviewer from *Variety*. "There isn't much shooting in *Thunder Mountain*, but all the way, the story is surcharged with action. Dialog pretty good."

The *New York Times* wrote: "The code of the West shall be preserved, so long as the stalwart George O'Brien rides the range, and danged if virtue doesn't triumph handsomely in *Thunder Mountain*, a minor horse opera from the Fox studios. It is chiefly concerned with feats of derringdo and winds up in a blaze of glory with the traditional hand-to-hand struggle between the hero and the villain on the edge of a cliff."

WHISPERING SMITH SPEAKS (1935)
20TH CENTURY FOX
PRODUCER: SOL LESSER
DIRECTOR: DAVID HOWARD
SCREENPLAY: Daniel Jarrett and Don Swift; Adaptation by Gilbert Wright and Rex Taylor, based on a story by Frank H. Spearman
LENGTH: 67 MINUTES
CAST: George O'Brien, Irene Ware, Kenneth Thomson, Maude Allen, Spencer Charters, Victor Potel, Frank Sheridan, William V. Mong, Edward Keane, and Maurice Cass. Actors appearing in unaccredited roles include Bess Flowers, John Ince, Si Jenks, J. P. McGowan, and Dick Rush.
SYNOPSIS: Gordon Harrington, the president of a railroad, sends his self-willed son to Colorado to work as a trackwalker to learn the business.

Frank S. Nugent, the reviewer in the *New York Times* liked the film, and wrote, "Back to Broadway, for what can scarcely be more than a passing visit, comes that dauntless combination of brawn and business acumen, George O'Brien in a railroading epic comparable to the construction of the siding for Kelly's brickyard. The production scarcely gives full play to the talents of this rugged actor. It's fine points are lost on Broadway, however."

(TOP) Irene Ware with George O'Brien in *Whispering Smith Speaks* (1935) and (BOTTOM) a studio advertising poster for *Whispering Smith Speaks*.

"*Whispering Smith Speaks* is an action item which the George O'Brien fans will accept," wrote a reviewer in *Variety*. "He-man star has laid his chaps aside this time, and no use of the fists but it's still a pretty fair picture for his following."

(LEFT) A studio advertising poster for *O'Malley of the Mounted* (1936).
(RIGHT) George O'Brien and Irene Ware in *O'Malley of the Mounted*.

O'MALLEY OF THE MOUNTED (1936)
20TH CENTURY FOX
PRODUCER: SOL LESSER
DIRECTOR: DAVID HOWARD
SCREENPLAY: Daniel Jarrett and Frank Howard Clark, from a story by William S. Hart
LENGTH: 59 MINUTES
CAST: George O'Brien, Irene Ware, Crauford Kent, James Bush, Victor Potel, Stanley Fields, Tom London, Reginald Barlow, Richard Cramer, Blackjack Ward. Actors appearing in unaccredited roles include Frank Ellis, Olin Francis, Charles King, Al Taylor, Emmett Vogan, Blackjack Ward, and Slim Whitaker.
SYNOPSIS: O'Malley, a Canadian Mountie, is sent to track down a gang of outlaws terrorizing American border towns.

A reviewer in *Variety* wrote, "Typical George O'Brien adventure thriller that will be aces with Western houses and subsequently hold up the second half of most dual spots. Original directorial touches and plot progression aid considerably in sustaining interest, with actual slam-bang action kept to a minimum. Some cowboy fans might voice objections to the limited amount of bronco galloping, but this should be a help in larger houses. George O'Brien gives an impressive performance as the daring O'Malley, displaying marked restraint both in comedy and action situations.

Frank S. Nugent, the *New York Times* reviewer, wrote, "With his bulging muscles straining at the seams of his form-fitting scarlet tunic, George O'Brien makes a striking figure in *O'Malley of the Mounted*.

(TOP) *The Border Patrolman* (1936) as advertised on a studio lobby card. (BOTTOM) Polly Ann Young and George O'Brien in *The Border Patrolman* (1936).

THE BORDER PATROLMAN (1936)
20TH CENTURY FOX
PRODUCER: SOL LESSER
DIRECTOR: DAVID HOWARD
SCREENPLAY: Daniel Jarrett and Bennett Cohen
LENGTH: 58 MINUTES
CAST: George O'Brien, Polly Ann Young, LeRoy Mason, Mary Doran, Smiley Burnette, Tom London, William P. Carleton, Al Hill, George MacQuarrie, John St. Polis, Cyril Ring. Actors appearing in unaccredited roles include Frank Campeau, Charles Coleman, Martin Garralaga, Lloyd Ingraham, and Chris-Pin Martin.
SYNOPSIS: A border patrolman hired to disciplin the spoiled daughter of a rich man chases her after she becomes unwittingly involved with a gang of jewel thieves, and he saves her in the nick of time.

A reviewer in the *New York Times* wrote, "A brave smile plays about the lips of patient George O'Brien as, cloaked this time in the dusty habit of a border ranger. Mr. O'Brien seems to bear up well enough, probably by hoping that Sol Lesser may have another *Sunrise* mixed in by mistake with his next batch of variations on the cops and robbers theme."

"The title stamps this one as one of those outdoor cop things from which certain audiences shy," wrote a reviewer in *Variety*. "Actually, *Border Patrolman* is a romantic piece, which little more than employs desert country for atmosphere. The script is away above the average for outdoor dramas, and David Howard's direction reduces it to very smooth telling on the screen."

DANIEL BOONE (1936)
RKO
PRODUCER: GEORGE A. HIRLIMAN
DIRECTOR: DAVID HOWARD
SCREENPLAY: Daniel Jarrett, based on a story by Edgecumb Pinchon
CAST: George O'Brien, Heather Angel, John Carradine, Ralph Forbes, Clarence Muse, George Regas, Dickie Jones, Huntley Gordon, Harry Cording, Aggie Herring, Crauford Kent, Keith Kenneth, Baron James Lichter. Actors appearing in unaccredited roles include Dick Curtis, John Merton, Edward Peil, Sr., and Tom Ricketts.

A studio advertising poster for *Daniel Boone* (1936).

A scene with George O'Brien and Heather Angel in *Daniel Boone* (1936).

SYNOPSIS: Daniel Boone shepherds settlers into newfound territory in Kentucky amid relentless Indian attacks of tremendous proportions.

The *New York Times* reviewer wrote, "Allegedly based on the life of Daniel Boone, frontiersman, this film loses all claim to authenticity or honest of purpose by giving a once-over-lightly to the matter of the sated Virginians who robbed Boone's band of hearty pioneers as rapidly as the latter found and settled new ground. Producer preferred to point his attention instead towards a lot of phony histrionics and make-believe hysterical Indian fighting. But maybe he was right. The first, honest way might have resulted in nothing more than another dull historical item; this way, he has a good Indian picture to sell. Boone is, of course, played by George O'Brien with Heather angel as the girl. John Carradine is the bad man. They all play their roles in the same manner as the story was written—phony, with loads of action. But the kids won't know the difference."

A reviewer in *Variety* wrote, "Further evidence of Hollywood's knack of distorting historical characters into stock figures of blood-and-thunder fiction. For all his physical prowess, George O'Brien manages to project Daniel Boone as a shy, unassuming adventurer, which is presumably what the man was.

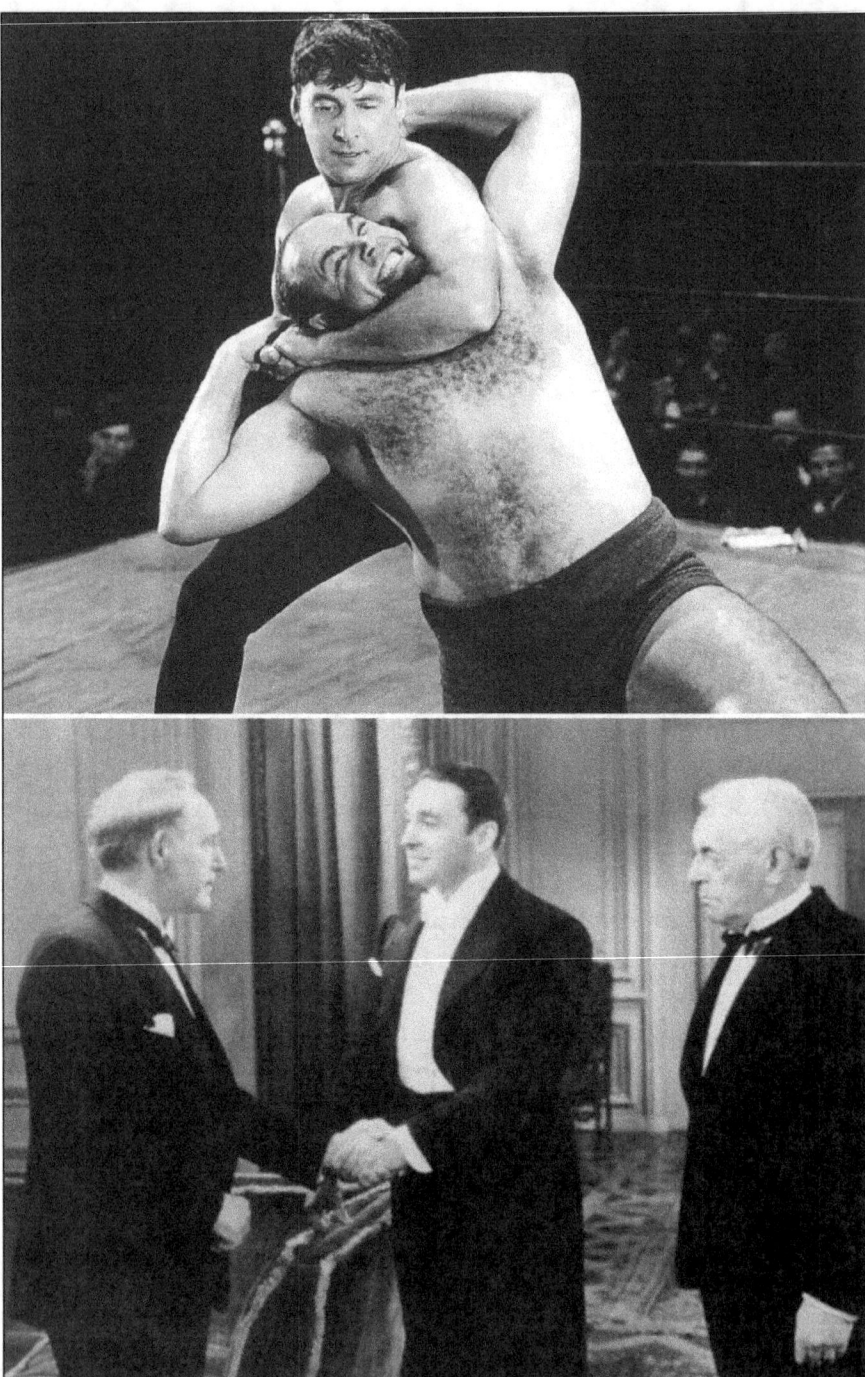

Two scenes from *Park Avenue Logger* (1937).

Park Avenue Logger (1937)
Also known as Millionaire Playboy in UK, and Tall Timber in USA
RKO
Producer: George A. Hirliman and Leonard Goldstein
Director: David Howard
Screenplay: Daniel Jarrett and Ewing Scott, based on a story by Bruce Hutchison
Length: 65 minutes
Cast: George O'Brien, Beatrice Roberts, Willard Robertson, Ward Bond, Bert Hanlon, Gertrude Short, Lloyd Ingraham, George Rosenor, Robert Emmett O'Connor. Actors appearing in unaccredited roles include Al Baffert, Lester Dorr, Frank Hagney, Otto Hoffman, Horace Murphy, Arthur Thalasso, and Dave Wengren.
Synopsis: Grant Curran, a young blueblood playboy, finds local fame as a professional wrestler on the sly. While working as a lumberman, Grant uncovers a plot to bilk his father of timberland. By using his brains and a lot of brawn, he bats down the scoundrels and wins the heroine's affection.

"With a bit more hokum, this woods romance of the great outdoors would be a satisfactory knock-down-drag-out thriller for double-deckers," advised *Variety* to exhibitors. "As it is now, *Park Avenue Logger* has little sentimental appeal, and rough stuff is just an appetizer. He-man O'Brien bulges his biceps and slaps the boys about like a dance-hall bruiser. *Park Avenue Logger* is mostly for juvenile matinees, but it has some striking logging shots."

Hollywood Cowboy (1937) Also known as Wings Over Wyoming
RKO
Producer: George A. Hirliman
Director: Ewing Scott
Screenplay: Daniel Jarrett and Ewing Scott
Length: 60 minutes
Cast: George O'Brien, Cecilia Parker, Maude Eburne, Joe Caits, Frank Milan, Charles Middleton, Lee Shumway, Walter De Palma, William Royle, Al Hill, Frank Hagney, Al Herman, Dan Wolheim, Slim Balch, Sid Jordan, Lester Dorr, Harold Daniels. Actors appearing

Cecilia Parker and George O'Brien in *Hollywood Cowboy* (1937).

in unaccredited roles include Arthur Millett, Hal Price, and Robert Walker.

SYNOPSIS: Jeffery Carson, a cowboy film star, discovers racketeers destroying a range fence. He bombs the site and aides in capturing the gang.

"*Hollywood Cowboy* makes for a highly pleasant hour," thought a reviewer for *Variety*. "It has just enough excitement to take it over the action hurdles, lots of smooth-running and up-to-the minute comedy passages and an ingratiating George O'Brien. O'Brien packs heaps of smiles and insouciance into the role of the screen cowboy."

The *New York Times* correspondent wrote, "*Hollywood Cowboy* transports the seeker-after-surcease to the painted majesties of the cattle country, and then reveals this charmed locale to be torn with labor strife and infested with metropolitan mugs trading on the strike situation to further a racket called the Cattlemen's Protective Association. Fine escape stuff! The insidious thing about this concoction is that after a few sips, you get to like it. It somehow imparts a rational appearance to a situation that calls for George O'Brien, as the Western star of a film company on location, to step out of his film-within-a-film role into that of a real-life ranch hand with a facility that seems to vindicate the oft-belittled Hollywood cowboys once and for all."

A studio advertising poster for *Windjammer* (1937).

WINDJAMMER (1937}
RKO
PRODUCER: DAVID HOWARD
DIRECTOR: EWING SCOTT
SCREENPLAY: Daniel Jarrett and James Gruen, based on a story by Raoul Haig
LENGTH: 84 MINUTES
CAST: George O'Brien, Constance Worth, William Hall, Brandon Evans, Gavin Gordon, Stanley Blystone, Lal Chand Mehra, Ben Hendricks, Jr., Lee Shumway, Frank Hagney, Sam Flint.
SYNOPSIS: In the middle of a yacht race, a Federal marshal is told to serve a subpoena on a gunrunner, and he proves himself to be just the muscle man nose-buster needed.

Constance Worth and George O'Brien in *Windjammer* (1937).

"High sea adventure fans will find *Windjammer* okay fare for a moderate evening," summarized a reviewer writing in *Variety*. "George O'Brien, mostly wished off in Westerns in the most recent tries, is put in polo shirts with ultra short sleeves to show off his biceps, which are about like Mr. Average Man's leg. He is shown swimming a bit, masquerading as a playboy, becoming a galley slave on a gun-runner, and a few other tidbits. He takes it easy and does a pretty fair job. He's best with the fights, of which there are several."

George O'Brien with Rita Oehman in *Gun Law* (1938).

GUN LAW (1938)
RKO
PRODUCER: BERT GILROY
DIRECTOR: DAVID HOWARD
SCREENPLAY: Oliver Drake
LENGTH: 60 MINUTES
CAST: George O'Brien, Rita Oehman, Ray Whitley, Paul Everton, Ward Bond, Francis McDonald, Edward Pawley. Actors appearing in

unaccredited roles include Bobby Barber, Hank Bell, Bob Burns, Neil Burns, Ken Card, Art Davis, Herman Hack, Lloyd Ingraham, Ray Jones, Ethan Laidlaw, James Mason, Eva McKenzie, Bill Patton, Robert Glecker, Frank O'Connor, Paul Fix, Willie Phelps, Earl Phelps, Norman Phelps.
SYNOPSIS: As Tom O'Malley, U.S. Marshal, George O'Brien is mistaken for an outlaw and dragged into the streets to be hanged. In a last minute rescue, the outlaws are arrested, and O'Malley reunites with the heroine. *Gun Law* was a remake of a 1928 film, *West of the Law*, which starred Tom Tyler.

"*Gun Law* is a good Western," wrote a reviewer in *Variety*, "short on romance, but long on intensity, nose-flattening fights, and hard riding. O'Brien, who batters convincingly when the air gets fist-clouded, looks like he could fight as well as he does."

The *New York Times* reviewer wrote, "George O'Brien takes over as the hard-hitting, two-fisted Marshall in an entertaining little Western . . . the film starts out rather slowly, but gathers melodramatic momentum as it goes along, and winds up in a blaze of gunfire. And what more can one ask of a horse opera?"

BORDER G-MEN (1938)
RKO
PRODUCER: BERT GILROY
DIRECTOR: DAVID HOWARD
SCREENPLAY: Oliver Drake, based on a story by Bernard McConville
LENGTH: 58 MINUTES
CAST: George O'Brien, Laraine Day, Ray Whitley, John Miljan, Rita La Roy, Edgar Dearing, William Stelling, Edward Keane, Ethan Laidlaw, Bob Burns, Hugh Sothern. Actors appearing in unaccredited roles include Hank Bell, Ken Card, Art Davis, Herman Hack, Lew Meehan, Earl Phelps, Norman Phelps, Willie Phelps, and Charles Sullivan.
SYNOPSIS: Jim Galloway, a border G-man, is sent to Texas to investigate the head of a smuggling outfit, ending with a confusion of swimming horses in the sea as they are being loaded on the ship. In this film, The Phelps Brothers introduced the popular song, "Back in the Saddle Again." Gene Autry later recorded the song and used it in his 1939 film, *Rovin' Tumbleweeds*. It became one of his biggest hits, and later his life-long theme song.

Laraine Day with George O'Brien in *Border G-Men* (1938).

Studio poster art for *Border G-Men* (1938).

"There are few new things about Westerns anymore, but there is one different approach offered this season in *Border G-Man*, which makes it come out more than usually interesting and a cinch entertainer," began a reviewer in *Variety*. "Credit goes to Oliver Drake and Bernard McConville, who have been turning out hoss operas by the dozens for years. They thumped out a neat screenplay and story, which, although obviously leading over the old routes, arrives at each point in slightly different manner . . . O'Brien has a full quota of riding, shooting and fighting. New femme, and appealing too, is Laraine Day, who is a touch play for O'Brien and gives him a rocky romance for the first three quarters of the pic. Whole film sums up as a tribute to the casting office, because there's no catch-as-catch can part filling."

George O'Brien in a scene from *Painted Desert* (1937).

PAINTED DESERT (1937)
RKO
PRODUCER: BERT GILROY
DIRECTOR: DAVID HOWARD
SCREENPLAY: Oliver Drake and John Rathmell, based on a story by Jack Cunningham
LENGTH: 58 MINUTES

Cast: George O'Brien, Laraine Day, Ray Whitley, Stanley Fields, Fred Kohler, Max Wagner, Harry Cording, Lee Shumway, Lloyd Ingraham, Maude Allen, William V. Mong. Actors appearing in unaccredited roles include Robert Burns, Fred Burns, Ken Card, Ray Jones, Lew Kelly, Jim Mason, Carl Miller, Frank O'Connor, Jack O'Shea, Earl Phelps, Norman Phelps, and Willie Phelps.

Synopsis: Bob McVey, as a young rancher, discovers a beautiful young girl and her grandfather have staked a claim on a mine that sits squarely on his property. Bob learns that the mine actually has rich deposits of tungsten, and makes a business and personal partnership with the girl

The *New York Times* review said the film ". . . falls short even of those modest standards we apply to the riding-shooting school of movie making. It is slow moving into action, hasn't much action to move into, and doesn't do especially well with the action it has."

Variety disagreed. "One of the better efforts, as Westerns go, but not strong enough to hold its own in solo," the publication detailed. "Packs plenty of action and suspense plus production and acting of tone not found often in the breed. Namby-pamby title leaves a lot of the load on O'Brien's broad shoulders, but it's likely that he can still draw 'em on his name. Fistically and histrionically, he's one of better outdoor types, who puts himself across without aid of trick riding, roping, and assorted trimmings. Star gets plenty of support."

The Renegade Ranger (1938)
RKO
Producer: Bert Gilroy
Director: David Howard
Screenplay: Oliver Drake, based on a story by Bennett Cohen
Length: 59 minutes
Cast: George O'Brien, Rita Hayworth, Ray Whitley, Tim Holt, Lucio Villegas, William Royle, Cecilia Callejo, Neal Hart, Monte Montague, Bob Kortman, Charles Stevens, Jim Mason, Tom London. Actors appearing in unaccredited roles include Hank Bell, Ken Card, Art Dillard, Chris-Pin Martin, Frank O'Connor, Jack O'Shea, Earl Phelps, Norman Phelps, Willie Phelps, Tom Steele, Frank M. Thomas, and Guy Usher.

George O'Brien with Rita Hayworth in *The Renegade Ranger* (1938).

SYNOPSIS: In a story of murder, political intrigue, and romance, Captain Jack Steel, a Texas Ranger, meets Judith Alvarez, a beautiful woman who rallies a band of renegades to regain her land.

Rita Hayworth had played in a number of films prior to co-starring with George in *The Renegade Ranger* as the feisty Judith Alvarez. She had been frequently typecast as a sensuous, Latin woman, and by 1938, her image had been painstakingly transformed into that of an

American girl as apple-pie as the names of the characters she played. Her last Latin role in this Western film was on lone-out to RKO. She shows spirit as the Spanish woman bent on revenging the wrong done to her rancher father, much like a female Robin Hood, and although the role was written as a Spaniard, no attempt was made to make her look like one. She has little to do in the film, other than look brave and proud while mounting and dismounting horses and changing costumes from trousers to dresses. Years later, George mentioned Rita had frequently asked for his advice when in doubt, never gave herself airs, and moved with admirable grace. He said she was "poetry in motion," a sentiment shared by many, as the young actresses quickly blossomed into one of Hollywood's stellar leading ladies.

Variety reviewed the film, reporting, "Reading between the lines of the law, as administered by crooked politicians, *Renegade* is a very good Western, filled with brawling, gunning, and outlawry. Good touch is given by having the leader of the so-called outlaws a girl, Rita Hayworth, a charmer, wearing the bathtub hair dress even in that early day. She's a vet of Columbia's action pic school. Direction by Dave Howard is good, and the screenplay by Oliver Drake is well done. Photography and sound is above the Western average."

"George O'Brien solves all problems, pardner, with a right hook to the jaw or a six-gun in the midriff," the *New York Times* reviewed. "Mr. O'Brien's technique, like his plots, is simple: he can take any number of villains, from one to ten, and reduce them to so many clunking noises on the sound track, the 'clunk' being as near as we can approach to the conventional sound of a cinematic sock in the jaw. Cold steel is resorted to only in the most extreme emergencies, and the bark of O'Brien's six-gun is inevitably fatal to wrongdoers."

LAWLESS VALLEY (1938)
RKO
PRODUCER: BERT GILROY
DIRECTOR: DAVID HOWARD
SCREENPLAY: Oliver Drake, based on a story by W. C. Tuttle
LENGTH: 59 MINUTES
CAST: George O'Brien, Walter Miller, Kay Sutton, Fred Kohler, Sr., Fred Kohler, Jr., George MacQuarrie, Lew Kelly, Earle Hodgins, Chill

(TOP) A studio lobby card for *Lawless Valley* (1938). (BOTTOM) George O'Brien with Fred Kohler, Sr. and cast in *Lawless Valley*.

Wills, Dot Farley. Actors appearing in unaccredited roles include George Chesebro, Ben Corbett, Kirby Grant, Dick Hunter, Jim Mason, Robert McKenzie, Carl Miller, Frank O'Connor, Jack Shea, Landers Stevens, Carl Stockdale, The Four Tunes.

SYNOPSIS: A double misfortune befalls George O'Brien when his father's death is a suicide, and charges George with the robbery. George forces a confession from the sheriff about the true murderer.

A *Variety* review thought the film was very entertaining. "George O'Brien gets into action and maintains it just short of an hour. He's either chased, chasing, or about to do one or the other all the time. The O'Brien style of cowboying is well known. He socks like he means it, and is big enough to take on all comers. A thoroughly satisfactory Western for both patron and box office."

ARIZONA LEGION (1939)
RKO-RADIO
PRODUCER: BERT GILROY
DIRECTOR: DAVID HOWARD
SCREENPLAY: Oliver Drake, based on a story by Bernard McConville
LENGTH: 61 MINUTES
CAST: George O'Brien, Laraine Day, Chill Wills, Carlyle Moore, Jr., Edward J. LeSaint, Harry Cording, Tom Chatterton, William Royle, Harry Cording, Glenn Strange, Monte Montague, and Bob Burns. Actors appearing in unaccredited roles include Fred Burns, John Dilson, Frank Ellis, Bob Kortman, Wilfred Lucas, Jim Mason, Lafe McKee, Bruce Mitchell, Art Mix, Frank O'Connor, Jack O'Shea, Bill Patton, Joe Rickson, Elliott Sullivan, and Guy Usher.

SYNOPSIS: In this exciting Western, Boon Yeager, an Arizona law officer, played by George O'Brien, takes on an assignment to infiltrate criminal activities by a gang of stagecoach thieves.

"Fast and exciting oat opera, about as good as Westerns go these days," wrote a reviewer in *Variety*. "Excellent work of George O'Brien and Chill Wills should please Western action fans and fill in nicely on double feature programs. Excellent casting, cutting, and general showmanship. O'Brien here has the advantage of being cast in a likeable, sympathetic part free of spurious heroics and over-exaggeration."

(TOP) George O'Brien with Laraine Day in *Arizona Legion* (1939). (BOTTOM) A studio advertising poster from the same film.

George O'Brien with Ray Whitley in *Trouble in Sundown* (1939).

TROUBLE IN SUNDOWN (1939)
RKO
PRODUCER: BERT GILROY
DIRECTOR: DAVID HOWARD
SCREENPLAY: Oliver Drake, Dorrell McGowan, and Stuart McGowan
LENGTH: 59 MINUTES
CAST: George O'Brien, Rosalind Keith, Ray Whitley, Chill Wills, Ward Bond, Cy Kendall, Howard Hickman, Monte Montague, John Dilson, Otto Yamaoka. Actors appearing in unaccredited roles include Bob Burns, Ken Card, Tom Chatterton, Lloyd Ingraham, Tom London, Frank O'Connor, Jack Perrin, Earl Phelps, Norman Phelps, Willie Phelps, and Carl Stockdale.
SYNOPSIS: George and the daughter of a local bank president follow a trail of clues to solve a bank robbery

"Best slugger in the Westerns, George O'Brien's stories are legitimately rough and ready, and *Trouble in Sundown* is no exception," proclaimed a reviewer in *Variety*. "It's a good action dish, with enough stuff on it to rate with all ages, however, O'Brien leans into his role with all of his near 200 pounds, and pulls no punches where the going is rugged. When he lays hand on 'em, he leaves calling cards on chins in black and blue. Authenticity is hard to get in most of these hussies when they reach the physical combat stage, but O'Brien looks better in a scrap than any other film land cowpoke."

George O'Brien with Marjorie Reynolds in *Racketeers of the Range* (1939).

RACKETEERS OF THE RANGE (1939)
RKO
PRODUCER: BERT GILROY
DIRECTOR: D. ROSS LEDERMAN
SCREENPLAY: Oliver Drake, based on a story by Bernard McConville
LENGTH: 61 MINUTES
CAST: George O'Brien, Chill Wills, Marjorie Reynolds, Ray Whitley, Gay Seabrook, Robert Fiske, John Dilson, Ben Corbett, Bud Osborne, Monte Montague, Cactus Mack, Frankie Marvin. Actors appearing in unaccredited roles include Stanley Andrews, Joe Balch, Harry Cording, Mary Gordon, Dick Hunter, Wilfred Lucas, Del Maggart, Frank O'Connor, Edward Peil, Sr., and Clint Sharp.

SYNOPSIS: Lovely but inexperienced Helen Lewis inherits her father's independent packing plant, and easily falls prey to the wheeling and dealing of a crooked lawyer until George O'Brien turns the tables on the scheme.

"Standard setup for a George O'Brien Western, providing plenty of fast riding, gunplay, rough-and-tumble fights, and the usual villainy," wrote a reviewer in *Variety*. "Final chase, in which O'Brien and his followers overtake the commandeered cattle train and dispose of the band of heavies, is thrillingly displayed aboard the moving train."

In the *New York Times*, one reviewer wrote, "A nice display of plain and fancy hip-shooting is provided. George O'Brien does it seriously with a six-gun. It is one of those tight-lipped, hard-riding Westerns ("You and the boys saddle up and get ready to ride!"), in which the rustlers introduce a novel trick by hijacking cattle in motor trucks. The gun-play is fierce, but harmless—just like the picture."

TIMBER STAMPEDE (1939)
RKO
PRODUCER: BERT GILROY
DIRECTOR: DAVID HOWARD
SCREENPLAY: Morton Grant, based on a story by Paul Franklin and Bernard MacConville
LENGTH: 59 MINUTES
CAST: George O'Brien, Marjorie Reynolds, Chill Wills, Morgan Wallace, Guy Usher, Earl Dwire, Frank Hagney, Monte Montague, Robert Fiske, and Bob Burns. Actors appearing in unaccredited roles include William Benedict, Eddie Borden, Ben Corbett, Sid Jordan, Bob Kortman, Elmo Lincoln, Tom London, Cactus Mack, Herman Nowlin, Frank O'Connor, and Hank Worden.
SYNOPSIS: A cattleman and a headstrong but naïve, young journalist rally friends to save their town from a cattle baron's land-stealing activities.

"Combining two phases of outdoor life that are surefire for action audiences, timber and cow country, this latest George O'Brien is above average for the red-blooded trade," reported a reviewer in *Variety*. "While the film itself is based on a stronger story than is to be found at the base of the usual Western, the telling of it suffers through O'Brien's overacting plus inept direction."

Marjorie Reynolds and George O'Brien in *Timber Stampede* (1939).

THE FIGHTING GRINGO (1939)
RKO
PRODUCER: BERT GILROY
DIRECTOR: DAVID HOWARD
SCREENPLAY: Oliver Drake
LENGTH: 59 MINUTES
CAST: George O'Brien, Lupita Tovar, Lucio Villegas, William Royle, Glenn Strange, Slim Whitaker, LeRoy Mason, Mary Field, Martin Garralaga, Dick Botiller, Lew Cody, Cactus Mack, Chris-Pin Martin. Actors appearing in unaccredited roles include Hank Bell, Ben Corbett, Billy Franey, Oscar Gahan, Al Haskell, Ben Johnson, Sid Jordan, and Forrest Taylor.
SYNOPSIS: A gang of gunslingers led by George O'Brien prevent a hostile takeover of a girl's ranch.

Lupita Tovar with George O'Brien in *The Fighting Gringo* (1939).

"*The Fighting Gringo* is a well-made Western in the George O'Brien series, based on a story that has a lot of meat, plenty of action, and better than average dialog," wrote a reviewer in *Variety*. "Picture is compact, has been carefully edited down to fifty-nine minutes, and will fit nicely on double bills."

THE MARSHAL OF MESA CITY (1939)
RKO
PRODUCER: BERT GILROY
DIRECTOR: DAVID HOWARD
SCREENPLAY: Jack Lait, Jr., based on a story, *The Peacemaker*, by Dudley Nichols
LENGTH: 60 MINUTES

George O'Brien with Leon Ames and henchmen in *The Marshal of Mesa City* (1939).

CAST: George O'Brien, Virginia Vale, Leon Ames, Henry Brandon, Harry Cording, Lloyd Ingraham, Slim Whitaker, Joe McGuinn, Mary Gordon, Frank Ellis. Actors appearing in unaccredited roles include Bob Burns, Jack Cheatham, Spade Cooley, Ben Corbett, Billy Franey, Aleth Hansen, Richard Hunter, Sid Jordan, Wilfred Lucas, Cactus Mack, Jim Mason, Monte Montague, Bill Patton, Edward Peil, Sr., Steve Pendleton, Stanley Price, Dick Rush, Rudy Sooter, Carl Stockdale, Harry Tenbrook, Blackie Whiteford

SYNOPSIS: A cowboy with a heart of gold and a loaded gun takes on a crooked judge and rids the town of his overbearing influence.

In this film, the 65th of George O'Briens career, Virginia Vale makes her first appearance. She teamed with George for his next five pictures, and their on-screen partnership ended only when George abruptly halted his film career to return to the US Navy during the early days of World War Two. Vale appeared in fifteen additional films from 1941 to 1945, before leaving the screen permanently.

Variety thought the film was an edge better than his previous ones, and noted the exceptional screenplay by Jack Lait, Jr.: "David Howard, who has handled O'Brien for a long time, directs him in an appropriately-paced vehicle. The film is in the upper bracket Western class, will go very well with the juvenile pasteboard sale, and has stuff for the family trade, generally."

Virginia Vale and George O'Brien in *Legion of the Lawless* (1940).

Legion of the Lawless (1940)
RKO
Producer: Bert Gilroy
Director: David Howard
Screenplay: Doris Schroeder, based on a Berne Giler
Length: 59 minutes
Cast: George O'Brien, Virginia Vale, Herbert Heywood, Norman Willis, Hugh Sothern, William Benedict, Eddy Waller, Delmar Watson, Bud Osborne, Monte Montague, Slim Whitaker, Mary Field. Actors appearing in unaccredited roles include Richard Cramer, John Dilson, Martin Garralaga, Lloyd Ingraham, Wilfred Lucas, Horace Murphy, Edward Peil, Sr., and Henry Willis
Synopsis: George O'Brien appears as an itinerant lawyer, Jeff Toland, who moves into town to set up practice only to face terrorism by a local vigilante group.

In 1940, a *Variety* reviewer told exhibitors the film was "... just another Western, made from a standard formula, with the horses running their heads off at about six furlongs in 1:10 flat and scores of shots going wild so that the whole cast won't be bumped off in the first hundred feet. As Westerns go, it is superior to the pack, and though he isn't in the juvenile class any more, George O'Brien of the block-wide shoulders has sufficient of a following to keep exchange bookers from getting on their knees to keep his stuff moving."

A reviewer writing for the *Bismark Tribune* thought, "Presenting a vivid and colorful tale of misrule in a little Western town by a band of masked desperados, *Legion of the Lawless* brings George O'Brien to the screen in another stimulating outdoor drama."

Bullet Code (1940)
RKO
Producer: Bert Gilroy
Director: David Howard
Screenplay: Doris Schroeder, based on a story by Bennett Cohen
Length: 60 minutes
Cast: George O'Brien, Virginia Vale, Slim Whitaker, Harry Woods, Robert Stanton, Walter Miller, William Haade, Kirby Grant. Actors appearing in unaccredited roles include Bob Burns, Billy Franey,

George O'Brien in *Bullet Code* (1940).

Cactus Mack, Robert McKenzie, Lew Meehan, Jack C. Smith, and Carl Stockdale.

SYNOPSIS: A cowboy wandering near the "Circle M" ranch overtakes the bad guys and restores peace to the troubled townfolk.

A reviewer in the *Soda Springs Sun* wrote, "Rated as the most popular of outdoor actors on the screen today, George O'Brien enacts the part of a border cattleman in his latest RKO Radio vehicle. The operation of a group of rustlers, the solution of a mystery regarding the death of a cowboy, and plenty of excitement are all woven into the story, which is said to give O'Brien one of his most thrilling pictures to date."

"Dealing with a young rancher's efforts to atone for a crime of which he is really innocent, George O'Brien's newest RKO Radio vehicle, *Bullet Code*, also presents vivid scenes of old-fashioned cattle-rustling in its exciting plot."

George O'Brien, Slim Whitaker, and Cy Kendall in *Prairie Law* (1940).

Prairie Law (1940)
RKO-Radio
Producer: Bert Gilroy
Director: David Howard
Screenplay: Doris Schroeder with Arthur V. Jones, based on a story by Bernard McConville
Length: 59 minutes
Cast: George O'Brien, Virginia Vale, Dick Hogan, J. Farrell MacDonald, Slim Whitaker, Cy Kendall, Paul Everton, Henry Hall, Monte Montague, Quen Ramsey. Actors appearing in unaccredited roles include Hank Bell, William Benedict, Edward Brady, Bob Card, Ben Corbett, Frank Ellis, Oscar Gahan, Ray Henderson, Darryl Hickman, Arthur Houseman, Lloyd Ingraham, Cactus Mack, Frank O'Connor, Bud Osborne, Jack O'Shea, Vester Pegg, Ferris Taylor, Ray Whitley, Hank Worden
Synopsis: Brill Austin, a cattleman, takes sympathy on incoming farmers and shares his springs with them, but when his cattle are stolen, slaughtered, and hung brazenly in the town's butcher shop, he takes on

the slaughters and finds romance with a beautiful girl.

"Although O'Brien is no kid, he is a particularly good outdoors opera type, and no doubt is the hero of plenty of Western fans. *Prairie Law* is the brawny star's latest and one of his best. In all departments, from production to photography and editing, this is a frontier drama that smacks of competency," wrote a reviewer in *Variety*. "Among other things, the dialog is excellent and stands out so far above the average from Westerns' adaptors that it is singularly noticeable. Nearly every line has punch. The only complaint that may be found is that the locale is supposed to be prairie country. It's anything but. However, most people won't know the difference anyway, presumably, so this is not an important an important point to consider in judging the picture. Action is in sufficient measure, including one outstanding fight in which several men figure."

STAGE TO CHINO (1940)
RKO-RADIO
PRODUCER: BERT GILROY
DIRECTOR: EDWARD KILLY
SCREENPLAY: Morton Grant and Arthur V. Jones, based on a story by Norton S. Parker
LENGTH: 60 MINUTES
CAST: George O'Brien, Virginia Vale, Hobart Cavanaugh, Roy Barcroft, William Haade, Carl Stockdale, Glenn Strange, Harry Cording, Martin Garralaga, Ethan Laidlaw, Tom London. Actors appearing in unaccredited roles include Hank Bell, William Benedict, Bob Burns, Jim Corey, John Dilson, Mike Donovan, Art Dupuis, Nellie Duran, Frank Ellis, Billy Franey, Herman Hack, Al Haskell, Dick Hunter, Pee Wee King, Elmo Lincoln, Nora Lou Martin, Lew Meehan, Frank Mills, Bruce Mitchell, Herman Nowlin, and Jack O'Shea.
SYNOPSIS: A postal inspector drives off bandits trafficking people and goods between the towns of Prescott and Chino.

"George O'Brien, smiling, debonair, and soft-spoken as ever, rides the US Mail to safety, and in taking him over the route, *Stage to Chino* spreads plenty of entertainment and excitement," buzzed a reviewer writing in *Variety*. "Little junior and his elders, who still enjoy the spectacle of hard-riding, punch-trading, and gun-blasting,

George O'Brien and Virginia Vale in *Stage to Chino* (1940).

won't find themselves let down by this O'Brien special. It's all carried out in the old tradition of the Hollywood horse opera, plus slick-production and direction. The pacing is especially good. Included is a hillbilly troupe that is billed as 'Pals of the Golden West.' The piece de resistance in their repertoire is an original by Fleming Allen, "Riding on the Stage to Chino." Radio hillbilly addicts may like the vocal interludes, others won't mind."

TRIPLE JUSTICE (1940)
RKO-RADIO
PRODUCER: BERT GILROY
DIRECTOR: DAVID HOWARD
SCREENPLAY: Morton Grant with Arthur V. Jones, based on a story by Arnold Belgard and Jack Roberts
LENGTH: 65 MINUTES
CAST: George O'Brien, Virginia Vale, Peggy Shannon, Harry Woods, Paul Fix, LeRoy Mason, Glenn Strange, Malcolm McTaggart, Robert McKenzie, Wilfred Lucas, The Lindeman Sisters. Actors appearing in

George O'Brien in *Triple Justice* (1940).

unaccredited roles include Frank O'Connor, Carlos Barbe, Bob Burns, Anne Cornwall, Jean Del Val, Fern Emmett, Paul Everton, Mabel Forrest, Billy Franey, Dick Hunter, Lloyd Ingraham, John Judd, Berta Lindeman, Clotilde Lindeman, Elena Lindeman, Max Lucke, Eva McKenzie, Lew Mehan, George Mendoza, Bruce Mitchell, Herman Nowlin, William J. O'Brien, Walter Patterson, Steve Pendelton, Joe Rickson, Henry Roquemore, Georgia Simmons, Henrique Valdez, Harry Weil, Betty West, and Hank Worden.

SYNOPSIS: In Star City, wedding bells are ringing for Sheriff Bill Gregory, but three outlaws secretly plan to rob the town's bank while the wedding is in progress. A cowboy confronts the bandits, and brings the conflict to an end.

In *Triple Justice*, Virginia Vale sings the song, "Lonely Rio." This film was the last film George O'Brien made before leaving his Hollywood career behind to answer the call to arms and re-enlist in the US Navy in World War Two. He never fully recovered his lost career.

Variety's review said, "The film is no slouch for Westerns which have been many and abused during the season just passed. *Triple Justice* is in the A-bracket for the open-spacers produced on relatively small budget, and ranks among the cream for the action places, just as the star-studded colossals go with deluxers. There's a lot of action in this story, considerable hard riding, and the photography, in the chases, etc., is nicely handled. Instead of allowing the horses to run directly at the rear of the camera car and be smothered in its dust, as is usual with the Westerns, the nags are made to run at the side, which gives a more legit appearance."

MY WILD IRISH ROSE (1947)
WARNER BROS.
PRODUCER: WILLIAM JACOBS
DIRECTOR: DAVID BUTLER
SCREENPLAY: Peter Milne, based on a novel by Rita Olcott, with additional dialogue by Sid Fields and Edwin Gilbert
LENGTH: 101 MINUTES
CAST: Dennis Morgan, Arlene Dahl, Andrea King, Alan Hale, George Tobias, George O'Brien, Sara Allgood, Ben Blue, William Frawley, Don McGuire, Charles Irwin, Clifton Young, Paul Stanton, George

A magazine advertisement for *My Wild Irish Rose* (1947) as it appeared in many magazines in 1947.

Cleveland, Oscar O'Shea, Ruby Dandridge, Grady Sutton, William B. Davidson, Douglas Wood, Charles Marsh, The Three Dunhills, Igor Dega, Pierre Andre, Lou Wills, Jr. Actors appearing in unaccredited roles include Rodney Bell, Monte Blue, Lilly Christine, Edward

George O'Brien in a scene from *My Wild Irish Rose* (1947).

Clark, Gino Corrado, Joe Devlin, Penny Edwards, Ross Ford, Sol Gorss, William Gould, Billy Greene, Winifred Harris, Brandon Hurst, Eddie Kane, Peggy Knudsen, Florence Lake, Robert Lowell, Phillo McCullough, Forbes Murray, Paul Panzer, Eddie Parker, Wally Ruth, Cy Shindell, Tom Stevenson, Andrew Tombes, and Emmett Votan.

SYNOPSIS: The life of Chauncey Olcott, an Irish singer, his relationship with the great star, Lillian Russel, and his rise to fame and fortune.

Variety's reviewer called the film a winner. "Whether this pic, a first-rate production in every department except big marquee names, lands first money, place or show, likely will depend on how well the distributor and exhibitor sells it. It's that sort of a picture. This handsomely mounted Technicolor musical on Chauncey Olcott's life needs to be smartly sold to land big openings because it will thrive on strong word-of-mouth. Film is the sort of vehicle that pleases right off the reel ... George O'Brien makes a rugged strong man."

The *New York Times* reviewer wrote, "Perhaps the Warner Bros., who produced this velvety-hued Technicolor hodgepodge of clichés, couldn't find sufficient dramatic incident in the life of the popular singer, actor, and composer of the beautiful melody after which the picture is named, to justify sticking to biographical facts. Granting that, one can only remark that the producers should have displayed sufficient respect for the man's memory and named the distressingly cute character played in the film by Dennis Morgan, something other than Chauncey Olcott. As an Irish tenor, Mr. Morgan's singing will hold best with the tone-deaf, and that brogue he affects, and let's not overlook Alan Hale either in this regard, is—just call it murderous. Indeed, the whole atmosphere of the film is so patronizing and professionally Irish in sentiment that it is downright embarrassing . . . George O'Brien is impressively muscular."

DECEMBER 7TH (1943)
DIRECTOR: JOHN FORD AND GREG TOLAND
SCREENPLAY: Budd Schulberg (unaccredited)
CAST: Walter Houston, Harry Davenport, Dana Andrews, Paul Hurst, George O'Brien, James Kevin McGuinness. Those appearing unaccredited include Philip Ahn, Addie Allen, Ralph Byrd, Hirohito, Adolf Hitler, James E. Kelley, Mrs. James E. Kelley, Mrs. William J. Leight, William J. Leight, Robert Lowry, Benito Mussolini, Irving Pichel, Joseph B. Poindexter, Henry L. Rosenthal, Mrs. Henry L. Rosenthal, Lionel Royce, William Schick, Jr., William Schick, Sr., Mrs. William Schick, Karl Swenson, Stephen Szabo, Mrs. Stephen Szabo, Jesus A. Tafoya, Mrs. Jesus A. Tafoya, and H. N. Wallin.
SYNOPSIS: A documentary produced for the U. S. Government. George O'Brien provided the voice-over narration.

PANTOMIME QUIZ (1949-1959)
HOST: MIKE STOKEY
DIRECTOR: PHILIPPE DE LACY
LENGTH: 30 MINUTES

Produced by CBS from October 4, 1949, to December, 1954. ABC produced the show from January 22, 1955, to March 6, 1955, and then brought it back from April 8, 1958, to October 4, 1959.

CAST: George O'Brien, Dorothy Hart, Angela Lansbury, Rocky Graziano, Carol Haney, Robert Clary, Hans Conried, Jackie Coogan, Milt Kamen, Howard Morris, Carol Burnet, Stubby Kaye, Denise Darcell, Tom Poston, Vincent Price, Colleen Gray, Robert Stack, Sandra Spence, Dave Willock, Fred Clark, George Macready, Frank DeVol, Beverly Tyler, Virginia Field.

SYNOPSIS: A game show, *Pantomime Quiz* featured two competing teams, Home and Visiting, each composed of four members. The host presents one member of a team with a charade topic. The player has to perform the charade, which has a two-minute time limit, to his team. The amount of time accumulated before the charade is identified is calculated. All remaining players compete in the same manner. Teams who accumulate the least amount of over-all time are the winners. Home viewers, who submit charades, receive merchandise prizes if the team fails to identify their charade.

Daily Variety reviewed the show in its July 1951 version: "Mike Stokey's *Pantomime Quiz* is another of those video charade games. However, with four regulars and four guests selected from among Hollywood thespers it has the lure of some film names. Additionally, the quotations the players have to act out were fairly cute on the preem Monday and the performers were adept at communicating without words. There was also some amusing banter among the various participants. Stokey keeps things rolling smoothly, giving each of the panelists—Jackie Coogan, Adele Jergens, Hans Conreid, and Fred Clark, for the regulars, and Beverly Tyler, George O'Brien, George Macready, and Virginia Field, for the guests—plugs for their upcoming pix. Kinescope was somewhat choppily edited, which destroyed the sense of being present. Commercially, linkup with Hollywood stars continues the Lux coy theme, and one plug had Stokey quiz Miss Jergens on the soap."

FORT APACHE (1948)
ARGOSY PICTURES-RKO RADIO
PRODUCER: MERIAN C. COOPER AND JOHN FORD
DIRECTOR: JOHN FORD
SCREENPLAY: Frank S. Nugent, suggested by a story, *Massacre*, by James Warner Bellah
CAST: John Wayne, Henry Fonda, Shirley Temple, John Agar, Ward

Henry Fonda, John Wayne, George O'Brien, and John Agar in *Fort Apache* (1948).

Bond, George O'Brien, Victor McLaglen, Pedro Armendáriz, Anna Lee, Irene Rich, Dick Foran, Guy Kibbee, Grant Withers, Jack Pennick, Ray Hyke, Movita, Miguel Inclán, Mary Gordon, Philip Kieffer, Mae Marsh, Hank Worden. Actors appearing in unaccredited roles include Cliff Clark, Frank Ferguson, Francis Ford, William Forrest, Fred Graham, Frank MacGrath, Mickey Simpson, Harry Tenbrook, and Archie Twitchell.

SYNOPSIS: The story follows Colonel Thursday, a demoted and embittered Cavalry Colonel assigned to a remote fort after a brilliant war record. His rulebook manners and inability to accept the advice of officers leads to a tragic and unnecessary death by massacre for himself and the majority of his command.

"Folks who are looking for action in the oldest tradition of the screen, observed through a genuine artist's camera, will find plenty of it here," wrote Bosley Crowther in the *New York Times*. "But also apparent in this picture, for those who care to look, is a new and maturing viewpoint upon one aspect of the American Indian wars. For here it is not the heathen Indian, who is the heavy of the piece, but a hard-bitten Army colonel, blind through ignorance and a passion for revenge. A handsome and thrilling outdoor drama of war on the American frontier. Mr. Ford is a genius at directing this sort of thing, and Frank S. Nugent has ably supplied him with a tangy and workable script. Henry Fonda is withering as the stiff with gallantry, and John Wayne is powerful as his captain, forthright and exquisitely brave. Ward Bond is stout, too, as a sergeant major and Victor McLaglen, Jack Pennick and Dick Foran honor the virtues of whisky and low humor as three Irish noncoms. Even Shirley Temple is ingratiating as the colonel's lass who falls in love with a noble young lieutenant, played patly by her husband, John Agar."

"*Fort Apache* undoubtedly will cause considerable critical pro and con because of the openly commercial approach John Ford has used on the subject," exclaimed a reviewer in *Variety*. "He has aimed the picture directly at the average theatergoer, bypassing non-profitable art effects. As a consequence, film has mass appeal, great excitement, and a potent box office outlook. For sheer seat-edge attention, Apache is socko. Mass action, humorous byplay in the Western cavalry outpost, deadly suspense, and romance are masterfully combined in the Ford-Merian C. Cooper production to stir the greatest number of filmgoers. Integrated with the tremendous action is a superb musical score by Richard Hageman. Score uses sound effects as tellingly as the music notes to point up the thrills. In particular, the massacre scene wherein the deadly drumming of the Indian ponies makes more potent the action that transpires."

SHE WORE A YELLOW RIBBON (1949)
ARGOSY PICTURES-RKO RADIO
PRODUCER: MERIAN C. COOPER, LOWELL J. FARRELL, AND JOHN FORD
DIRECTOR: JOHN FORD
SCREENPLAY: Frank S. Nugent and Laurence Stallings, based on stories *War Party* and *The Big Hunt* by James Warner Bellah
LENGTH: 103 MINUTES
CAST: John Wayne, Joanne Dru, John Agar, Ben Johnson, Harry Carey, Jr., Victor McLaglen, Mildred Natwick, George O'Brien, Arthur Shields, Michael Dugan, Chief John Big Tree, Fred Graham, Chief Sky Eagle, Tom Tyler, Noble Johnson. Actors appearing in unaccredited roles include Rudy Bowman, Lee Bradley, Paul Fix, Francis Ford, Ray Hyke, Billy Jones, Fred Kennedy, Fred Libby, Cliff Lyons, Frank McGrath, Post Park, Jack Pennick, Irving Pichel, Mickey Simpson, William Steele, Don Summers, Dan White, and Harry Woods.

Victor McLaglen, Ben Johnson, and John Wayne with George O'Brien in John Ford's *She Wore a Yellow Ribbon* (1949).

SYNOPSIS: The story follows Cavalry men pitted against Indians. At an undermanned post far out in the Indian country, a veteran, Captain Brittles, faces wild Indians who outride the Army, an operation on a wounded man, a dazzling stampede by whooping troopers through a startled Indian camp, and a romance between two younger commissioned officers over a newly arrived girl at the fort."

Bosley Crowther of the *New York Times* wrote with elation, "For in this big, Technicolor Western, Mr. Ford has superbly achieved a vast and composite illustration of all the legends of the frontier cavalryman. He has got the bold and dashing courage, the stout masculine sentiment, the grandeur of rear-guard heroism, and the brash bravado of the barrack-room brawl. And, best of all, he has got the brilliant color and vivid detail of those legendary troops as they ranged through the silent Indian country and across the magnificent Western plains. No one could get more emotion out of a thundering cavalry charge or an old soldier's farewell departure from the ranks of his comrades than he. To be sure, he is ably assisted in his achievement by a fine outdoor cast, which boasts the experienced John Wayne in the tough Captain Brittles role. Mr. Wayne, his hair streaked with silver and wearing a dashing mustache, is the absolute image and ideal of the legendary cavalryman. *She Wore a Yellow Ribbon* is a dilly of a cavalry picture. Yeehooooo!"

"RKO has a real moneymaker," beamed a reviewer for *Variety*, "Several scenes have been developed into real tear-jerkers, while the barroom drinking scene of McLaglen is the roughest, yet most hilarious seen on the screen in months. The river crossing is one of several vivid outdoor scenes that combine action with remarkable color. Much of the outdoor color photography is awe-inspiring. Outstanding femme role is played by Mildred Natwick as the wife of Major George O'Brien. Not a looker, she epitomizes the Army officer's wife of the West in that era. O'Brien suffices as the major, while Arthur Shields does well as the troop's medico. Trooper Cliff is played with fidelity by Cliff Lyons, who with Major Philip Kieffer was a technical advisor on the production."

GOLD RAIDERS (1951) ALSO KNOWN AS STOOGES GO WEST
UNITED ARTISTS
PRODUCER: JACK SCHWARZ AND BERNARD GLASSER
DIRECTOR: EDWARD BERNDS
SCREENPLAY: Elwood Ullman and William Lively
LENGTH 56 MINUTES
CAST: George O'Brien, Moe Howard, Shemp Howard, Larry Fine, Sheila Ryan, Clem Bevans, Monte Blue, Lyle Talbot, John Merton, Al Baffert, Hugh Hooker, Bill Ward, Fuzzy Knight, Dick Crockett, Roy Canada, Rene Paquet.
SYNOPSIS: George O'Brien plays himself in the guise of a gang-busting, ex-marshal working as an insurance agent bringing the insurance system to the West. He encounters the Three Stooges in his campaign to clean up the area from raiders hijacking mine shipments.

"*Gold Raiders* is grooved for the Saturday matinee market. Antics of the Three Stooges are strictly on a juvenile level, and the plot is pretty much spelled out in words of one syllable. It's a mediocre low-budgeter," assessed a reviewer writing in *Variety*. "O'Brien, who hasn't been too active in recent years, is somewhat stiff as the gun-toting agent, but casting him as insurance man makes it easier to accept. Three Stooges take a lot of slopping around, both from the raiders and from Sheilah

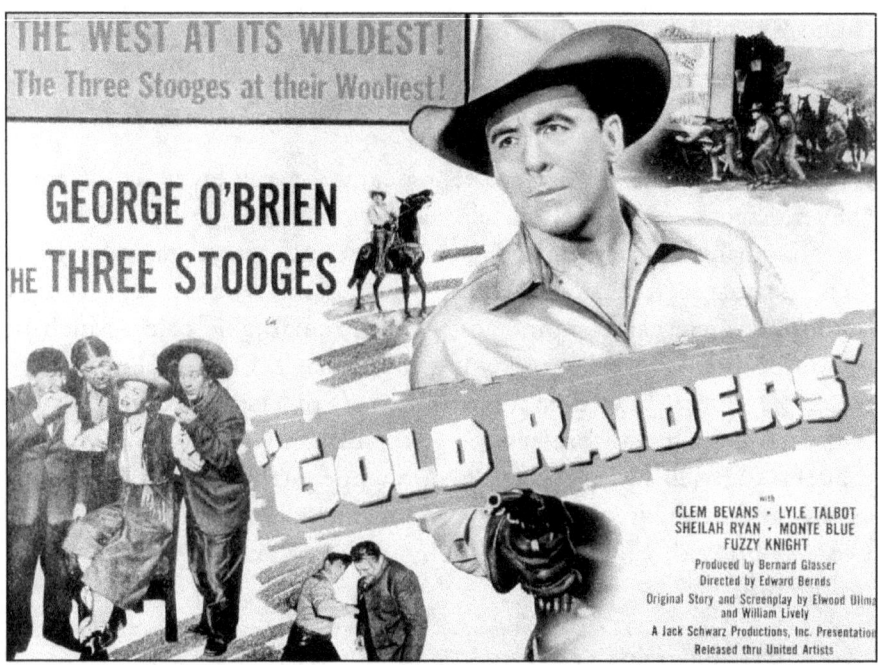

A studio lobby card for *Gold Raiders* (1951).

Ryan, who plays the old physician's granddaughter. Slapstick stuff is purely for the elementary school set."

HEINZ STUDIO 57 (1957)
TYPHOON
REVUE PRODUCTIONS, INC.
COPYRIGHT DATE DEC 30, 1956
AIR DATE: SEPT 8, 1957
CAST: George O'Brien

This filmed, half-hour anthology series on the struggling DuPont network was sponsored by Heinz Foods. It was also known as *Heinz 57 Playhouse* during its run from 1954-1955, and then the name was changed to *Studio 57*, which ran until 1957. During its third year, several episodes that were previously shown were again aired on the *Fireside Theatre*. This was due to the crumbling DuPont Network, which carried this last, regularly scheduled show to its end. Stories were generally melodramas or mysteries. The episode with George O'Brien titled *Typhoon* appears to be lost.

KOREA: BATTLEGROUND FOR LIBERTY (1959)
DIRECTOR: JOHN FORD
CAST: George O'Brien (Narrator)
SYNOPSIS: *Korea: Battleground for Liberty* was a short film commissioned by the Office of Armed Forces Information and Education to counteract Communist propaganda about American imperialism. The documentary was designed to coordinate better relations between Americans and friendly Asian countries. George O'Brien served as project officer and Narrator.

CHEYENNE AUTUMN (1964)
WARNER BROS.
PRODUCER: BERNARD SMITH AND JOHN FORD
DIRECTOR: JOHN FORD
SCREENPLAY: James R. Webb, based on the novel, *Cheyenne Autumn*, by Mari Sandoz, and the novel, *The Last Frontier*, by Howard Fast.
LENGTH: 90 MINUTES
CAST: Richard Widmark, Carroll Baker, James Stewart, Edward G. Robinson, Karl Malden, Sal Mineo, Dolores del Rio, Ricardo Montalban, Gilbert Roland, Arthur Kennedy, Patrick Wayne, Elizabeth Allen, John Carradine, Victor Jory, Mike Mazurki, George O'Brien, Sean McClory, Judson Pratt, Carmen D'Antonio, Ken Curtis. Actors appearing in unaccredited roles include Walter Baldwin, Willis Bouchey, Lee Bradley, Harry Carey, Jr., Dan Carr, Jeannie Epper, Stephanie Epper, Shug Fisher, James Flavin, William Forrest, Donna Hall, Sam Harris, Chuck Hayward, William Henry, Harry Hickox, Harry Holcombe, Nancy Hsueh, Ben Johnson, Steven Manymules, Ted Mapes, Mae Marsh, Philo McCullough, John McKee, David Miller, Louise Montanna, Nanomba Morton, Many Muleson, James O'Hara, Denver Pyle, John Qualen, Walter Reed, Chuck Roberson, Bing Russell, Charles Seel, Mary Statler, and Carleton Young.
SYNOPSIS: A small band of Cheyenne attempt to escape from their barren Oklahoma reservation to their own lush Yellowstone River lands in Wyoming, from which they were transported after having surrendered to the army in 1877. Weak but determined, the Indians begin a painful trek back to their homeland 1,500 miles away.

Variety wrote in their review, "*Cheyenne Autumn* is a rambling, episodic account of a reputedly little-known historic Cheyenne Indian migration. The original premise of the Mari Sandoz novel is lost sight of in a wholesale insertion of extraneous incidents which bear no little relation to the subject. As a result, picture lacks forceful qualities. While there is excitement in the various US Cavalry and Indian skirmishes and the overall benefits of exquisite Technicolor photography in picturesque settings, the film emerges as an uneven piece of filmmaking. Physically, it is filled with excellent production values. These, however, are dissipated in effect by the script never cleaving to a direct line. Detracting considerably are several long comedy sequences which in striking slapstick proportions evoke laughs but project no valid reason for them other than to drag James Stewart for marquee lure as a clownish and totally unconvincing Wyatt Earp."

The *New York Times* wrote in their review, "An epic frontier film. It is a beautiful and powerful motion picture that stunningly combines a profound and passionate story of mistreatment of American Indians with some of the most magnificent and energetic cavalry-and-Indian lore ever put upon the screen. It is a stark and eye-opening symbolization of a shameful tendency that has prevailed in our national life—the tendency to be unjust and heartless to weaker peoples who get in the way of manifest destiny. On a huge screen (Super-Panavision 70) and in color that does full justice to the awesome beauty of Monument Valley and other desert and hill country of the southwest, Mr. Ford has spread a rumbling, throbbing drama of the stoicism and self-sufficiency of the Indian who is an alien in his own country, of the meanness and perfidy of the whites, and of the compassion and heroism of some good people who try to see that justice is done. *Cheyenne Autumn* is a strong film, grandly directed and expertly played by a large cast."

George O'Brien played the small role of Major Braden, and was not mentioned in major reviews. It was his final screen appearance.

Part 3
PORTRAIT GALLERY

During his first four years as a star of motion pictures, George O'Brien appeared in eighteen films: five in 1924, three in 1925, six in 1926, and four in 1927. Because of this constant exposure to audiences around the world, his personality became quickly familiar, and audiences developed intimate feelings for him, as if he were a well-known personal friend. They wanted to extend their love beyond the local movie theater, and large numbers of people began writing the Fox Studio requesting photographs along with their constant questions about physical fitness, offers of proposals of marriage, and questions seeking advice on breaking into movies.

Typically, the studio answered most of this kind of mail, and filled requests for copies of the latest photos. Specialists employed by the studio created these portraits. Known as "still men," they often took as many as a hundred photographs of scenes staged for the motion picture camera. In addition to these on-the-set photographers, portrait specialists carefully staged reenactments of various scenes against white or black backgrounds for advertising purposes. They also took close-up poses known as "glamour portraits" for use in a variety of ways. These glamour portraits were most often the poses sent to fans when a photo was requested.

Those photographers who furnished photographs to the Fox Studio of their stars in the 1920s and 1930s include Hal Duvee, Alexander Kahle, Hal Phyfe, Max Mun Autry, and Albert Witzel. The photographs they took of George O'Brien remain among the best examples of their work, and many of their portraits are still traded and admired today.

The pictures in this gallery represent George O'Brien from his beginnings in the early 1920s through his personal appearances in the 1970s, a span of half a century. They capture him in the flush of youth, the maturity of middle age, and as a stalwart elder gentleman in his later years.

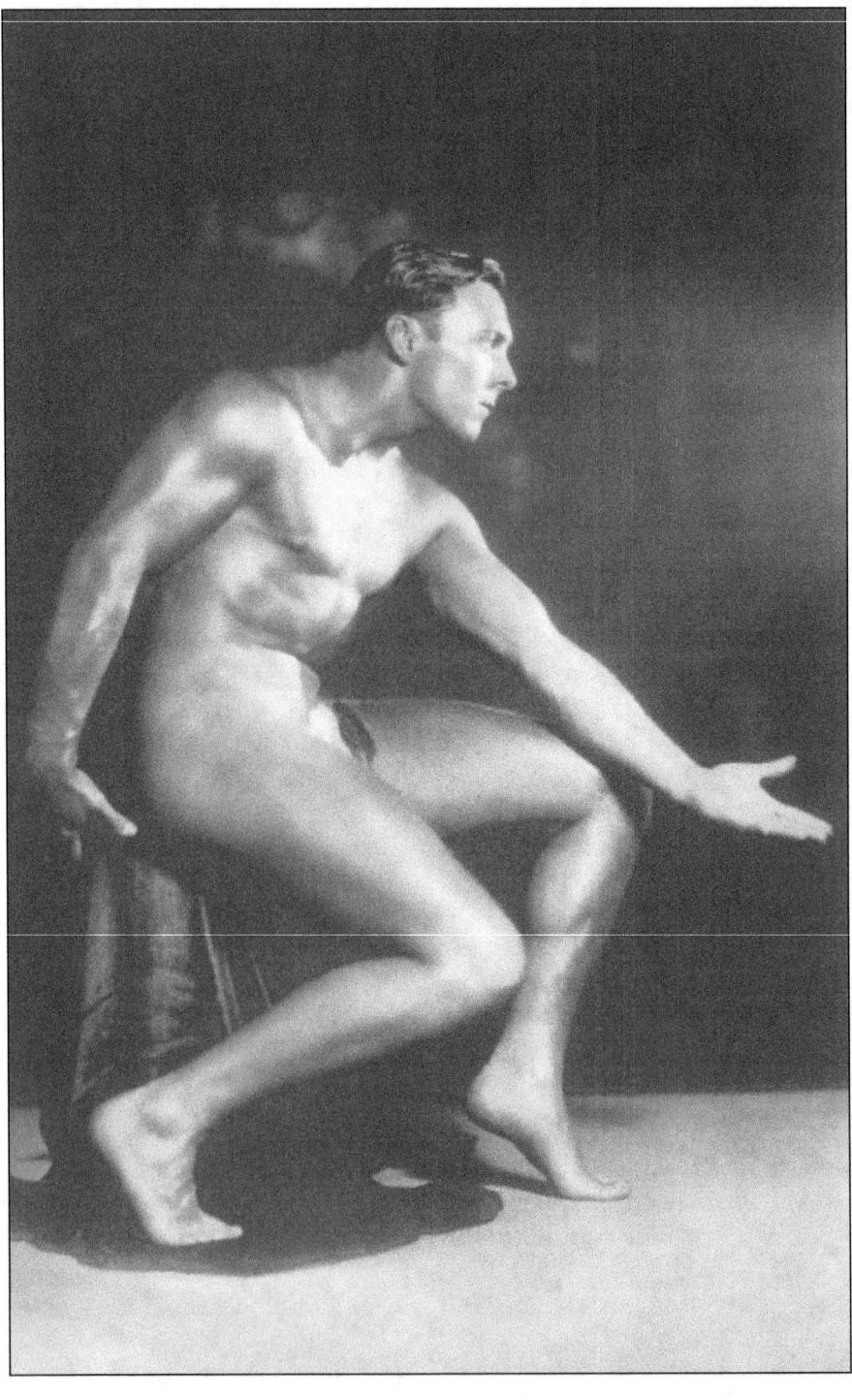

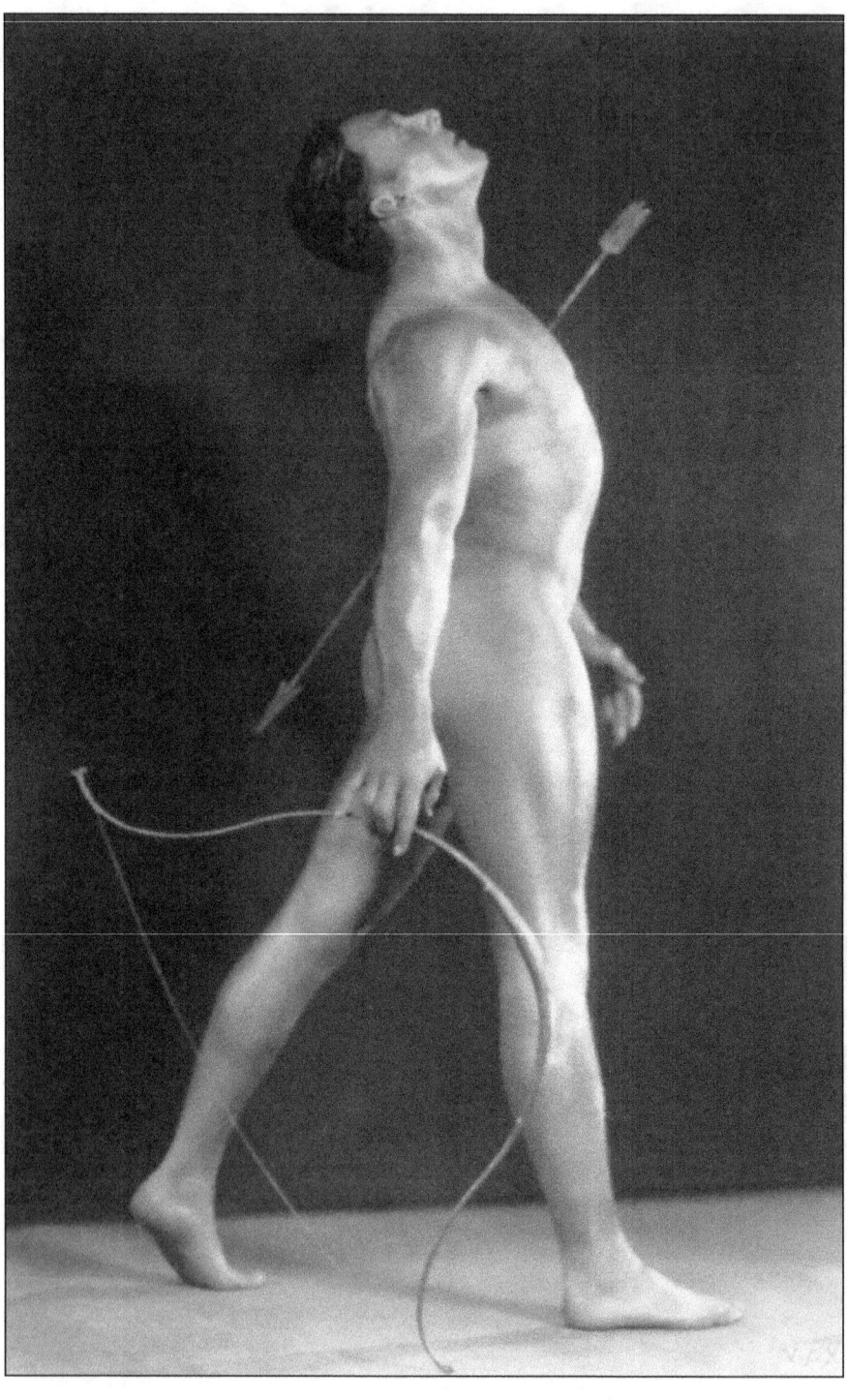

Appendix
"George O'Brien Defends Movies for Chldren"

In December 1933, *Movie Classic* answered charges from those contributing writers to a book, *Our Movie-Made Children*, which received tremendous publicity in the *New York Times*. The book reported on four-year study on the effects of movies on children, and concluded films had a bad effect on the home, school, and church in molding young minds. Hollywood answered with an intelligent denial penned by George O'Brien in an interview with Sonia Lee. His comments are reprinted here:

"I disagree with anyone who declares that crime films distort children's values and give them destructive patterns of behavior. The exploits of outlaws have always been recorded in books avidly read by children. The vivid screen invariably shows that CRIME DOESN'T PAY.

"I consider pictures such as *Little Caesar, Scarface*, and others similar a powerful deterrent to lawlessness, rather than an impetus. The pay-off, the finale, lingers in the young mind, no matter what the professors say. *Without exception*, in the movies, wrong-doing carries its punishment. That lesson is minimized only when courts of law set criminals free; when Al Capone is deified in the public prints; when society shows itself powerless to cope with gangster's organization and his activities.

"Our civilization is geared to excitement. To say that a child is emotionally over-stimulated because of a certain motion picture, and to ascribe certain psychological reactions *to the movies only* is unfair and untrue. Amusement parks with their merry-go-rounds, their loop-the-loops, roller coasters and airplane rides, are a far greater excitant than any movie could be.

"We live in a world of contrary impulses. If it were possible to segregate a group of children from infanthood, to expose them only to books of ethical teachings, to mold their environment so that the baser human emotions and activities remained unrevealed to them, to keep them in a vacuum where every action had only a certain definite effect—then, and then only, could we justly test the influence for bad or good that the movies might exert.

"But the world is not so simple as that. And our children cannot be raised in seclusion. If children can read at all, they read the newspapers. Certainly, our recent crime waves and racket killings, with many of the guilty ones never caught, must induce the consequent thought in young minds that evil is not always punished. But the movies never show success attending any wrong emotion, any wrong act. On the contrary, here are vivid textbooks—which, without preaching, set patterns for right behavior.

"Granted, a very small proportion of the produced motion pictures might induce misplaced admiration. It is shortsighted to condemn an entire industry because it doesn't always maintain a high plane of conduct for every character in every drama.

"You might as well condemn the art of printing because newspapers tell of crimes. Or condemn magazines because they publish stories of intrigue and of love that are removed from the reality of everyday experience. But it would be foolish to say that only books with a high moral be permitted to be printed; that newspapers must feature only those stories that contribute to high thinking and right living.

"The educators who select a dozen pictures and say to the motion picture industry, 'You're misusing this great invention because you're not making *all* pictures like these,' automatically close their eyes to the fact that life isn't all a thing of beautiful ideals that the evil and the good are part of existence; that human nature expresses itself in hundreds of different ways.

"Hollywood is the kindergarten, the high school and the university of the world. I know through the thousands of letters I have received that children of every age look to Hollywood and to the actors and actresses whom they have dignified with hero-worship, for the answers to many of their problems.

"My conclusions about the effect of motion pictures on Young America are not based on speculation. I have the tangible facts contained in almost a half-million letters, which are a cross-section of the child and the adolescent mind of today."

"Hero-worshiping youngsters will frequently take advice form an actor because they happen to admire some character he has played. They regard his every activity, his every work with a tremendous seriousness. Their eating habits, their routine of sleep, exercise, their manners, their dress and their codes are all vitally influenced by the characters they idealize. Hollywood sets valuable standards for youth. Particularly is this true when they are supported and intensified by home or school environment.

"Children, it is pointed out, live in a movie world. They collect pictures of stars, read avidly of their daily routines, and give them a collective importance and worship. Suppose they do. Outside of President Roosevelt and Lindbergh, we haven't had a national hero whom we could idolize in the past two decades. Our statesmen haven't kept faith; government officials have been proved bribe-takers; our spectacular financiers have been faithless. What other heroes—except those on the screen—remain to the young for worship? Isn't it natural, then, that the shadows of the screen usurp the place of these men in the growing, avid mind, which demands its idols?"

"And suppose some of them don't always come up to scratch in their characterizations—or even their personal lives? What of it? History tells us that the youth of Greece sat at the feet of Socrates. But his teachings weren't nullified by the fact that he quarreled with his wife. I have reason to think that our young people are as selective today."

"Educators say that motion pictures create prejudices. But even the great teachers—those very philosophers who have always been approved—wrote and spoke with prejudice."

"Unquestionably, there are delinquent girls and boys who ascribe their rules of conduct to the movies. But why blame the movies only? We've always had delinquents. Blame, instead, inadequate schools, poverty, and unstable social conditions."

"That doesn't mean that the movies have no responsibility toward Young America. They have. So do the players. That's part of the game of pictures. The actor is not so much a public figure as he is a symbol. A politician or a statesman, or an office holder, or a professor—all these are judged only by what they do in public. They set their example by their acts. An actor has to do more than that—he has to turn the searchlight on his individual habits, on his private life."

"He belongs to his audiences. He has not—and should not have—a right to his private life. If someone wants to know what I eat, whether or not I'm happily married, what I do with my leisure, or how many hours I sleep, it is not an infringement of my privacy. As a matter of fact, if you're in the public eye, people are privileged to come in when you're taking a shower and ask you what soap you're using. It's an indication of interest and a measure of success for which we work."

"Motion pictures are a vital educational system. Their teachings are persuasive and widespread. Hollywood doesn't overlook its duties to the Young America that looks to it for guidance, for inspiration, for a pattern of living and deportment."

"George O'Brien Defends Movies For Children." By Sonia Lee in *Movie Classic*, December 1933, pages 5, 84, 85.

BIBLIOGRAPHY

"3 Bad Men." *The Sheboygan Press,* October 9, 1926, page 19.

"3 Bad Men — Review." *Variety,* August 25, 1926.

"A Child of the Frisco Earthquake Is George O'Brien." By Dorothy Donnell in *Motion Picture Classic,* August 1925, 24-25, 81.

Aitken, Frank, and Edward Hilton. *A History of the Earthquake and Fire.* San Francisco: E. Hilton Co., 1906.

"All Eligibles Face Military Service." The *Elvira Evening Telegram,* July 30, 1917, page 9.

"A new stage for Murnau in the glowing splendor of his 'Sunrise.'" The *New York Times,* November 29, 1927.

"Antonio Moreno." By DeWitt Bodeen in *Films in Review,* June-July, 1967.

"A Physically Perfect Young Man." By Alma Talley in *Picture Play,* October 1927, pages 74, 114.

"Arlene Dahl." By Ronald L. Davis in the *New York Times Oral History Program,* No. 82, September 24, 1975.

"Another Movie Miracle — William Fox, Now Owner of Roxy Theater, Predicts Talking Photoplays. The *New York Times,* April 3, 1927.

"Antonio Moreno." By DeWitt Bodeen in *Films in Review*, June-July, 1967.

"Arizona Legion – Review." *Variety*, July 5, 1939.

Banks, Charles E. and O. Read. *The History of the San Francisco Disaster and Mount Vesuvius Horror*. San Francisco: C. E. Thomas Co., 1906.

Barrymore, John. *Confessions of an Actor*. Indiana: The Bobs-Merrill Company, 1926.

"Behind the Scenes in Hollywood." By Harrison Carroll in the *Monessen Daily Independent*, June 21, 1935, page 11.

Berry, James. *The Earthquake of 1906*. Privately printed, 1907.

"Blindfold." The *Lima News*, February 5, 1929, page 8.

"Blindfold." The *Bismark Tribune*, April 8, 1929, page 4.

"Blindfold." *Variety*, February 20, 1929.

"Blue Eagle." *Picture Show*, April 2, 1927, page 14.

Blum, Daniel. *A Pictorial History of the Silent Screen*. New York: G. P. Putnam's Sons, 1953.

"Border G-Men." *Variety*, July 20, 1938.

"Border Patrolman." The *New York Times*, July 29, 1936, page 11.

"Border Patrolman." *Variety*, July 1, 1936.

Bronson, William. *The Earth Shook, the Sky Burned*. New York: Doubleday, 1959.

Brownlow, Kevin. *The Parade's Gone By*. New York: Ballentine Books, Inc., 1968.

Brundidge, Harry T. *Twinkle, Twinkle, Movie Star!* New York: Garland Publishing, 1977.

"Bullet Code." The *Soda Springs Sun*, July 18, 1940, page 5.

"Bullet Code." The *Times Recorder*, July 31, 1940, page 2.

"Bullet Code." *Variety*, February 28, 1940.

Caruso, Dorothy. *Enrico Caruso: His Life and Death*. London: J. Werner Laurie Ltd., 1946.

"Caruso Hears His Voice." The *New York Times*, January 15, 1917.

Casanova, Eve. "I Married the World's Greatest Lover." *True Story*. New York: True Story Publishing Company, February, 1935.

Chambliss, William H. *Chambliss' Diary*. New York: Chambliss & Co., 1895.

Chaplin, Charles. *My Autobiography*. New York: Simon and Schuster, 1964.

"Child Stars Are Guarded Until They Reach 18." The *Lima News*, July 10, 1938, page 30.

"Cheyenne Autumn." Bosley Crowther in the *New York Times*, December 24, 1964, page 8.

"Cheyenne Autumn." *Variety*, October 7, 1964.

"Col. Selig's Stories of Movie Life — Wallace Reid." *Screenland*. Chicago: Screenland Publishing Company, April 1923.

"Cowboy Millionaire, The." The *Hammond Times*, October 11, 1935, page 56.

"Cowboy Millionaire, The." *Variety*, June 5, 1935.

"Cut in Movie Stars' Salaries Starts in a Few Months." The *Reno Evening Gazette*, November 28, 1931, page 9.

"Dancers, The." *Variety*, January 7, 1925.

"Dancers, The." By Mordaunt Hall in the *New York Times*, January 26, 1925, page 22.

"Daniel Boone." The *New York Times*, October 24, 1936, page 23.

"Daniel Boone." *Variety*, October 28, 1936.

"December 7th." The *Chronicle Telegram*, Tuesday, November 16, 1999, page 23.

DeMille, Cecil B. *The Autobiography of Cecil B. DeMille*. New Jersey: Prentice-Hall, Inc., 1959.

"Dan O'Brien Leaves Less Than $10,000." *Nevada State Journal*, January 7, 1934, page 2:

Dickelmann, William. *San Francisco Earthquake Fire,* April 18, 1906. San Francisco: 1906.

"Down Nostalgia Trails with George O'Brien." By Buck Rainey in *Western Film Collector*, March — May 1974, Vol. 2, pages 24-39.

"Dude Ranger." The *New York Times*, October 2, 1934, page 18.

"Dude Ranger." *Variety*, October 2, 1934.

Duke, Thomas S. *Synopsis of the San Francisco Police and Municipal Records of the Greatest Catastrophe in American History.* California: Board of Police Commissioners, 1910.

"Earthquake and Fire — San Francisco in Ruins." The *Call-Chronicle-Examiner*, April 19, page 1.

"East Side, West Side." By Mordaunt Hall in the *New York Times*, October 18, 1927, page 33.

"East Side, West Side." *Variety*, October 19, 1927.

"East Side, West Side." The *Wisconsin Rapids Daily Tribune*, August 21, 1928, page 7.

Eisner, Lotte. *Murnau.* Berkley: University of California Press, 1973.

"Ever Since Eve." By Mordaunt Hall in the *New York Times*, March 28, 1934, page 27.

"Ever Since Eve." *Variety*, April 3, 1934.

Eyman, Scott. *Print the Legend The Life and Times of John Ford.* New York: Simon & Schuster, 1999.

Eyman, Scott. *The Speed of Sound.* New York: Simon and Schuster, 1997.

"Fair Warning." The *Lima News*, April 24, 1931, page 5.

"Fair Warning." *Variety*, February 18, 1931.

Fennin, George N. with William K. Everson. *The Western From Silents to the Seventies.* New York: Grossman Publishers, 1973.

"Fibbed a little article to get the job but made good in it." The *Zanesville Signal*, June 25, 1933, page 12.

"Fig Leaves." The *Sheboygan Press*, October 9, 1926, page 19.

"Fig Leaves." *Variety*, July 7, 1926.

"Fighting Gringo, The." *Variety*, November 29, 1939.

"Fighting Heart, The." The *Bridgeport Telegram*, August 29, 1925, page 12.

"Fighting Heart, The." The *Mansfield News*, December 14, 1925, page 14.

"Fighting Heart, The." *Photoplay*, November 1925, page 125.

"Film Fan Monthly Interviews George O'Brien." By Leonard Maltin in *Film Fan Monthly*, May 1971, pages 19-27.

"First Son Born to Film Couple." The *Nevada State Journal*, July 17, 1939, page 1.

"Flo Ash Fan Dance." The *Nevada State Journal*, September 25, 1934, page 6.

"Fort Apache." By Bosley Crowther in the *New York Times*, June 25, 1948, page 26.

"Fort Apache." *Variety*, March 10, 1948.

"Forty-two Cameras Used on Scenes for Ben-Hur." The *New York Times*, November 1, 1925.

"Fox Leading Lady Switches Film Parts." The *Nevada State Journal*, November 30, 1930, page 5.

Franklin, Joe and William K. Everson. *Classics of the Silent Screen*. New York: Citadel Press, 1971.

"From Assistant Cameraman to Motion Picture Star." By John Parker in *American Cinematographer*, July 1929, pages 23-24.

"Frontier Marshal." The *New York Times*, January 31, 1934, page 20.

"Frontier Marshal." The *New York Times*, January 30, 1934.

"Frontier Marshal." *Variety*, February 6, 1934.

Froude, James Anthony. *Oceana, or England and Her Colonies*. New York: Charles Scribner's Sons, 1896.

"Gay Caballero, The." The *New York Times*, March 26, 1932, page 17.

"Gay Caballero, The." *Variety*, March 29, 1932.

"George As He Is." By Margaret Reid in *Picture Play*, May 1929, pages 34, 112.

"George O'Brien." By Maury Daly in *Films In Review*, May/June 1994, pages 50-52.

"George O'Brien Defends Movies For Children." By Sonia Lee in *Movie Classic*, December 1933, pages 5, 84, 85.

"George O'Brien — His Silent Years Part One." By Joe Collura in *Westerns and Western Serials #26*. Minnesota: Favorite Westerns & Serial World, 1987, pages 9-11.

"George O'Brien – His Silent Years Part Two." By Joe Collura in *Westerns and Western Serials #27*. Minnesota: Favorite Westerns & Serial World, 1988, pages 48-51.

"George O'Brien in Zane Grey Story." *Picture Show*, September 21, 1929, page 3.

"George O'Brien – Movie Actor. The *New York Times*, September 6, 1985.

"George O'Brien Movie Muscle Man!" By Lew Pike in *Strength and Health*, March 1948, pages 18, 19, 29, 30, 31.

"George O'Brien Stars as Fighting Barrister — Legion of the Lawless." The *Bismark Tribune*, October 1, 1940, page 10.

"Ghost Breaker, The." *Film Fun*, November 1922, page 47.

"Ghost Breaker, The." The *New York Times*, September 11, 1922, page 20.

"Ghost Breaker, The." *Variety*, September 15, 1922.

"Giant at 76. Ford Directing Film With Capra." The *Dallas Times Herald*, November 24, 1971.

Gish, Lillian. *The Movies Mr. Griffith and Me.* New Jersey: Prentice-Hall, Inc., 1969.

"Golden West, The." The *Monessen Daily Independent*, November 12, 1932, page 3.

"Golden West, The." The *Bedford Gazette*, November 25, 1932, page 7.

"Gold Raiders." *Variety*, June 18, 1952.

"Graphic Description French Battlefields as Seen by South Carolina Lady." The *Gastonia Daily Gazette*, September 6, 1920, page 6.

Greely, Adolphus W. *Earthquake in California*, April 18, 1906. Washington: U. S. Government Printing Office, 1906.

"Great Athletes of the Screen." By Hal K. Wells in *Motion Picture Classic*, September 1926, pages 40, 41, 70.

"Gun Law." The *New York Times*, June 24, 1938, page 15.

"Gun Law." *Variety*, June 29, 1938.

"Hard Rock Harrigan." The *New York Times*, January 30, 1935, page 16.

"Hard Rock Harrigan." *Variety*, July 31, 1935.

"Havoc." *Photoplay*, November 1925, page 51.

"Havoc Scores Triumph." The *Helena Independent*. March 8, 1926, page 3.

"He Might Be the Richest Man in the World." By Frederick James Smith in *Photoplay*, December 1926, page 30-31, 106.

Henry, Neil. *Complete Story of the San Francisco Earthquake*. Chicago: The Bible House, 1906.

"He-Man With Brains." By John K. Newnham in *Film Weekly*, March 11, 1939, page 26.

"He's a Travelin' Man." By Franc Dillon in *Modern Screen*, March 1936, pages 52, 81.

"Heroes on Horseback." By Katherine Hartley in *Movie Mirror*, January 1939, pages 48, 76.

"He Was Their Stage Coach." By Michael F. Blake in the *Los Angeles Times*, May 28, 1999.

"Hickman Hill Press Release." *CBS Television Network*, February 20, 1964.

"Holy Terror, A." The *New York Times*, July 20, 1931, page 20.

"Holy Terror, A." *Variety*, July 21, 1931.

Holland, Larry Lee. "Lou Tellegen." *Films in Review*. April, 1988, pages 222-229.

"Hollywood Cowboy." By Frank S. Nugent in the *New York Times*, July 24, 1937, page 12.

"Hollywood Cowboy." *Variety*, July 28, 1937.

"Hollywood High Lights — The Old, Old, Story." By Edwin and Elza Schallert in *Picture-Play*, November 1927, pages 55, 108.

"Hollywood on the Wing — RKO Seeks a Sure-Fire Formula." The *New York Times*, January 23, 1938.

"Hollywood Star Attends Global Strategy Talks." The *Newport Daily News*, June 3, 1959, page 8.

"Honor Bound." By Mordaunt Hall in the *New York Times*, April 30, 1928, page 18.

"Honor Bound." *Variety*, May 9, 1928.

"How A Formal Gown Can Help Your Morale." By Mrs. Penrose Lyly in the *Wisconsin Rapids Daily Tribune*, April 29, 1933, page 7.

"How George O'Brien of the Movies Keeps Fit." By George Lowther in *Your Physique*, October 1947, pages 8, 9, 44.

"I Knew Him When — What Richard Dix Says of George O'Brien." By Helen Klumph in *Picture-Play*, March 192, pages 61, 110-111.

"Illness Forces Ford to Halt Film Work. The *Dallas Times Herald*, August 4, 1964.

"In Hollywood." By Erskin Johnson in the *Helena Independent Record*, January 16, 1948.

"In Hollywood." By Paul Harrison in the *Ironwood Daily Globe*, October 19, 1938.

"In Hollywood." By Paul Harrison in the *Wisconsin Rapids Daily*, March 3, 19337, page 10.

"Iron Horse, The." The *New York Times*, August 29, 1924. Page 6.

"Iron Horse, The." *Variety*, September 3, 1924.

"Is Zat So?" The *New York Times*, May 17, 1927, page 27.

"Is Zat So?" *Variety*, May 18, 1927

Jensen, Larry. The *Movie Railroads*. California: Darwin Publications, 1983.

"John Ford — An Epic Half-Century of American Filmmaking." The *Christian Science Monitor*, September 13, 1973.

"Johnstown Flood, The." The *Bridgeport Telegram*, February 26, 1926, page 19.

"Johnstown Flood, The." *Variety*, March 17, 1926.

"Just Tony." *Lima News*, February 1, 1929, page 10.

"Just Tony." The *New York Times*, August 7, 1922.

"Just Tony." *Variety*, August 11, 1922.

Katchmer, George A. *Eighty Silent Film Stars*. Jefferson, N.C.: McFarland & Company, Inc., 1991.

Key, Pierre V. R. *Enrico Caruso: A Biography*. Boston: Little, Brown, & Co., 1922.

Kobal, John. *Rita Hayworth The Time, the Place and the Woman.* London: A Howard & Wyndham Company, 1977.

Kotsilibas-Davis, James. *The Barrymores The Royal Family in Hollywood.* New York: Crown Publishers, Inc., 1981.

"KFRC Opening Justifies 'Known for Radio Clearness' Title — Broadcasting Station at Whitcomb Crowded." By Earle Ennis in the *San Francisco Bulletin*, September 25, 1924, page 2.

Lafler, Henry A. *How the Army Worked to Save San Francisco.* San Francisco: Calkins Newspaper Syndicate, 1906.

Lasky, Jesse L. *I Blow My Own Horn.* New York: Doubleday & Company, Inc., 1957.

"Last of the Duanes." The *New York Times*, September 13, 1930, page 9.

"Last of the Duanes." *Variety*, September 17, 1930.

"Last Trail, The." *Variety*, January 23, 1934.

"Legion of the Lawless." *Variety*, February 28, 1940.

"Lawless Valley." *Variety*, June 7, 1939.

"Life in the Raw." The *Delta Herald Times*, August 24, 1933, page 3.

"Life in the Raw." *Variety*, November 7, 1933.

"Lois Moran Now to Be Seen in Blindfold." In *Picture Show*, July 13, 1929, page 14.

"Lone Star Ranger." *Variety*, January 22, 1930.

"Lou Tellegen Stabs Self to Death With Shears; Feared Insanity." The *New York Tribune*, October 30, 1934.

Macgowan, Kenneth. *Behind the Screen*. New York: Delacorte Press, 1965.

"Madge Bellamy Held in Shooting." *Lethbridge Herald*, January 20, 1943, page 3.

"Man Afraid of his Wardrobe." *Motion Picture News*. September 25, 1915, page 16.

"Man Who Came Back, The." The *New York Times*, September 1, 1924, page 9.

"Man Who Came Back, The." The *New York Times*, September 1, 1924.

"Manhattan Medley." By Alma Talley in *Picture-Play*, January 1928, page32.

"Marriage Hasn't Changed Him." By Whitney Williams in *Picture-Play*, January 1934, pages 18, 56.

"Marshal of Mesa City, The." *Variety*, December 27, 1939.

Martin, Mary. *My Heart Belongs*. New York: Quill, 1984.

"Masked Emotions." The *Lima News*, November 22, 1929, page 27.

"Masked Emotions." *Picture Show*, December 7, 1929, page 9.

Matthews, Leonard. *History of Western Movies*. New York: Crescent Books, 1984.

Maturi, Richard J. and Mary Buckingham Maturi. *Francis X. Bushman A Biography and Filmography*. Jefferson, NC.: McFarland & Company, Inc., 1998.

McBride, Joseph. *Searching For John Ford A Life*. New York: St. Martin's Press, 2001.

McCarthy, Todd. *Howard Hawks The Grey Fox of Hollywood.* New York: Grove Press, 1997.

McLaughlin, Robert. *Broadway and Hollywood.* New York: Arno Press, 1974, pages 52-80.

Miller, Lee O. *The Great Cowboy Stars of Movies & Television.* New York: Arlington House Publishers, 1979.

Mix, Olive Stokes with Eric Heath. *The Fabulous Tom Mix.* New York: Prentice-Hall, Inc., 1957.

Mix, Paul E. *The Life and Legend of Tom Mix.* New York: A. S. Barnes and Company, 1972.

"Moran of the Lady Letty." The *Gettysburg Times,* May 3, 1922, page 6.

"Moran of the Lady Letty." The *Manitoba Free Press*, February 24, 1922, page 18.

"Moran of the Lady Letty." The *Mexia Evening News*, April 23, 1922, page 7.

"Moran of the Lady Letty." The *New York Times*, February 6, 1922.

"Moran of the Lady Letty." *Variety*, February 10, 1922.

"Movie Veterans of the War." By Alice L. Tildesley in *Motion Picture Magazine*, November 1925, page 97.

"Mr. Columbus Dix." By Dorothy Herzog in *Photoplay*, July 1926, page 118.

Murnau, F. W. "Films of the Future." In *Hollywood Directors 1914-1940*, by Richard Koszarski. New York: Oxford University Press, 1976.

"Murnau II: Sunrise." By Robin Wood in *Film Comment*, May-June 1976, page 17.

'My Wild Irish Rose." The *New York Times*, December 25, 1947, page 32.

"My Wild Irish Rose." *Variety*, December 10, 1947.

"Mystery Ranch." The *New York Times*, July 30, 1932, page 26.

"Mystery Ranch." *Variety*, July 5, 1932.

"Ne'er-Do-Well, The." *Variety*, May 3, 1923.

"Ne'er-Do-Well, The." The *New York Times*, May 1, 1923, page 24.

"New Production Set-Up at Fox." The *New York Times*, November 24, 1940.

"Niblo Talks About Work in Filming Ben-Hur." The *New York Times*, January 3, 1926.

"Noah's Ark." By Arline De Haas in *Screen Book*, March 1929, page 21-44.

"Noah's Ark." By Mordaunt Hall in The *New York Times*, March 13, 1929, page 28.

"Noah's Ark." The *Santa Cruz Morning Sentinel*, May 23, 1928, page 4.

"Noah's Ark." The *Reno Gazette*, July 14, 1928, page 6.

"Noah's Ark." *Variety*, November 7, 1928.

"Noah's Ark Co. Depart. Fox Unit Finishing New Play." The *Santa Cruz Morning Sentinel*, May 26, 1928, page 8.

"O'Brien, Mackaill Reunite. 37 Years Since Last Picture." The *Manitowoc Herald Times*, August 2, 1968, page 8.

"O'Brien Within Five Minuts of Being South Sea Islander Instead of Star in Pictures." *The Fighting Heart Press Book*, page 6.

"Old Time Stars Recall Heyday." By Bob Thomas in the *Newark Advocate*, August 2, 1968, page 17.

"Olive Borden Dead." The *Coshocton Tribune*, October 2, 1947, page 1.

"Olive Borden Death." The *Joplin Globe*, October 12, 1947, page 34:

"O'Malley of the Mounted." By Frank S. Nugent in the *New York Times*, April 6, 1936, page 18.

"O'Malley of the Mounted." *Variety*, April 8, 1936.

On the Mexican Border — The Gay Caballero Review." The *New York Times*, Mrch 26, 1932.

"Paid to Love." The *New York Times*, July 25, 1927, page 25.

"Paid to Love." *Variety*, July 27, 1927.

"Painted Desert." The *New York Times*, September 14, 1938, page 26.

"Painted Desert." *Variety*, September 21, 1938.

"Painted Lady." The *Nevada State Journal.* March 15, 1925, page 11.

"Park Avenue Logger." *Variety*, April 7, 1937.

"Parties Galore." By Doris Denbo in *The New Movie*, October 1932, pages 61, 83.

"Prairie Law." *Variety*, July 3, 1940.

"Racketeers of the Range." The *New York Times*, June 8, 1939, page 31.

"Racketeers of the Range." *Variety*, May 31, 1939.

"Pantomime Quiz." Daily *Variety*, July 4, 1951.

"Picture Star Skilled Boxer." The *Lima News*, March 20, 1937, page 5.

"Pleasure Crazed." The *Zanesville Signal*, December 18, 1929, page 13.

"Rainbow Trail, The." The *New York Times*, January 30, 1932, page 13.

"Rainbow Trail." The *Zanesville Signal*, January 20, 1932, page 6.

"Rainbow Trail, The." *Variety*, February 2, 1932.

"Ramon The Recluse." By Margaret Chute in *Picture Show*, May 21, 1927, page 9.

Ramsaye, Terry. *A Million and One Nights*. New York: Simon and Schuster, 1926.

"Renegade Ranger, The." The *New York Times*, February 17, 1939, page 17.

"Renegade Ranger, The." *Variety*, October 5, 1938.

"Riders of the Purple Sage." The *Nevada State Journal*, November 29, 1931, page 8.

"Riders of the Purple Sage." The *New York Times*, September 26, 1931, page 25.

"Riders of the Purple Sage." *Variety*, September 29, 1931.

"Robbers Roost." By Eleanor Barnes in the *Illustrated Daily News*. February 3, 1933.

"Robbers Roost." *Film Daily*, March 18, 1933.

"Robbers Roost." *Variety*, March 21, 1933.

"Rough Romance." The *Nevada State Journal*, January 18, 1931, page 10.

"Rough Romance." The *New York Times*, June 16, 1930, page 25.

"Rough Romance." *Variety*, June 18, 1930.

"Roughneck, The." The *Bridgeport Telegram*, February 7, 1925, page 10.

"Roughneck, The." The *New York Times*, December 3, 1924, page 14.

"Roughneck, The." *Variety*, December 3, 1924.

"Rustlin' For Cupid." *Variety*, June 23, 1926.

"Salute." The *Bee Register*, December 12, 1927, page 6.

"Salute." The *New York Times*, October 5, 1929, page 22.

"Salute." *Variety*, October 9, 1929.

"Sea Hawk, The." The *New York Times*, June 2, 1924.

"Sea Hawk, The." *Variety*, June 11, 1924.

"Seas Beneath, The." The *New York Times*, January 31, 1931, page 15.

"Seas Beneath, The." *Variety*, February 4, 1931.

"Shadows of Paris." The *New York Times*, February 18, 1924, page 13.

"Sharp Shooters." The *New York Times*, January 23, 1928, page 18.

"Sharp Shooters." *Variety*, January 25, 1928.

"She Likes Outdoor Life." The *Appleton Post-Crescent*, November 15, 1930, page 11.

"She Wore a Yellow Ribbon." By Bosley Crowther in the *New York Times*, November 18, 1949, page 35.

"She Wore a Yellow Ribbon." *Variety*, July 27, 1949.

"Silver Treasure, The." The *Appleton Post Crescent*, November 6, 1926, page 13.

"Silver Treasure, The." *Variety*, July 28, 1926.

Sinclair, Andrew. *John Ford*. New York: The Dial Press, 1979.

"Singing Important Police Recruit Training." By Daniel O'Brien in the *San Francisco Bulletin*, September 8, 1925.

Smith, Albert E. *Two Reels and a Crank*. New York: Doubleday & Company, Inc., 1952.

"Smoke Lightning." The *Monessen Daily Independent*, February 25, 1933, page 3.

"Smoke Lightning." The *Newark Advocate*, February 20, 1933, page 9.

"Stage to Chino." *Variety*, August 21, 1940.

"Stage Tradition Hit By Pictures." The *Reno Evening Gazette*, November 28, 1931, page 9.

Stovall, Peter. *John Ford*. Boston: Twayne Publishers, 1986.

"Sunrise: A Film Meets Its Public." *Quarterly Review of Film Studies 2*, August 1977, page 327-338.

"Sunrise: A Murnau Masterpiece." By Dorothy B. Jones in the *Quarterly of Film, Radio, and Television*, Spring 1955, page 258.

"Sunrise." *Motion Picture Classic*, September 1926, page 3.

"Sunrise." *Motion Picture Classic*, October 1925, page 25.

"Sunrise." *Moving Picture World*, March 5, 1927, page 35.

"Sunrise." *Moving Picture World*, April 2, 1927, page 267.

"Sunrise." *Moving Picture World*, June 25, 1927, page 589.

"Sunrise." *Moving Picture World*, July 17, 1926, page 51.

"Sunrise." *Moving Picture World*, July 23, 1927, page 244.

"Sunrise." *Moving Picture World*, August 6, 1927, page 402.

"Sunrise." *Photoplay*, December 1927, page 53.

"Sunrise Synchronized by Fox Movietone To Show Here." The *Sheboygan Press*, November 3, 1928, page 21.

"Sunrise." The *New York Times*, December 7, 1926, page 21.

"Sunrise." The *New York Times*, September 24, 1927, page 15.

"Sunrise." The *New York Times,* December 24, 1927, page 15.

"Sunrise — Song of Two Human Beings." The *New York Times*, January 29, 1928, Section 8, page 6.

"Sunrise." *Variety*, March 27, 1927, page 4.

"Sunrise." *Variety*, September 28, 1927.

"Sunrise," excerpt from "Box Office Record," *The Motion Picture Almanac — 1929*, Chicago: The Quigley Publishing Company, p. 207.

Swanson, Gloria. *Swanson on Swanson*. New York: Random House, 1980.

Taraborrelli, J. Randy. *Laughing Til It Hurts The Complete Life and Career of Carol Burnett*. New York: William Morrow and Company, Inc., 1988.

"Tellegen Dead Alone With Faded Glory." The *Evening Herald and Express*, October 30, 1934.

"Tellegen, Former Stage Idol, Stabs Himself to Death." The *Los Angeles Examiner*, October 30, 1934.

Tellegen, Lou. *Women Have Been Kind*. New York: The Vanguard Press, 1931.

Terrace, Vincent. *The Complete Encyclopedia of Television Programs Vol. 2*. New York: A. S. Barnes and Company, 1976.

"Thank You." By Mordaunt Hall in the *New York Times*, October 6, 1925, page 30.

"Thank You." *Variety*, October 7, 1925.

"The Career of Rudolph Valentino." By Theodore Huff in *Films in Review*. New York: National Board of Review of Motion Pictures, Inc., April 1952. Pages 145-149.

"The Case of Mr. Fox." *Fortune*, May 1930, page 49.

"The Catch of Hollywood." By Ivan St. Johns in *Photoplay*, March 1925, 48, 94.

"The German Goose—Or the Golden Eggs?" *Moving Picture World*, July 24, 1926, page 151.

"The O'Brien Boy Gets a Kick Out of Life." By Scott Pierce in *Motion Picture Classic*, August 1926, page 56, 86.

"The Path of Glory — Is Hard Work and the Strain Attendant Upon Fame Killing our Screen Stars?" By Helen Carlisle in *Motion Picture*, January 1927, pages 23,108.

"The Screen: The Railroad Pioneers." The *New York Times*, August 29, 1924, page 6.

"The Shadow Stage — Sunrise." *Photoplay*, December 1927, page 52.

"The Super Cowboy." By Tom Kennedy in *Screenland*, September 1936, page 61, 93.

"They Join Western Wall of Fame." *People*, September 23, 1953, page 37-38.

Thomas, Gordon and Max Morgan Witts. *The San Francisco Earthquake*. New York: Stein and Day, 1971.

"Thunder Mountain." The *New York Times*, October 2, 1935, page 27.

"Thunder Mountain." *Variety*, October 2, 1935.

"Timber Stampede." *Variety*, October 25, 1939.

"Tragic Mansions." By Cal York in *Photoplay*, September 1929. Pages 33-34, 128.

"Triple Justice." *Variety*, October 9, 1940.

"Trouble in Sundown — Review." *Variety*, July 5, 1939.

"True Heaven." *Screenbook*, May 1929 page 12.

"True Heaven." The *New York Times*, February 11, 1929, page 26.

"True Heaven." *Variety*, February 13, 1929.

Tuska, Jon. *The Filming of the West*. New York: Doubleday & Company, 1976, pages 347-352.

"Two Opera Stars in Silent Films." The *New York Times*, November 25, 1918, page 11.

"Valentino, the Immortal." By Evans J. Casso in the *Italian-American Digest*, Fall, 1985.

Vermilye, Jerry. *The Films of the Twenties*. New York: The Citadel Press, 1985.

"Virginia Valli." *Picture Show*, June 11, 1927, pages 8-9.

Wagenknecht, Edward. *Fifty Great American Silent Films*. New York: Dover Publications, Inc., 1980.

"Wallace Reid Dies in Fight on Drugs." The *New York Times*, January 19, 1923.

"What Price Film Fame?" *Picture Show*, June 11, 1927, pages 14-15.

"What Price Glory?" By Harrison Carroll in the *Bradford Era*, March 22, 1949, page 5.

"What Price Glory?" In "Looking at Hollywood." By Hedda Hopper in the *Portland Press Herald*, February 25, 1949, page 23.

"What Price Glory?" The *Zanesville Signal*, January 29, 1949, page 8.

"When a Man's a Man." The *New York Times*, February 22, 1935.

"When a Man's a Man." *Variety*, February 27, 1935.

"Whispering Smith Speaks." By Frank S. Nugent in the *New York Times*, February 17, 1936, page 21.

"Whispering Smith Speaks." *Variety*, February 19, 1936.

"White Hands." The *Gettysburg News*, March 4, 1922, page 8.

"White Hands." The *Lima News,* April 27, 1922, page 10.

"White Hands." *Variety*, February 10, 1922.

"Whoa!" by S. R. *Mook in Silver Screen*, September 1934, pages 29, 58.

"William Fox Presents Sunrise." By Robert C. Allen in *Quarterly Review of Film Studies*, August 1977.

"Windjammer." *Variety*, October 20, 1937.

"Woman Proof." The *New York Times*, October 30, 1923, page 16.

"Why a Straight Shooter Wins." By Bernarr Macfadden in *Physical Culture*, April 1939, pages 22, 23, 34.

Zukor, Adolph. *The Public is Never Wrong.* New York: G. P. Putnam's Sons, 1953.

INDEX

3 Bad Men 82-84, 103, 112, 158, 171, 172, 208, photo 84, advertisement and photos 209
4 Devils 104, 113
Abel, Alfred 41
Accord, Art 49, photo 44
Adams, Claire 175
Adams, Ernie 244
Adams, Sam 257
Adamson, Ewart 231
Ade, George 183
Adrian, Gilbert 78
Agar, John 317, 319, photo 318
Agnew, Robert 183
Ahlm, Philip 241, 316
Alba, Maria 231
Alberni, Luis 265
Albertson, Frank 235
Albright, Wally 269
Alcatraz 175
Alexander, Dick 237
Alexander, Richard 237
Allen, Addie 316
Allen, Elizabeth 323
Allen, Maude 272, 277, 294
Allgood, Sara 313
Allsworth, Frank 221
American Biograph Company 86
American West of John Ford, The 171
Ames, Leon 305, photo 305
Amram, David 173
And Now, Goodbye 146
Anderson, William "Bronco Billy" 42, 163
Andre, Pierre 314
Andrews, Dana 316
Andrews, Stanley 301
Angel, Heather 281, photo 283
Anthony, Stuart 265, 266, 268
Apfel, Oscar 234
Arizona Legion 146, 147, 298, photo 299
Arlen, Richard 58, 81, 166, 179
Armendáriz, Pedro 318
Armour, Jean 221
Armstrong, Paul 268
Armstrong, Robert 159
Arness, James 168
Arnold, Eddie 220
Ash, Flo 70
Assignment Underwater 166
Astor, Gertrude 181
Astor, Mary 173, 183
Ates, Roscoe 251
Atkinson, Frank 262
Atlas, Charles 2
Austin, William 205
Autry, Gene 163

Autry, Max Mun 325
Ave, Maryon 194
Baffert, Al 285, 321
Bailey, Frankie 201
Bailey, William N. 276
Baker, C. Graham 224
Baker, Carroll 167, 323
Baker, Silver Tip 269
Balch, Joe 301
Balch, Slim 285
Baldwin, Walter 323
Barbe, Carlos 313
Barber, Bobby 290
Barcroft, Roy 310
Barlow, Reginald 279
Barnes, Al G. 64
Barringer, Barry 269
Barrows, Henry 186
Barrymore John 9, 10, 11, 16, 17, 19, 23, 168, photo 10
Barrymore, Ethel 23
Barrymore, Lionel 113
Baxter, Warner 124
Beach, Rex 181
Beaumont, Gerald 210
Becker, Fred 208
Beery, Noah 225
Beery, Noah 225, 248
Beery, Wallace 173, 186
Begley, Ed 159
Belgard, Arnold 311
Bell, Bell 269
Bell, Hank 237, 290, 294, 303, 309, 310
Bell, Rex 98, 235
Bell, Rodney 314
Bellah, James Warner 317, 319
Bellamy, Madge 198
Bellamy, Madge 64, 155, 187, 195, photos 76, 189, 199
Belmore, Lionel 186

Benedict, William 302, 309, 310
Ben-Hur (film) 54, 56, 57, 64, 119, photos 55
Ben-Hur (play) 54
Bennett, Al 241
Bennett, Chester 155, 192
Bennett, Enid 186
Bentley, Irene 266
Benton, Dean 272, 275
Beranger, André 205
Berke, Ruth Ellen 164
Bernds, Edward 321
Bernhardt, Sarah 83
Bethea, Jack 224
Better 'Ole, The 97
Bevans, Clem 321
Big Boy 97
Big Hunt, The 319
Big Trail, The 115, 116
Bing, Herman 127, 218
Bingham, Edfrid 203
Birth of a Nation, The 54
Blake, Larry 159
Blake, Michael F. 160
Blandick, Clara 241
Blindfold 99, 102, 231, photo 231
Block, Ralph 246
Blue Eagle, The 171, 173, 210, advertisement 211, photos 212
Blue, Ben 313
Blue, Monte 314, 321
Blystone, John G. 223
Blystone, Stanley 257, 271, 287
Blythe, Betty 268
Bogart, Humphrey 246
Boland, Eddie 220
Bolder, Robert 186
Boles, John 159
Bond, Ward 116, 159, 160, 235, 237, 266, 285, 289, 300, 318, 319, photo 236

Index

Bonner, Priscilla 208
Bonomo, Joe 226
Booth, John Hunter 237, 302
Borden, Eddie 239
Borden, Mrs. Sybil 159
Borden, Olive 6, 74, 75, 78, 205, 208, death 158, photos 76, 84, 206, 209
Border G-Man 145, 290, photos 291, advertisement 292
Border Patrolman, The 281, advertisement 280, photos 280
Borzage, Dan 187
Borzage, Frank 85, 89, 96
Bostock, Evelyn 138, 272
Bostwick, Edith 201
Bosworth, Hobart 1, 50, 176, photo 177
Boteler, Wade 198
Botiller, Dick 303
Bouchey, Willis 323
Bow, Clara 96
Bowman, Earl Wayland 241
Bowman, Rudy 319
Boyd, William 163
Boyer, Charles
Bracey, Sidney 220
Bradbury, James Jr. 241
Bradley, Lee 319, 323
Brady, Edward 257, 309
Brand, Bill 241
Brand, Harry 234
Brand, Max 175, 244, 246
Brandon, Henry 305
Breeden, John 235
Breese, Edmund 257
Brendel, El 265
Brenon, Herbert 53, 54, 184
Brent, George 244
Brian, Mary 268, photo 268
Brinley, Charles 178

Brock, Ralph 246
Brown, Clarence 96
Brown, Joe 248
Brown, Johnny Mack 163
Brown, Lucille 240, photo 241
Browning, Tod 96
Brownlow, Kevin 90, 111
Bruce Mitchell, Bruce 310
Brundidge, Harry 25, 62
Bull, Charles Edward 187
Bullet Code 307, photo 308
Burnet, Carol 317
Burnette, Smiley 281, photo 280
Burns, Bob 290, 298, 300, 302, 305, 307, 310, 313
Burns, Edward 251
Burns, Fred 294, 298
Burns, Marion 257, photo 259
Burns, Neil 290
Burns, Robert 294
Burton, George 251, 262
Bush, James 279
Bushman, Francis X., 55, photo in *Ben-Hur* 55
Butler, David 156, 157, 198, 210, 234, 235, 313
Butler, Jimmy 271
Butts, Billy 237
Byrd, Ralph 316
Cabinet of Dr. Caligari, The 85
Cactus, My Paul 33
Caits, Joe 285
Caldwell, Captain H. H. 92, 218
Callejo, Cecilia 294
Calvert, Captain E. H. 198
Cameo Kirby 60
Camille 50
Campeau, Frank 83, 175, 208, 241, 281
Canada, Roy 321
Cannon, Maurice 184

Canyon Walls 262
Capone, Al 385
Capra, Frank 164
Carco, Francis 184
Card, Bob 309
Card, Ken 290, 294, 300
Carewe, Arthur 179
Carey, Harry Jr. 160, 161, 319, 323, 163
Carey, Harry, Sr. 163, 169
Carleton, William P. 281
Carlisle, Richard 271
Carmen (opera) 9, 11
Carol, Sue 139, 237, photo 237
Carr, Dan 323
Carr, Harry 100, 215
Carradine, John 281, 323
Carrillo, Leo 163
Carroll, Harrison 38, 160
Cartwright, Pegg 187
Caruso, Enrico 8-11, 15, 16, photo 10
Case, Theodore 94
Cass, Maurice 277
Cavanaugh, Hobart 310
Chadwick, Cyril 187, 190, 201, 213, photo 189
Chadwick, Helene 269
Chandler, George 246
Chandler, Helen 235, 239
Chandler, Janet 132, 257
Chaney, Lon 100
Chaplin, Charlie 66, 80, 97, 180
Chaplin, Sid 97
Chapman, Cyril 198
Chapman, Edythe 198
Charters, Spencer 277
Chase, Alden 272
Chase, Colin 187, 237
Chatterton, Ruth 113
Chatterton, Tom 300

Cheatham, Jack 305
Cheron, André 234
Chesebro, George 298
Chester, Alma 269
Cheyenne Autumn 2, 167, 323
Chief Big Tree 187, 257, 319
Chief Sky Eagle 319
Chief White Spear 187
Christine, Lilly 314
Church, Fred 257
Churchill, Berton 266
Churchill, Marguerite birth 29, 32, 74, 116, 117, 124, 127, 128, marriage to George O'Brien 131, 133, death of son Brian 133, birth of daughter Orin 133, birth of son Darcy 133, 136, 137, 146, 153, 154, 157, divorce 166, 248, photos 31, 115, 123, 129, 135, 136, 249, 250
Chute, Margaret 57
Cinecon Film Festival 171
Circle D Ranch Wild West Show 28
Clark, Cliff 318
Clark, Dan 45, 47
Clark, Edward 315
Clark, Frank Howard 279
Clark, Fred 317
Clark, Harvey 190, 194, 198, 208
Clarke, Kenneth B. 239
Clary, Robert 317
Clayton, Gilbert 208
Clegg, Sy 251
Clemente, Steve 256, 257
Cleveland, George 314
Cline, Edward F. 269, 271, 272
Clopton, Betty 146
Clothier, William 167
Clyde, Andy 231
Clyde, David 275
Cody, Iron Eyes 251, 257

Cody, Lew 159, 303
Coe, Charles Francis 231
Cohen, Bennett 281, 294, 307
Cohn, Alfred A. 246, 256
Coldeway, Anthony 225
Coleman, Charles 281
Collier, Warren Sr. 241
Collier, William Jr. 9, 186
Collure, Joe 78, 118
Collyer, June 221
Compson, Betty 53
Compton, Joyce 235
Congedo, Father Joseph H. 81
Conklin, Heinie 205
Connelly, Erwin 244
Connors, Barry 248, 251, 254
Conquering Power, The 50
Conrad, Joseph 207
Conried, Hans 317
Conroy, Frank 266
Conselman, William 215, 266
Conway, Jack 194
Coogan, Jackie 317
Cook, Jesse 13
Cooley, Frank 224
Cooley, Spade 305
Cooper, Gary 4, 64, 163
Cooper, Ken 271
Cooper, Merian C. 317, 319
Corbett, Ben 298, 301-303, 305, 309
Corbett, Jim 28
Cordell, Frank 260
Cording, Harry 239, 281, 294, 298, 301, 305, 310
Corey, Jim 310
Cornwall, Anne 194, 313
Corrado, Gino 220, 315
Corrigan, Emmett 257
Cortez, Ricardo 57, 60, 137
Costello, Dolores 104, photo 106, 107

Costello, Dolores 4, making *Noah's Ark* 104-112, 108, 109, 111, 225, photos 228, 229
Covered Wagon, The 61, 116
Cowboy Millionaire 138, 140, 272
Cowles, Jules 181
Cradle Snatchers, The 103
Cramer, Richard 279, 307
Crawford, Joan 96
Crockett, Dick 321
Crosby, Bing 90
Crowder, General 33
Cummings, Irving 78, 79, 203, 204, 246,
Cummins, Dwight 232
Cunningham, Jack 179, 298
Curran, Thomas A. 272
Currier, Frank 186
Curtis, Dick 281
Curtis, Ken 323
Curtiz, Michael 105, 108, 109, 111, 225, 227, 229, photo 106
Curwood, James Oliver 138
Cushing, Tom 201
D'Algy, Helena 208
D'Antonguolla, Rodolfo Alfonza Raffaelo Pierre Filibert Guglielmi *(see Rudolph Valentino)*
D'Antonio, Carmen 323
Dahl, Arlene 156, 313
Dalton, Dorothy 52, 178, photo 178
Dana, Muriel Frances 176
Dancers, The 73, 121, 171, 195, advertisement 196
Dandridge, Ruby 314
Daniel Boone 141, 281, advertisement 282, photos 283
Daniels, Harold 285
Darcell, Denise 317
Davenport, Harry 316
Davidson, Dore 221

Davidson, Leonard 241
Davidson, Max 204
Davidson, William B. 314
Davis, Art 290
Davis, Donald 239
Davis, Edwards 186
Davis, Richard Harding 9
Day, Laraine 190, 294, 298, photos 291, 299
Dazey, Frank Mitchell 271
De Brulier, Nigel 225, 265
De Grasse, Sam 224
De Grey, Sidney 208
De Lacy, Philippe 316
De Lacy, Phillip 213
De Palma, Walter 285
De Putti, Lya 41
De Silva, Fred 186
Dearing, Edgar 290
December 7th 316
Dega, Igor 314
Del Rio, Dolores 96, 167, 323, photo 76
Del Val, Jean 313
DeLeon, Walter 179
Demarest, William 223
DeMille, Cecil B. 52, 58, 96, 104
Dempsey, Clifford 235
Denny, Reginald 60
Depew, Joseph 241
Devlin, Joe 315
DeVol, Frank 317
Dickey, Paul 179
Dickey, Will A 28
Dictator, The 9
Dillard, Art 294
Dillon, Edward 257
Dillon, Franc 140
Dilson, John 298, 300, 301, 307, 310
Dinan, Jeremiah 9, 11, 19
Dinner at Eight (film) 127

Dinner at Eight (play) 127
Dione, Rose 184
Diplomats, The 116
Dix, Richard 53, 54, 56-58, 60, 68, 79, 80, 147, photo 44
Dixon, Jr., Thomas 192
Dodge, Frank 221
Don Juan 97
Donlin, Mike 183
Donnell, Dorothy 14
Donnelly, Ruth 251
Donohue, Margaret L. *(see Margaret O'Brien)*
Donovan, Mike 310
Dooley, John 221
Doran, Mary 281
Dorr, Lester 248, 271, 185
Dove, Billie 137, 194, 199, 289
Drake, Oliver 290, 293, 298, 300, 301, 303
Dresden, Curley 275
Dresser, Louise 183
Drew, John 23, 24
Dru, Joanne 319
Du Brey, Claire 186
Dude Ranger, The 269, advertisement 270, photos 270
Dugan, Michael 319
Dugan, Tom 223
Dumbrille, Douglas 262
Dunne, Irene 147
Dupuis, Art 310
Duran, Nellie 310
Durant, Thomas 187
Duse, Eleonora 83
Duvee, Hal 325
Dwan, Allan 221, 222
Dwire, Earl 269, 302
East Side, West Side 99, 101, 221, 222, photos 222
Eburne, Maude 260, 285

Eckert, Jules 190
Eckhardt, Oliver 237
Edeson, Robert 210
Edwards, Alan 265, 266
Edwards, Penny 315
Edwards, Ralph 166
Edwards, Snitz 179
Eichor, Edna 194
Eilers, Sally 147, 220, 246, photos 247
Eisenhower, Dwight 161, 164, 165
Elinor, Carli 93, 96
Elliott, Frank 192
Elliott, John 246
Ellis, Dione 213
Ellis, Frank 271, 279, 298, 305, 309, 310
Emmett, Fern 313
Enemies of the Law 121
Epper, Jeannie 323
Epper, Stephanie 323
Erickson, A. F. 237, 239
Ethier, Alphonz 244
Evans, Brandon 287
Evans, Larry 192, 199
Evans, Madge 127
Ever since Eve 268, photos 268
Everton, Paul 289, 309, 313
Fagan, Myron C. 246
Fair Warning 244, advertisement 245
Fair, Elinor 176
Fairbanks, Douglas Sr. 72, 137
Fairbanks, Douglas Jr. 147, 173, 213
Falstaff 103
Farley, Dot 298
Farnum, William 96, 163
Farrar, Geraldine 83
Farrell, Charles 79, 89, 96, photo 76
Farrell, Lowell J. 319

Fast, Howard 323
Faust 85
Fawcett, George 201
Faye, Randall H. 223
Fazenda, Louise 225, photo 229
Feld, Fritz 231
Feldman, Charles 148
Fenton, Leslie 198
Fergus, Barney 118, 119
Ferguson, Bob 37
Ferguson, Frank 318
Fetchit, Stepin 235
Field, Mary 303, 307
Field, Virginia 317
Fields, Sid 313
Fields, Stanley 246, 248, 279, 294
Fig Leaves 74, 75, 76, 78, 158, 205, advertisement and photos 206
Fighting Gringo, The 303, photo 304
Fighting Heart, The 73, 199, advertisement and photos 200
Fine, Larry 321
Fireside Theater 322
Fisher, Shug 323
Fiske, Robert 301, 302
Fitzroy, Emily 190
Fix, Paul 290, 311, 319
Flavin, James 323
Fleming, Bob 237
Flint, Sam 287
Flowers, Bess 277
Flynn, Emmett J. 69, 190, 195
Foch, General Ferdinand 36
Fog 231
Fonda, Henry 317, photo 318
Foran, Dick 318
Forbes, Ralph 281
Ford, Daniel Sergeant 171
Ford, Eddie 66
Ford, Francis 33, 199, 241, 265, 318, 319

Ford, John 1, 33, 60, 61, 62, 64, 66, 68, 73, 82, 83, 85, 90, 96, 124, 125, 127, 147, 152, 157-161, 163-165, 167-169, 171, death 172, 187, 189, 199, 201, 210, 235, 236, 241, 316, 317, 319, 320, 323, photos 65, 126
Ford, Philip 210
Ford, Robert 241
Ford, Ross 315
Ford, Wallace 159
Forrest, Mabel 313
Forrest, William 318, 323
Fort Apache 1, 157, 173, 317, photo 318
Foster, Jerry 266
Four Horsemen of the Apocalypse, The 50
Four Sons 96
Four Tunes, The 298
Fox, Earl 231, photo 231
Fox, William 39, 61, 64, 68, 79, 85, 86, 88, 89, 94, 98, 109, 110, 116, 124, 175, 187, 190, 192, 194, 195, 198, 199, 203, 204, 205, 207, 208, 210, 213, 215, 218, 221, 223, 224, 231, 232, 234, 235, 237, 239, 240, 241, 244, 246, 248, 254, 256, 257
Foxe, Earle 231
Francis, Alec B. 201, 208, photo 201
Francis, Noel 239
Francis, Olin 275, 279
Francisco, Betty 256
Franey, Billy 269, 303, 305, 307, 310, 313
Franz, Joel 237
Frawley, William 313
Frazer, Robert 251
Frederici, Blanche 241
Fredericks, William 221

French, Charles K. 178
Fritchie, Barbara 275, photo 276
Frontier Marshal 138, 266, photo 266, advertisement 267
Fuerberg, Hans 241
Fung, Willie 237
Funston, Brigadier General 18, 22
Furthman, Charles 275
Gable, Clark 4, 140
Gahan, Oscar 303, 309
Gainor, Laura Augusta *(see Janet Gaynor)*
Garbo, Greta 119, 127
Garcia, Al Earnest 254
Garralaga, Martin 254, 281, 303, 307, 310
Garvey, Edward 221
Gay Caballero, The 131, 254, photo 255
Gaynor, Janet 76, 78, 79, 88, 92, 95, 96, 173, 203, 204, 210, 220, 326, photos 87, 217, 219
Gebhart, Charles *(see Buck Jones)*
Generaux, Al 241
Geraghty, Tom 183
Ghost Breaker, The 58, 179
Gibson, Hoot 163
Gilbert, Edwin 313
Gilbert, Florence 204
Giler, Berne 307
Gill, Tom 254
Gillette, Bob 241
Gillette, Ruth 266, photo 266
Gilroy, Bert 289, 290, 293, 294, 298, 300, 301, 303, 304, 307, 309, 310, 311
Giraud, Wesley 254
Girl Who Wasn't Wanted, The 239
Glasser, Bernard 321
Glazer, Benjamin 100, 215
Gleason, James 213

Glecker, Robert 290
Goddard, Charles W. 179
Gold Raiders 321, advertisement 322
Golden West, The 131, 257, advertisement 258, photos 142, 259
Golden, George 241
Golden, John 201
Goldstein, Leonard 285
Goldwyn, Samuel 83, 103
Golem, The 94
Gombell, Minna 132, 251
Gonder, William 183
Goodman, Jules Eckert 69
Goodrich, John F. 248
Gordon, C. Henry 254
Gordon, Gavin 287
Gordon, Grace 208
Gordon, Huntley 184, 281
Gordon, James 187, 190, 234
Gordon, Julia Swayne 257
Gordon, Mary 301, 305, 318
Gorss, Sol 315
Gould, William 275, 315
Goulding, Edmund 190, 195, 198
Gowland, Gibson, 220
Graf, Max 176
Graham, Fred 318, 319
Grainger, Edmund 246, 257
Grant, Cary 147
Grant, Frances 275
Grant, Kirby 298, 307
Grant, Morton 310, 311
Grassby, Bertram 198
Gray, Colleen 317
Graziano, Rocky 317
Green, Alfred E. 179, 181, 183, 224
Greene, Billy 315
Gregory, Paul 173
Greig, Robert 260
Grey, Tippy 195

Grey, Zane 138, 237, 240, 248, 251, 257, 260, 262, 265, 269, 275
Griffith, D. W. 86
Gripp, Harry 224
Gruen, James 287
Gun Law 289, advertisement and photo 289
Gunsmoke 168
Guy, Eula 269
Haade, William 307, 210
Hack, Herman 290, 310
Haggin, James 11, 16
Hagney, Frank 234, 285, 287, 302
Haig, Raoul 287
Hale, Alan Jr. 313
Hale, Alan Sr. 159
Hall, Ben 241, 257
Hall, Donna 323
Hall, Henry 269, 309
Hall, Mordaunt 94, 201, 223, 257, 269
Hall, William 287
Haney, Carol 317
Hanlon, Bert 257, 285
Hansen, Aleth 305
Hard Rock Harrigan 138, 274, 275, photo 274
Hardy, Oliver 159
Hare, Lumsden 235
Harlan, Marion 201
Harlan, Otis 208
Harold and Maude 173
Harris, George 204, 208, 241
Harris, Mitchell 244
Harris, Sam 323
Harris, Winifred 315
Harrison, Paul 137
Harron, Robert 82
Hart, Al 224
Hart, Dorothy 317
Hart, Jeanne 269

Hart, Neal 294
Hart, William S. 42, 163, 279
Hartford, David 239
Hartmann, Paul 41
Harvey, Forrester 256
Haskell, Al 303, 310
Haver, Phyllis 205, 208
Havoc 73, 155, 198, advertisement 199
Hawks, Howard 74, 75, 100, 101, 205, 215, 232
Hawks, J. G. 186
Hawks, Kenneth 234
Hayes, George F. "Gabby" 275
Hayward, Chuck 323
Hayward, Lillie 199
Hayworth, Rita 294, photo 295
Hearn, Hamilton 251
Heinz 57 Playhouse 322
Heinz Studio 57 166
Heir to the Hoorah, The 268
Heirs, Walter 179
Henderson, Ray 309
Hendricks, Ben Jr. 287
Henry IV 34
Henry, William 323
Herbert, Dr. G. S. 58
Herbert, Holmes 221, 222
Herdman, Virginia 256
Herman, Al 285
Herrick, Jack 213
Herring, Aggie 281
Hertz, Alfred 9, 15, 16
Hervey, Irene 269, 275, photos 270, 274
Herzog, Dorothy 60
Heywood, Herbert 307
Hickman, Darryl 309
Hickman, Howard 300
Hickox, Harry 323
Higgins, Colin 173

Hill, Al 281, 285
Hill, Kickman 168
Hilliker, Katherine 92, 218
Hillman, Eddie 137
Hillyer, Lambert 176
Hirliman, George A. 141, 281, 285, 413
Hirohito (Emperor Shōwa) 316
Hitler, Adolf 316
Hodgins, Earle 296
Hoffman, Otto 226, 285
Hofmann, Ernst 41
Hogan, Dick 309
Holcombe, Harry 323
Holland, Cecil 178
Hollister, Alice 195
Hollywood Cowboy 172, 285, photo 286
Holmes, Gilbert 260
Holt, Tim 149, 153, 294
Holy Terror, A 103, 121, 246, photos 247
Homans, Robert E. 231
Honor Bound 99, 224, photo 225
Hooker, Hugh 321
Hopper, Hedda 160, 208
Hopper, James 11
Horwood, Robert 231
House of Shadows, The 116
Houseman, Arthur 220, 309
Houston, Walter 316
Howard, David 153, 251, 256, 257, 260, 262, 275, 277, 279, 281, 285, 287, 289, 290, 293, 294, 298, 300, 303, 304, 307, 309, 311, photo 142
Howard, Moe 321
Howard, Shemp 321
Howard, William K. 127
Howell, Hazel 199
Hoyt, Arthur 262

Hsueh, Nancy 323
Hughes, Gareth 184
Hughes, Lloyd 186
Hulce, Edward 171, 172
Hulette, Gladys 64, 187
Humbert, George 275
Hunt, Jay 208
Hunter, Dick 248, 251, 260, 298, 301, 305, 310, 313
Huntington, Louise 244
Hurst, Brandon 315
Hurst, Paul 316
Hutchison, Bruce 285
Hutton, Lucille 192
Hyams, Leila 224
Hyke, Francis Ray 318, 319
Hymer, Warren 237, 241
I Blow My Own Horn 58
Imhof, Roger 268
Ince, John 269, 277
Inclán, Miguel 318
Ingham, Leonard 9, 11, 18, 20
Ingraham, Lloyd 241, 269, 276, 281, 285, 290, 294, 300, 305, 307, 309, 313, photo 284
Inside Story, The 127
Iron Horse, The 1, 4, 61, 64, 65, 66, 68, 69, 173, the making of 82-83, 103, 155, 168, 171, 172, 187
Irving, George 208, 224
Irwin, Charles 313
Is Matrimony a Failure? 53
Is Zat So? 99, 213, photo 214
Jackson, Frank 184
Jacobs, William 313
Janney, William 235
Jannings, Emil 119
Jarrett, Daniel 272, 275, 277, 279, 281, 285, 287
Jazz Singer, The 95, 97, 104
Jefferson, Thomas 215

Jenks, Si 265, 269, 277
Jennings, Al 186
Jensen, Eulalie 198, 205
John A. Campbell 12
John War Eagle 257
Johnson, Agnes Christine 271
Johnson, Ben 303, 319, 323, photo 320
Johnson, Erskin 156
Johnson, Henry 268
Johnson, John Lester 269
Johnson, Lorraine 146
Johnson, Noble 195, 226, 259, 319
Johnston, Andrew 186
Johnstown Flood, The 78, 173, advertisement and photos 203
Jolson, Al 97, 104
Jones, Arthur V. 309-311
Jones, Billy 319
Jones, Buck 45, 61, 82, 118, 138, 141, death 155, 163
Jones, Dickie 281
Jones, Ray 290, 294
Jordan, Sid 204, 269, 271, 276, 285, 302, 303, 305
Jorgenson, Emil 178
Jory, Victor 167, 323
Judd, John 313
Judith 232
Just Tony 45, 175, 176
Kahle, Alexander 325
Kaliz, Armand 225
Kamen, Milt 317
Kane, Eddie 315
Katterjohn, Monte M. 178
Kaufman, Al 176
Kaye, Stubby 317
Keane, Edward 275, 277, 290
Kearney, John 221
Keckley, Jack 237
Keith, Rosalind 300

Kelley, James E. 316
Kelley, Mrs. James E. 316
Kelly, George 32
Kelly, John 231
Kelly, Lew 294, 296
Kelly, Paul 271
Kelly, Reynolds "Ren" 32
Kelly, Walter C. 241
Kemper, Charles 159, 160
Kendall, Cy 300, 309, photo 309
Kennedy, Arthur 323
Kennedy, Edgar 272
Kennedy, Fred 319
Kennedy, Hester Titman 35, 36
Kenneth, Keith 281
Kent, Crauford 231, 279, 281
Kent, Larry 241
Kentucky Pride 60
Kenyon, Charles 187, 194
Kerrigan, J. M. 251
Kerry, Norman 72
Key, Kathleen 186
Kibbee, Guy 318
Kieffer, Philip 318
Killer, The 256
Killy, Edward 310
King, Andrea 313
King, Charles 279
King, Henry 124
King, Lewis 265
King, Louis 260
King, Pee Wee 310
Kipling, Edward 184
Kirby, David 190
Kirk, Jack 269, 275
Kirkland, Hardee 183
Kirkwood, James 246, 251
Klein, Charles 231
Klein, Philip 213, 224, 248, 251, 254
Klöpher, Eugene 41
Klumph, Helen 53

Knight, Fuzzy 321
Knudsen, Peggy 315
Kohler, Fred 62, 187, 275, 294
Kohler, Fred Sr. 296, photo 297
Korea: Battleground for Liberty 164, 323
Kortman, Robert 294, 298, 302, 220
Krauss, Werver 41
Krueger, Stubby photo 120
Kuwa, George 178, 208
Kyle, Bob 241
La Roy, Rita 246, 290
La Verne, Lucille 265
Laidlaw, Ethan 290, 310
Lait, Jack Jr. 304
Lake, Florence 315
Lake, Stuart N. 266
Lane, Nora 234
Lanning, Frank 239
Lansbury, Angela 317
Lasky, Jesse 58
Last Frontier, The 323
Last Laugh, The 85
Last of the Duanes, The 240
Last Trail, The 265
Laurel, Stan 159
Lawless Valley 296, photos 297
Leather Pushers, The 60
Lederman, D. Ross 301
Lee, Anna 318
Lee, Duke R. 175
Lee, Gwen 223
Lee, Lila 53, 179, 181, 183, photo 180
Lee, Robert N. 207
Lee, Rowland V. 198, 207
Lee, Sonia 385
LeFever, Ralph 237
Legion of Terror 146
Legion of the Lawless 307, photo 306
Leight, Mrs. William J. 316

Leight, William J. 316
LeRoy, Mervyn 58, 64, 81, 96, 179
LeSaint, Edward J 265, 266, 275, 298
Lesser, Sol 138, 141, 172, 260, 262, 265, 266, 268, 269, 271, 272, 275, 277, 279, 281
Lessing, Marion 124, 241, photo 243
Lester, Elliott 239
Levett, Harold 221
Levine, Nat 153
Lewis, Ralph 190
Libby, Fred 319
Lichter, Baron James 281
Lieberman, Natalie Behrman 154
Life in the Raw 130, 132, 265, photos 264
Lighton, Louis D. 74, 205
Lincoln, Elmo 302, 310
Lindbergh, Charles 94, 387
Lindeman Sisters, The 311
Lindeman, Berta 313
Lindeman, Clotilde 313
Lindeman, Elena 313
Little Caesar 385
Littlefield, Lucien 192
Lively, William 321
Livingston, Janet 92
Livingston, Margaret 88, 95, 96, 198, 210, 220, photos 87, 88, 95, 96 217, 326, photo 87
Lloyd, Doris 213, 260
Lloyd, Frank 62, 186
Lloyd, Harold 137
Lockney, J. P. 175
Loder, John 241
Logan, Jacqueline 201
London, Jack 138
London, Tom 279, 281, 294, 300, 302, 310
Lone Star Ranger, The 118, 139, 237, photo 237

Long, Walter 52, 178
Longi, Joe 164
Lorch, Theodore 186
Lord, Robert 203
Lord's Referee, The 210
Loring, Hope 74, 205
Lost Jungle, The 153
Lou Martin, Nora 310
Lowe, Edmund 213
Lowell, Robert 315, 316
Loy, Myrna 173, 225, 240, photo 241
Lucas, Wilfred 298, 301, 305, 307, 311
Lucey, Frank 155
Lucke, Max 313
Lund, Arthur 66
Luther, Johnny 251
Lydon, Jimmy 159
Lyons, Cliff 248, 251, 319
MacDermott, Mark 186
MacDonald, J. Farrell 66, 179, 187, 199, 201, 208, 215, 220, 221, 234, 309, photo 235
MacDonald, Wallace 186
Macfadden, Bernarr 73
MacFadden, Hamilton 248
MacGrath, Frank 318
Mack, Cactus 301-303, 305, 308, 309
Mackaill, Dorothy 70, 168, 190, 192, photos 191
MacKenna, Kenneth 116
MacKenzie, Donald 234
MacQuarrie, George 281, 296
MacQuarrie, Murdock 269
Macready, George 317
Madame X 113
Madden, Jerry 210
Madison, Cleo 194
Maggart, Del 301
Maitland, Richard 213

Makerenko, Daniel 208
Malden, Karl 323
Maltin, Leonard 60, 62, 88, 116
Man Who Came Back, The 69, 70, 79, 98, 168, 190
Manion, Jack 38
Mann, Delbert 187
Mann, Hank 215
Manning, Aileen 201
Manslaughter 52
Manymules, Steven 323
Mapes, Ted 323
Marcus, James 187, 199
Marion, Frances 201
Maris, Mona 241
Markson, Benjamin 234
Marsh, Charles 314
Marsh, Mae 318, 323
Marshal of Mesa City, The 171, 304, photo 305
Marshall, George 268
Marshall, William 52
Marstini, Rosita 184
Martin, Chris-Pin 281, 294, 303
Martin, Duke 234
Martin, Jack 241
Marvin, Frankie 301
Masked Emotions 99, 116, 234, photo 235
Mason, James 241, 269, 290
Mason, Jim 241, 294, 298, 305
Mason, LeRoy 265, 269, 281, 303, 311
Massacre 317
Mathis, June 54
Matieson, Otto 208
Mattimore, Richard van *(see Richard Arlen)*
Mattox, Martha 183
Max Reinhardt School 41
Mayer, Carl 86, 218
Mayer, Louis B. 57

Maynard, Ken 163
Mayo, Walter 256
Mazurki, Mike 323
McAllister, Paul 104, 225
McClory, Sean 323
McConville, Bernard 290, 298, 301, 309
McCoy, Tim 68, 163
McCrea, Joel 98
McCullough, Phillo 315, 323
McDaniel, Hattie 257
McDaniel, Sam 257, 265
McDonald, Francis 289
McGlynn, Frank Jr. 204, 248, photo 250
McGowan, Dorrell 300
McGowan, J. P. 277
McGowan, Stuart 300
McGrail, Walter 195, 198, 237, 241, 260
McGrath, Frank 251, 260, 319
McGuiness, James Kevin 237, 316
McGuinn, Joe 305
McGuire, Don 313
McHugh, Matt 265
McKee, John 323
McKee, Lafe 269, 276, 298
McKenzie, Eva 290, 313
McKenzie, Robert 298, 308, 311
McKim, Robert 50, 176
McLaglen, Victor 199, 254, 318, 319, photos 200, 320
McRae, Gordon 221
McTaggart, Malcolm 311
McWade, Margaret 192
Meehan, Lew 290, 308, 310
Meeker, George 268
Mehan, Lew 313
Mehra, Lal Chand 287
Meighan, Thomas 58, 59, 68, death 146, 181, 183, photo 182

Melford, George 52, 178
Memphis Western Film Festival 172
Mendoza, George 313
Menjou, Adolphe 184
Merchant, George 32
Meredith, Frank 248
Mersch, Mary 269
Merton, John 281, 321
Metropolis 85
Middleton, Charles B. 256, 258, 285
Milan, Frank 285
Milasch, Robert 201
Milestone, Lewis 47
Miljan, John 192, 290
Millard, Bailey 8, 12
Miller, Brother 190
Miller, Carl 294, 298
Miller, David 323
Miller, Diana 199
Miller, Lee O. 154
Miller, Seton I. 100, 101, 215, 237, 238
Miller, Walter 296, 307
Miller, Winston 187
Millett, Arthur 286
Millionaire Playboy (see Park Avenue Logger)
Mills, Frank 310
Milne, Peter 313
Miltern, John 181, 221
Mineo, Sal 167, 323
Miracle Man, The 59
Miracle, The 34
Mirande, Thomas 127
Mitchell, Bruce 298, 313
Mitchell, Sidney 262
Mix, Art 298
Mix, Ruth 148
Mix, Tom 1, 4, 8, 28, 29, 39, 42, 43, 44, 45, 46, 49, 61, 82, 96, death 148, 118, 121, 159, 163, 168, 175, photos 44, 47, 48

Modoc 18
Mohr, Hal 108
Mon Hommes 184
Mong, William V 225, 277, 294
Monkey Talks, The 103
Montague, Charles Edward 232
Montague, Monte 294, 298, 300, 301, 302, 305, 307, 309
Montalban, Ricardo 167, 323
Montanna, Louise 323
Montenegro, Conchita 254
Montgomery, George 163, 251
Montgomery, Robert 137
Montt, Christina 186
Mook, S. R. 139
Moon of Israel 105
Moon, Heran 164
Moore, Carlyle Jr. 298
Moore, Colleen 96, 111, 112, 137
Moore, Ida 201
Moran of the Lady Letty 51, 52, 178
Moran, Lois 102, 103, 223, 231, 231, 234, photos 84, 231
Moreno, Antonio 159, 239
Morey, Harry T. 192, 194
Morgan, Dennis 156, 157, 313
Morris, Chester 147
Morris, Colonel Charles 20
Morris, Howard 317
Morrison, L 186
Morton, Charles 104, 112
Morton, Nanomba 323
Mount, Harry 241
Movita 318
Muleson, Many 323
Mundin, Herbert 268
Murnau, Friedrich Wilhelm 5, 34, 41, 70, 79, 85, 86, 88-91, making *Sunrise* 86-93, 95-99, 101, 103, 104, 113, 116, 125, death 127, 139, 217-219, photos 87, 326

Murphy, Horace 285, 307
Murphy, Jack 241
Murphy, Maurice 201, 241
Murphy, Ralph 160
Murphy, Stanwood 155
Murray, Forbes 315
Muse, Clarence 281
Mussolini Benito, 94
Mussolini, Benito 316
My Wild Irish Rose 156, 157, 313, advertisement 314, photo 315
Mystery Ranch 131, 172, 256, photo 256
Mystery Squadron 153
Nagel, Conrad 225
Nail, Shirley 248
Naish, J. Carol 265
Natwick, Mildred 319
Ne'er-Do-Well, The 58, 59, 181
Negri, Pola 1, 4, 53, 184, photo 185
Neill, James 201
Nelson, Bob 241
Nelson, Frank 184
Nestrell, Bill 260
New York Metropolitan Opera 9
Newton, Charles 187
Niblo, Fred 57
Nichols, Dudley 241, 260, 304
Nicholson, Paul 204
Nissen, Greta 265, photo 264
Nixon, Marion 137
Noah's Ark 4, 104, 105, 108, 110, 111, 112, 163, 171, 225, advertisement 226, photos 227, 228, 229
Nodalsky, Sonia 221
Norris, Frank 178
Norton, Barry 104, 112, 220
Norton, Edgar 183, 271
Novarro, Ramon 57, 64, 119, photo in *Ben-Hur* 55

Walsh, George 64
Nowlin, Herman 248, 251, 302, 310, 313
Nugent, Frank S. 317, 319
O'Brien, Daniel Joseph birth 7, marriage 7, 8, 9, in San Francisco earthquake 12-26, 27, 28, 29, 34, 38, 40, 41, 43, 53, 68, 125, death 132, 167, photos 10, 31, 33, 48, 129
O'Brien, Darcy 4, 5, 133, 164, 166, 173, photo 135
O'Brien, Daniel James "Jack" Jr. birth 8, in San Francisco earthquake 12-26, 13, 14, 17, 18, 27, 28, 125, 154, 167, 187, photo 33
O'Brien, George birth records 1, in San Francisco earthquake 12-26, in grammar school 27-28, in Polytechnic High School 30, in World War One 1, 4, 6, 34-37, in Santa Clara College 40-43, with Tom Mix 43-47, discovered by Hobart Bosworth 50, doubling for Rudolph Valentino 52-53, testing for *Ben-Hur* 54, making *The Iron Horse* 61-66, making *The Man Who Came Back* 70, making *Fig Leaves* 74-78, making *The Johnstown Flood* 78-79, making *The Iron Horse* 82-83, making *Sunrise* 86-93, *Sunrise* premiere 96, making *Noah's Ark* 104-112, first sound film 111, making first full length sound film 118-119, marriage to Marguerite Churchill 131, death of son Brian 133, birth of daughter Orin 133, birth of son Darcy 133, in World War Two 1, 4, 6, 151-155, in *What Price Glory?* play 159-161, divorce from

Marguerite Churchill 166, in Korean conflict 4, 6, 161-163, death 173, photos 30, 31, 32, 33, 46, 47, 56, 63, 65, 71, 76, 77, 84, 87, 88, 106, 107, 114, 120, 122, 123, 126, 129, 130, 134-136, 142-145, 149, 151, 152, 165, 170, 189, 191, 194, 197, 199, 200, 201, 203, 205, 206, 209, 212, 214-219, 222, 224, 225, 227-229, 231, 233, 235, 237, 239, 241, 243, 244, 247, 249, 250, 253, 255, 256, 259, 261, 264, 266, 268, 270, 271, 273, 274, 276, 278-280, 283, 284, 286, 288, 289, 291, 295, 297, 299, 300, 301, 303-306, 308-310, 312, 315, 318, 326-384

O'Brien, Margaret marriage 7, 8, 10, in San Francisco earthquake 12-26, 27, 38, 68, 125, photo 33

O'Brien, Orin 1, 4, 133, 137, 154, 164, 166-168, photo 135

O'Brien, Pat 159, 160

O'Brien, Turlough 6

O'Brien, William J. 313

O'Connor, Frank 290, 294, 298, 300, 301, 302, 309, 313

O'Connor, Robert Emmett 285

O'Day, Nell 132, 262

O'Feeney, Sean *(see John Ford)*

O'Hara, James 323

O'Hara, Maureen 159

O'Malley of the Mounted 279, advertisement 279, photos 279

O'Malley, Charles 187

O'Neill, Henry 159

O'Shea Jack 294, 298, 309, 310

O'Shea, Oscar 314

O'Sullivan, Maureen 132, 137, 260, photos 261

Oehman, Rita 289, photo 289

Ogden, Vivian 201

Olcott, Chauncey 157, 315

Olcott, Rita 313

Oliver, Ted 260

Olmstead, Gertrude 62

Once to Every Man 73, 199

Orth, Marion 223

Osborne, Bud 208, 301, 307, 309

Over the Border 208

Owen, Reginald 260

Padjan, John 187

Paid to Love 99, 100, 215, photos 215, 216

Painted Desert, The 146, 293

Painted Lady, The 70, 155, 192, advertisement 193

Pantomime Quiz 316

Panzer, Paul 204, 265, 315, 321

Park Avenue Logger 285, photos 284

Park, Post 319

Parker, Cecilia 131, 132, 172, 251, 254, 256, 285, photos 253, 286

Parker, Eddie 315

Parker, James Jr. 241

Parker, John 43, 49, 53

Parker, Norton S. 310

Parsons, Hubert 195

Pascal, Ernest L. 240, 244

Patterson, Elizabeth 237

Patterson, Walter 313

Patton, Bill 290, 298, 305

Pawley, Edward 289

Pawley, William 260

Peacemaker, The 304

Peck, Gregory 159, 160

Pegg, Vester 208, 269, 309

Peil, Edward 234, 281, 301, 305, 307

Pelletier, Yvonne 248

Pendelton, Steve 313

Pendleton, Nat 240, 241, 244
Pendleton, Steve 241, 265, 305
Pennick, Jack 235, 318, 319
Perrin, Jack 237
Perrin, Jack 300
Perry, Kathryn 213
Perry, Walter 204, 208
Phelps, Earl 290, 294
Phelps, Lee 275
Phelps, Norman 290, 294, 300
Phelps, Willie 290, 294, 300
Phyfe, Hal 325
Physical Culture 73
Pichel, Irving 316, 319
Pickford, Mary 42, 80, 91, 180
Piel, Edward 187, 190, 199, 241
Pierce, Scott 75
Pierson, Arthur 257
Pike, Lew 29, 72
Pinchon, Edgecumb 281
Pine, Little 251
Pinegree, Earle 246
Plantation Act, A 97
Pleasure Crazed 116
Plummer, Rose 271
Poff, Lon 237
Poindexter, Joseph B. 316
Poston, Tom 317
Potel, Victor 275, 277, 279
Powell, Russ 257
Powell, Russell 256
Powell, William 101, 173, 215
Powers, Francis 187
Prairie Law 308, photo 309
Pratt, Judson 323
Price, Hal 276, 286
Price, Stanley 265, 305
Price, Vincent 317
Prior, Herbert 204
Prisco, Albert 186
Pyle, Denver 323

Qualen, John 323
Queen Elizabeth 83
Quested, Jay 168
Racketeers of the Range 301, photos 301
Radzina, Medea 186
Rainbow Trail, The 121, 131, 153, 172, 251, advertisement 252, photos 253
Rainey, Buck 46, 124, 155, 168
Ramsey, Quen 309
Ranch Life in the Great Southwest 28
Randolf, Anders 108, 204, 225
Range Riders, The 28
Rankin, Caroline 237
Rathmell, John 293
Raven 49, 50
Ray, Terrance 241
Raymond, Frances 179
Reed, George 257, 265
Reed, Walter 323
Regas, George 257, 281
Reicher, Hedwig 234
Reid, Wallace 1, 4, 6, 54, 58, death 59, 60, 69, 82, 179, photos 44, 180
Remington, Frederick 158
Renee, Joan 208
Renegade Ranger, The 294, photo 295
Reynolds, Lynn F. 175
Reynolds, Marjorie 301, 302, photos 301, 303
Reynolds, Vera 183, 184
Ricard, André 184
Rice, Frank 256, 260, 275
Rich, Irene 318
Richmond, Warner P. 265
Ricketts, Tom 281
Ricksen, Lucille 192
Rickson, Joe 237, 298, 313

Riders of the Purple Sage 120, 121, 123, 128, 131, 153, 248, photos 249, 250
Riesenberg, Felix 221
Riesenfeld, Hugo 94, 95
Rigby, Gordon 257, 262
Rigby, L. G. 204, 210
Rinaldi, Billy 201
Ring, Cyril 181, 281
Rivero, Julien 246
Roan, Vinegar 248
Roan, Vinegar 251, 260
Robber's Roost 131, 260, advertisement 260, photos 261
Roberson, Chuck 323
Roberts, Beatrice 285
Roberts, Jack 311
Robertson, Willard 241, 244, 254, 285
Robins, Walt 175
Robinson, Edward G. 167, 323
Roche, Charles De 184
Rodin, Auguste 72, 83
Rogers, Roy 4, 163
Rogers, Walter 187
Rogers, Will 137, 163
Roland, Gilbert 167, 323
Rollins, Jack 208
Romain, George E. 186
Rome, Stewart 208
Roosevelt, Theodore 24, 387
Roquemore, Henry 313
Rosenor, George 285
Rosenthal, Henry L. 316
Rosenthal, Mrs. Henry L. 316
Rosher, Charles 86, 88, 90, 91, 96, 218
Rosing, Bodil 220
Ross, Betsy King 262
Rough Romance 121, 239, photos 84, 239

Roughneck, The 73, 79, 194, advertisement 194
Roy, Gloria 269
Royce, Lionel 316
Royle, William 285, 294, 303
Rubens, Alma 121, 195
Rush, Dick 269, 277, 305
Russell, Bing 323
Russell, John 187
Russell, Lillian 315
Russell, William 210
Rustlin' For Cupid 204, advertisement and photos 205
Ruth, Del 111
Ruth, Wally 315
Ryan, Jim 64
Ryan, Sheila 321
Sabatini, Rafel 186
Sainpolis, John 183
Sale, Virginia 262
Salute 116, 139, 235, photos 236
Sandoz, Mari 167, 323
Sandrock, Adele 41
Santley, Clifford 260
Santschi, Tom 83, 208, 224
Sarno, Hector V. 186
Saxe, Templar 195
Saylor, Sid 269
Scarface 385
Schick, Mrs. William 316
Schick, William 316
Schmitz, E. E. 19, 20, 21
Schrock, Raymond L. 275
Schroeder, Doris 307, 309
Schulberg, Budd 316
Schultz, Harry 241
Schumann-Heink, Ferdinand 241
Schwarz, Jack 321
Scott, Ewing 285, 287
Scott, Vernon 171
Sea Hawk, The 62, 186

Seabrook, Gay 301
Seas Beneath, The 124, 241, photos 243
Seel, Charles 323
Seigfried 85
Seiler, Lewis 266
Selbie, Evelyn 208
Selig, William 28
Sellon, Charles A. 183, 194
Semels, Harry 262
Sennett, Mack 159
Service, Robert W. 194
Seventh Heaven (film) 79, 96
Seventh Heaven (play) 89
Shadows of Paris 53, 184
Shamrock Handicap, The 60
Shannon, Peggy 311
Sharp Shooters 99, 103, 223, photo 224
Sharp, Clint 251, 260, 301
Sharpe, David 234
She Goes To War 121
She Wore a Yellow Ribbon 1, 319, 320, photo 320
Shea, Jack 298
Shearer, Norma 96
Shechter, Marvin 241
Sheehan, John 244
Sheehan, Winifield 116, 205
Sheik, The 50
Shepherd, Robert 241
Sheridan, Frank 277
Sherwood, Yorke 269
Shields, Arthur 319
Shindell, Cy 315
Short, Gertrude 285
Short, Lew 210
Shumway, Lee 237, 275, 285, 287, 294
Sills, Milton 62, 186, photo 186
Silver Treasure, The 83, 112, photos 207

Simmons, Georgia 313
Simpson, Mickey 318, 319
Simpson, Russell 204, 237, 266, 268
Sinatra, Frank 160, 161
Sipperly, Ralph 210, 220
Skidding 116
Smalley, Phillips 231, 234
Smith, Bernard 323
Smith, Buddy 194
Smith, Jack C. 308
Smith, Sid 181
Smith, Winchell 201
Smoke Lightning 131, 262, advertisement 263
Son of Anuk, A 234
Son of the Sheik, The 81
Sooter, Rudy 305
Sothern, Hugh 290, 307
Spearman, Frank H. 277
Spence, Sandra 317
Spencer, Robert 186
Spider, The 124
Spitz, Leo 146
SS Luzon 125
St. Polis, John 281
Stack, Robert 317
Stage to Chino 310, photo 310
Stallings, Laurence 319
Standing, Joan 195
Stanton, Paul 313
Stanton, Robert 307
Stanton, Will 234
Star is Born, A 78
Statler, Mary 323
Steele, Tom 294
Steele, William 237, 319
Stella Dallas 103
Stelling, William 290
Sterling, Merta 215
Stevens, Charles 256, 257, 294
Stevens, Landers 251, 298

Stevens, Louis 181
Stevens, Onslow 257
Stevenson, Tom 315
Stewart, Anita 204, photo 205
Stewart, James 160, 167, 323
Stewart, Roy 237, 239, 256
Stockdale, Carl 276, 298, 300, 305, 308, 310
Stokey, Mike 316
Stone, George E. 266
Stone, John 308, 235
Stooges Go West (see Gold Raiders)
Storm, The 100
Strang, Harry 241
Strange, Glenn 275, 298, 303, 310, 311
Stranger, The 60
Strauss, Karl 218
Street Angel 95, 96
Strength and Health 29
Struss, Karl 88, 90, 96
Studio 57 322
Subchaser 297 113
Sudermann, Hermann 86
Sullivan, C. Gardner 176
Sullivan, Charles 290
Sullivan, Elliott 298
Sullivan, John 160
Summers, Don 319
Sunrise: A Song of Two Humans 2, 4, 5, 79, 85, 86, 88, 92, 94-97, 103, 169, 171-173, 217, photos 217-219
Sutherland, Eddie 66
Sutton, Arthur 120
Sutton, Grady 314
Sutton, Kay 296
Svenson, Captain 12
Swanson, Gloria 138
Swenson, Karl 316
Swickard, Joseph 223

Swift, Don 275, 277
Szabo, Mrs. Stephen 316
Szabo, Steph 316
Taber, Richard 213
Tabu 98, 125
Tafoya, Jesus A. 316
Tafoya, Mrs. Jesus A. 316
Tai Yang 124
Taiwan – Island of Freedom 164
Talbot, Lyle 321
Tall Timber (see Park Avenue Logger)
Talley, Alma 73, 101-103
Talmadge, Constance 119
Talmadge, Norma 119
Tapis, Father Estevan 131
Taylor, Al 279
Taylor, Estelle 224
Taylor, Ferris 309
Taylor, Forrest 303
Taylor, Rex 277
Taylor, William Desmond 82
Tchechowa, Olda 41
Teague, Frances 187
Tell, Anton 241
Tellegen, Lou 6, 83, 112, 119, 121, suicide 133, 208, photos 84, 207
Temple, Shirley 317
Templeton, George 241
Ten Commandments, The 52, 54, 104
Tenbrook, Harry 210, 235, 241, 305, 318
Terry, Don 231
Thalasso, Arthur 276, 285
Thalberg, Irving 57, 96
Thalberg, Irving 96
Thank You 73, 201, advertisement 201
Thirty Days 58
This is Your Life 166
Thomas, Frank M. 294
Thompson, Lady 78

Thomson, Kenneth 277
Thorne, William L. 251
Thorns of Passion 73
Three Dunhills, The 314
Three Naval Rascals (see Sharp Shooters)
Thunder Mountain 140, 172, 275, photo 276
Timber Stampede 302, photo 303
Tinling, James 265
Tobias, George 313
Todd, James 248
Toland, Gred 316
Tombes, Andrew 315
Toones, Fred 260, 269, 271
Torchy 70
Torena, Juan 254
Tovar, Lupita 303, photo 304
Tracy, Lee 235
Trailin' 246
Trevor, Claire 132, 265, photo 130
Trip to Tilsit, A 86
Triple Justice 149, 153, 311, photo 312
Trouble in Sundown 300, photo 300
True Heaven 99, 232, photo 233
Tucker, Forrest 159
Tucker, Richard 246
Tupper, Tristram 235
Twitchell, Archie 318
Tyler, Beverly 317
Tyler, Tom 72, 319
Typhoon 166, 322
Ullman, Elwood 321
Ulmer, Edgar 127
Uncharted Seas 50
Unknown, The 100
Unsell, Eve 184
Untamed, The 244
Usher, Guy 294, 298, 302
USS Chicago 24

Valdez, Henrique 313
Vale, Virginia 305, 307, 309, 310, 311, photos 306, 310
Valentino, Rudolph 1, 4, 6, 32, 50, 52, 54, 80, death 81, 84, photos 51, 178
Valli, Virginia 99, 100, 101, 215, 221, photos 215, 222
Veidt, Conrad 41
Victor, Henry 241
Villegas, Lucio 294, 303
Vogan, Emmett 279
Volpe, Nick 163
Von Fuerberg, Kurt 241
Votan, Emmett 315
Waggner, George 187, 272
Wagner, Max 294
Wagon Train 149
Waite, Malcolm 225
Walker, Robert 286
Wallace, Morgan 262, 275, 302
Wallace, Richard 49
Waller, Eddy 307
Wallin, H. N. 316
Walling, Will 187
Walsh, George 57, 72, photo in *Ben-Hur* 55
Walsh, Raoul 85, 115, 116
Walton, Frank 241
Wang, James 269
War Party 319
Ward, Alice 251
Ward, Bill 321
Ward, Blackjack 279, 279
Ward, Dorothy 257
Ware, Irene 277, 279, photos 278, 279
Warner, Jack 111, 156, 157
Warren, E. Allen 262
Warren, Ruth 265
Warwick, Robert 246

Washer, Bed 173
Watkins, Linda 132, 254
Wayne, John 115, 116, 159, 160, 163, 167, 235, 239, 317, 319, photos 236, 318, 320
Wayne, Maude 178
Wayne, Patrick 168, 323
Webb, James R. 323
Weil, Harry 241, 313
Weinberg, Gus 181
Weismuller, Johnny photo 120
Welch, Jame 187
Welch, Niles 251
Wengren, Dave 285
Werker, Alfred 240, 244, 254
West, Betty 313
West, Sam 257
Westmore, Bud 107
Westmore, Frank 107
Westmore, Wally 107
What Price Glory? (play) 103, 159, 160
Wheat, Larry 181, 269
Wheatcroft, Stanhope 187
When a Man's a Man 171, 271, photo 271
Whispering Smith Speaks 138, 140, 277, advertisement 278, photos 278
Whitaker, Herman 208
Whitaker, Slim 246, 271, 279, 303, 305, 307, 309, photo 309
White Hands 50, 176
White, Dan 319
White, Stewart Edward 256
Whiteford, Blackie 305
Whitley, Ray 289, 290, 294, 300, 301, 309, photo 300
Widmark, Richard 167, 323
Wild Man of Borneo, The 116
Wilhelm, Kaiser II 103

Wilhelmina 49
Wilkinson, Walter 186, 190
Williams, Ben 234
Williams, Guinn 225, photo 229
Williams, Kathlyn 29
Williams, Whitney 127
Willis, Harry 307
Willis, Norman 307
Willock, Dave 317
Wills, Chill 298, 300, 301, 302
Wills, Lou Jr. 314
Wilson, Clarence 271
Wilson, Dorothy 271, photo 271
Wilson, Fred 262
Wilson, Jay 246
Wilson, John Fleming 190
Windjammer 168, 287, advertisement 287, photos 288
Windom, Lawrence 121
Wings 95-97
Wings Over Wyoming (see *Hollywood Cowboy*)
Winterhalder, Hans 241
Winters, Laska 251
Winton, Jane 220
Withers, Grant 318
Witzel, Albert 325
Wolheim, Dan 285, 221
Woman Proof 59, 183
Woman With Four Faces, The 53
Wood, Douglas 314
Wood, Freeman 176, 195
Woodruff, Bert 186, 199
Woods, Harry 271, 307, 311, 319
Worden, Hank 302, 309, 313, 318
Worth, Constance 287, photo 288
Wright, Gilbert 277
Wright, Harold Bell 271
Wurtzel, Sol 64, 118, 139
Wyatt Earp Frontier Marshal 266
Yamaoka, Otto 300

Yorke, Edithe 204
Young Cassidy 168
Young, Carleton 323
Young, Clifton 313
Young, Noah 223
Young, Polly Ann 280, 281, photos 280
Youngston, Robert 163
Zanft, John 272
Zanft, Major 138
Zann, Nancy 186
Zanuck, Darryl F. 108, 137, 225
Ziegfeld Follies 70
Zukor, Adolph 61, 181, 183

WESTERN Clippings
by Boyd Magers
1312 Stagecoach Rd. SE
Albuquerque, NM 87123
(505) 292-0049
www.westernclippings.com

- Exclusive B-western and TV Cowboy News and Photos
- Film Festival Reports/Updates
- Westerns of...(B-western stars' films)
- Western Movie Book Reviews
- Upcoming Westerns
- Candid Film/TV/DVD Reviews
- Cowboy Quotes
- Old Pros In New Shows
- Western Boo Boos
- Best of Western TV Selections
- TV Series Histories
- Comic Book Cowboys
- Rare Historic Photos
- Empty Saddles w/comments by co-stars on the passing of the stars
- Characters and Heavies (Profiles)

Sample Issue $4

- Regular Columns by
  WILL ("Sugarfoot") HUTCHINS
  TY ("Bronco") HARDIN
  JOHNNY WESTERN—"Filmland Horsemen"
  NEIL SUMMERS—Forgotten Western Classics
  BILL RUSSELL—Silent Cowboy Profiles
  CARLO GABERSCEK/KEN STIER—Western movie sites
  O. J. SIKES—Western music reviews
  BOBBY COPELAND "Cowboy Commentary" Western star quotes
  TOM AND JIM GOLDRUP—Actor profiles and filmmaking in early California
  BOB NAREAU "Reel Lore" Facts and Figures on western stars
  TOM WEAVER—Character Actress/Actor Interviews
  JOHN BROOKER—Historic B-Western Star Interviews
  PHIL LOY—"Hoofprints on the Trail" real and reel history

INTRODUCTORY SPECIAL
Regular annual subscription $29.20
(6 issues)

Introductory Special
(U.S. only)

$25
(6 issues)

Now in our 15th year of publication!   Now 32 pages   Published Bi-Monthly!

WESTERN CLIPPINGS   6 issues (1 Year)

NAME: _____

ADDRESS: _____

CITY/STATE/ZIP: _____

- ☐ 1st Class Air Mail $29.20   ☐ Bulk Mail $25.20   ☐ Canada $33.50   ☐ Foreign $47.00
- ☐ 1st Class Air Mail (2 yrs.) $56   ☐ Bulk Mail (2 yrs.) $48.50   (In U.S. Funds Only)